Praise for *Au Revoir to All That*

"*Au Revoir to All That* is a fascinating and knowledgeable valedictory to the greatest food and wine culture the world has ever known. Michael Steinberger is a great gourmand and a great storyteller, and he will make you care about the fate of Camembert and other endangered traditions."

—Jay McInerney, author of *A Hedonist in the Cellar*

"Steinberger has done remarkably thorough research to detail just what has gone wrong in French gastronomy. Drawing on astonishing tidbits ... Steinberger convincingly explains why so many of its greatest chefs have grown complacent, its greatest gastronomic guide so off-track, and its winemakers just plain broke. In spite of all the bad news, the book is a ripping fun read and is even a little optimistic, as Steinberger points out a few key men and women bucking the trends."

—*Food and Wine*

"Steinberger fingers everything from a bloated, micromanaging bureaucracy to the new creative cooking wave out of Spain and England to the rise of the celebrity chef and the tyranny of the Michelin Guide."   —*Washington Post*

"One of the greatest books I've read."   —Marco Pierre White

"If you have lamented or questioned the downfall of French cuisine, or just need a good gustatory puzzler to mull over, this is a great read."   —*Sauce* magazine

"If you've ever wondered why eating in France is so often disappointing, Michael Steinberger can explain. His delicious account draws not just on his amazing gastronomic expertise, but on a sophisticated understanding of French politics and history as well. Three stars: This one really is worth a special trip."

—Jacob Weisberg, author of *The Bush Tragedy* and editor of *Slate*

"Most books on food and wine are misty-eyed memoirs of great meals and happy times. Michael Steinberger's book is different; he is trying to understand the decline and fall of France as the center of the world's great cuisine. Of course, in his explorations, Steinberger takes us to the kitchens of great chefs, describes extraordinary food, and evokes fond memories. The result turns out to be intelligent, interesting, and complicated. You will have to read the book to get it—and you will read it with much pleasure."

—Fareed Zakaria, author of *The Post-American World*

"Informative ... [Steinberger's] fascinating profiles of influential French chefs and restaurateurs include Paul Bocuse, Alain Ducasse, and the late Alain Chapel and Jean-Claude Vrinat of Taillevent in Paris ... [An] excellent narrative."

—*Pittsburgh Tribune-Review*

"Steinberger makes many bold claims throughout the book ... Regardless of if you agree or disagree that France is no longer the epicenter of all things gourmet, Steinberger makes a convincing argument."

—Eats.com

"Michael Steinberger pulls off the magic trick of throwing a funeral you want to go to: The elegy is unflinching but heartfelt and celebratory; the guests are the most interesting people; the food (and wine) couldn't get any better; and—get this—the deceased shows signs of rising again."

—Benjamin Wallace, author of *The Billionaire's Vinegar*

"An offering of fresh and engaging insights for foodies and Francophiles alike."

—*Kirkus Reviews*

"[Steinberger's] descriptions of treats ... are shown in the true voice of a passionate Francophile. Steinberger's love for the country is tangible through his descriptions of the food he eats and remembers eating, and somehow it makes sense that he fell in love with his future wife over a French meal. It's not an adolescent love that Steinberger has for the country, but more like adoration mixed with a dose of reality."

—*Minneapolis Star Tribune*

Au Revoir to All That

Food, Wine, and the End of France

Michael Steinberger

BLOOMSBURY

NEW YORK · BERLIN · LONDON

Published by Bloomsbury USA, New York

Excerpt from *Auguste Escoffier: Memories of My Life* (Hoboken, NJ: John Wiley &
Sons, 1996), by Auguste Escoffier, reprinted by permission of the publisher.

Excerpt from "The Coming of Age of American Restaurants," *New York
Times*, December 30, 1998, reprinted by permission of Ruth Reichl.

Excerpt from *Camembert: A National Myth* (Berkeley: University of California
Press, 2003), by Pierre Boisard, reprinted by permission of the publisher.

Excerpt from "Enter a New French Superchef," by Craig Claiborne from the *New York Times*,
January 20, 1988. © 1988 the New York Times. All rights reserved. Used by permission and
protected by the copyright laws of the United States. The printing, copying, redistribution,
or retransmission of the material without express written permission is prohibited.

All papers used by Bloomsbury USA are natural, recyclable products made
from wood grown in well-managed forests. The manufacturing processes
conform to the environmental regulations of the country of origin.

Library of Congress Cataloging-in-Publication Data

Steinberger, Michael.
Au revoir to all that: food, wine, and the end of France/Michael
Steinberger.—1st U.S. ed.
p. cm.
ISBN-13: 978-1-59691-353-0 (hardcover)
ISBN-10: 1-59691-353-3 (hardcover)
1. Gastronomy—History. 2. Cookery—France. 3. Food habits—France.
I. Title.

TX637S67 2009
641.01´3—dc22
2008054504

First published by Bloomsbury USA in 2009
This paperback edition published in 2010

Paperback ISBN: 978-1-59691-506-0

1 3 5 7 9 10 8 6 4 2

Typeset by Hewer Text UK Ltd, Edinburgh
Printed in the United States of America by Worldcolor Fairfield

To Kathy, James, and Ava

CONTENTS

Introduction

O N AN UNCOMFORTABLY WARM September evening in 1999, I swapped my wife for a duck liver. The unplanned exchange took place at Au Crocodile, a Michelin three-star restaurant in the city of Strasbourg, in the Alsace-Lorraine region of France. We had gone to Crocodile for dinner and, at the urging of our waiter, had chosen for our main course one of Chef Émile Jung's signature dishes, *Foie de Canard et Écailles de Truffe en Croûte de Sel, Baeckeofe de Légumes*. Baeckeofe is a traditional Alsatian stew made of potatoes, onions, carrots, leeks, and several different meats. Jung, possessed of that particular Gallic genius for transforming quotidian fare into high cuisine, served a version of *baeckeofe* in which the meats were replaced by an entire lobe of duck liver, which was bathed in a truffled bouillon with root vegetables and cooked in a sealed terrine. The seal was broken at the table, and as soon as the gorgeous pink-gray liver was lifted out of its crypt and the first, pungent whiff of black truffles came our way, I knew our palates were about to experience rapture. Sure enough, for the ten minutes or so that it took us to consume the dish, the only sounds we emitted were some barely suppressed grunts and moans. The *baeckeofe* was outrageously good—the liver a velvety, earthy, voluptuous mass, the bouillon an intensely flavored broth that flattered everything it touched.

We had just finished dessert when Jung, a beefy, jovial man who looked to be in his mid-fifties, appeared at our table. We thanked him profusely for the meal, and my wife, an editor for a food magazine, asked about some of the preparations. From the look on his face, he was smitten with her, and after enthusiastically fielding her questions, he invited her to tour the kitchen with him. "We'll leave him here," he said, pointing at me. As my wife got up from the table, Jung eyed her lasciviously and said, "You are a mango woman!" which I took to be a reference to her somewhat exotic looks (she is half-American, half-Japanese). She laughed nervously; I laughed heartily. As Jung squired her off to the kitchen, I leaned back in my chair and took a sip of Gewürztraminer.

By now, it was midnight, the dining room was almost empty, and the staff had begun discreetly tidying up. After some minutes had passed, Madame Jung, a lean woman with frosted blonde hair who oversaw the front of the restaurant, approached my table, wearing a put-upon smile which suggested this wasn't the first time her husband had taken a young female guest to see his pots and pans. Perhaps hoping to commiserate, she asked me if everything was okay. "*Bien sûr*," I immediately replied, with an enthusiasm that appeared to take her by surprise. I was in too much of a stupor to engage in a lengthy conversation, but had I been able to summon the words, I would have told her that her husband had just served me one of the finest dishes I'd ever eaten; that surrendering my wife (in a manner of speaking) was a small price to pay for such satisfaction; and that I'd have gladly waited at the table till daybreak if that's what it took to fully convey my gratitude to Monsieur Jung.

In the end, I didn't have to wait quite that long. After perhaps forty-five minutes, Jung returned my wife to the table. She came back bearing gifts: two bottles of the chef's own late-harvest Tokay Pinot Gris and, curiously, a cold quail stuffed with foie gras, which had been wrapped in aluminum foil so that we could take it with us. We thanked him again for the memorable dinner and his generosity, and then he showed us to the door. There, I received a perfunctory handshake, while my wife got two drawn-out pecks, one to each cheek. She got two more out in front of the restaurant, and as we walked down the street toward our hotel, Jung joyfully shouted after her, "You are a mango woman!" his booming voice piercing the humid night air.

Early the next morning, driving from Strasbourg to Reims in a two-door Peugeot that felt as if it was about to come apart from metal fatigue, my wife and I made breakfast of the quail. We didn't have utensils, so we passed it back and forth, ripping it apart with our hands and teeth. As we wound our way through the low, rolling hills of northeast France, silently putting the cold creature to an ignominious end, I couldn't help but marvel at what had transpired. Where but in France could a plate of food set in motion a chain of events that would find you whimpering with ecstasy in the middle of a restaurant; giving the chef carte blanche to hit on your wife, to the evident dismay of his wife; and joyfully gorging yourself just after sunrise the next day on a bird bearing the liver of another bird, a gift bestowed on your wife by said chef as a token of his lust? The question answered itself: This sort of thing could surely only happen in France, and at that moment, not for the first time, I experienced the most overwhelming surge of affection for her.

I first went to France as a thirteen-year-old, in the company of my parents and my brother, and it was during this trip that I, like many other visitors there, experienced the Great Awakening—the moment at the table that changes entirely one's relationship to food. It was a vegetable that administered the shock for me: Specifically, it was the baby peas (drowned in butter, of course) served at a nondescript hotel in the city of Blois, in the Loire Valley, that caused me to realize that food could be a source of gratification and not just a means of sustenance—that mealtime could be the highlight of the day, not simply a break from the day's activities.

A few days later, while driving south to the Rhône Valley, my parents decided to splurge on lunch at a two-star restaurant called Au Chapon Fin, in the town of Thoissey, a few miles off the A6 in the Mâcon region. I didn't know at the time that it was a restaurant with a long and illustrious history (among its claims to fame: It was where Albert Camus ate his last meal before the car crash that killed him in 1960), nor can I recollect many details of the meal. I remember having a pâté to start, followed by a big piece of chicken, and that both were excellent, but that's about it. However, I vividly recall being struck by the sumptuousness of the dining room. The tuxedoed staff, the thick white tablecloths, the monogrammed plates, the heavy silverware, the ornate ice buckets—it was the most elegant restaurant I'd ever seen. Every table was filled with impeccably attired, perfectly mannered French families. I hadn't yet heard of Baudelaire, but this was my first experience of that particular state of bliss he described as *luxe, calme, et volupté* (richness, calm, and pleasure), and I found it enthralling.

Other trips to France followed, and in time, France became not just the place that fed me better than any other, but an emotional touchstone. In low moments, nothing lifted my mood like the thought of Paris— the thought of eating in Paris, that is. When I moved to Hong Kong in 1994, I found a café called DeliFrance (part of a local chain by the same name) that quickly became the site of my morning ritual; reading the *International Herald Tribune* over a watery cappuccino and a limp, greasy croissant, I imagined I was having breakfast in Paris, and the thought filled me with contentment. Most of the time, though, I was acutely aware that I was not in Paris. On several occasions, my comings and goings from Hong Kong's airport coincided with the departure of Air France's nightly flight to Paris. The sight of that 747 taxiing out to the runway always prompted the same thought: Lucky bastards.

In 1997, a few months after I moved back to the United States, the *New Yorker* published an article by Adam Gopnik asking, "Is There a Crisis in French Cooking?" The essay was vintage Gopnik—witty, well observed, and bristling with insight. Gopnik, then serving as the magazine's Paris correspondent, suggested that French cuisine had lost its sizzle: It had become rigid, sentimental, impossibly expensive, and dull. The "muse of cooking," as he put it, had moved on—to New York, San Francisco, Sydney, London. In these cities, the restaurants exuded a dynamism that was now increasingly hard to find in Paris. "All this," wrote Gopnik, "makes a Francophile eating in Paris feel a little like a turn-of-the-century clergyman who has just read Robert Ingersoll: you try to keep the faith, but Doubts keep creeping in."

I didn't share those Doubts: To me, France remained the *orbis terrarum* of food, and nothing left me feeling more in love with life than a sensational meal in Paris. I refused to entertain the possibility that French cuisine had run aground; I didn't see it then, and I still didn't see it when Émile Jung took off with my wife two years later during that Lucullan evening at Au Crocodile. Sure, I knew that it was now pretty easy to find bad food in France if you went looking for it. I was aware, too, that France's economic difficulties had made it brutally difficult for restaurants like Au Crocodile to keep the stoves running. In 1996, Pierre Gagnaire, a three-star chef in the industrial city of Saint-Étienne, near Lyon, had gone bankrupt, and the same fate had almost befallen another top chef, Marc Veyrat. I also recognized that I was perhaps prone to a certain psychophysical phenomenon, common among France lovers, whereby the mere act of dining on French soil seemed to enhance the flavor of things. Even so, as far as I was concerned, France remained the first nation of food, and anyone suggesting otherwise either was being willfully contrarian or was eating in the wrong places.

It was the swift and unexpected demise of Ladurée just after the turn of the millennium that caused the first Doubts to creep in. Ladurée was a Paris institution, a charmingly sedate tea room on the rue Royale, in the eighth arrondissement. It was famous for its *macarons* and pastries, and it also served one of the best lunches in Paris. I usually went with the artfully composed, perfectly dressed salade niçoise, which I chased down with a glass or two of Marcel Lapierre's violet-scented Morgon (a Beaujolais) and a deliciously crusty roll. At some point, I discovered Ladurée's praline mille feuille, which was also habit-forming: I would finish every lunch with this ethereal napoleon consisting of almond pralines, praline cream, caramelized pastry dough, and crispy hazelnuts. Of all the things that I routinely ate in France, it was the praline mille feuille that made me the happiest.

But returning to Ladurée, after a year's absence, I walked into a restaurant whose pilot light had been extinguished. The first sign of trouble was the lack of familiar faces: The endearingly gruff waitresses who had given the restaurant so much of its character had been replaced by bumbling androids. Worse, the menu had changed, and many of the old standbys, including the salade niçoise, were gone (so, too, the Morgon), replaced by a clutch of unappetizing dishes. The perpetrators of this calamity had the good sense to leave the praline mille feuille untouched, but I had to assume that it would soon be headed for history's flour bin. While Ladurée was an adored institution, it had no standing in the gastronomic world—no famous chef, no Michelin stars, no widely mimicked dishes. Even so, I now began to wonder if the French really were starting to screw things up—if French cuisine was genuinely in trouble. You might say it was the moment the snails fell from my eyes.

A few days after my dismaying visit to Ladurée, I was in the Mâcon area, this time with my wife and a friend of ours. As the three of us kicked around ideas for dinner late one afternoon, I felt pangs of curiosity. Did it still exist? If so, was it still any good? I quickly began leafing through the Michelin Guide, found Thoissey, and there it was: Au Chapon Fin. It was now reduced to one star, but the fact that it still had any was mildly encouraging. Several hours later, we were en route to Thoissey. By then, however, my initial enthusiasm had given way to trepidation. For the dedicated feeder, the urge to relive the tasting pleasures of the past is constant and frequently overwhelming. But restaurants change and so do palates; trying to recreate memorable moments at the table is often a recipe for heartache (and possibly also heartburn). And here I was, exactly two decades later, hoping to find Chapon Fin just as I had left it.

Well, the parking lot hadn't changed a bit—it was as expansive as I remembered it, and most of the spaces were still shaded by trees. Sadly, that was the high point of the visit. One glance at the dining room told the tale. The grandeur that had left such a mark on me had given way to decrepitude. Those thick, regal tablecloths were now thin, scuffed sheets. The carpet was threadbare. The plates appeared ready to crack from exhaustion. The staff brightened things a bit. The service was cheerful and solicitous—perhaps overly so—but they were doing their best to compensate for the food, which was every bit as haggard as the room. The evening passed in a crestfallen blur. What the hell was going on here?

En route back to Paris, my wife and I stopped in the somniferous village of Saulieu, at the northern edge of Burgundy, to eat at La Côte d'Or, a three-star restaurant owned by Bernard Loiseau. He was the peripatetic clown prince of French cuisine, whose empire included the three-star mother ship, three bistros in Paris, a line of frozen dinners, and a listing on the Paris stock exchange. Loiseau's brand-building reflected his desire to emulate the venerated chef Paul Bocuse, but it was later learned that it was also a matter of survival: Business in Saulieu had become a struggle, and Loiseau was desperate for other sources of revenue. The night we had dinner in Saulieu, the food was tired and so was he. It was another discouraging meal in what had become a thoroughly dispiriting trip. Maybe the muse really had moved on.

In 2003, the *New York Times Magazine* published a cover story declaring that Spain had supplanted France as the culinary world's lodestar. The article, written by Arthur Lubow, heralded the emergence of *la nueva cocina*, an experimental, provocative style of cooking that was reinventing Spanish cuisine and causing the entire food world to take note. El Bulli's Ferran Adrià, the most acclaimed and controversial of Spain's new-wave chefs, was the focus of the article and graced the magazine's cover. Lubow contrasted Spain's gastronomic vitality with the French food scene, which he described as ossified and rudderless. "French innovation," he wrote, "has congealed into complacency ... as chefs scan the globe for new ideas, France is no longer the place they look." For a Francophile, the quote with which he concluded the article was deflating. The Spanish food critic Rafael García Santos told Lubow, "It's a great shame what has happened in France, because we love the French people and we learned there. Twenty years ago, everybody went to France. Today they go there to learn what not to do."

But by then France had become a bad example in all sorts of ways.

Since the late 1970s, its economy had been stagnant, afflicted with anemic growth and chronically high unemployment. True, France had a generous welfare state, but that was no substitute for creating jobs and opportunity. By the mid-2000s, hundreds of thousands of French (among them many talented chefs) had moved abroad in search of better lives, unwilling to remain in a sclerotic, disillusioned country. France's economic torpor was matched by its diminished political clout; although prescient in hindsight, its effort to prevent the Iraq war in 2003 struck even many French as a vainglorious blunder that served only to underscore the country's weakness.

A sense of decay was now pervasive. For centuries, France had produced as much great writing, music, and art as any nation, but that was no longer true. French literature seemed moribund, ditto the once-mighty French film industry. Paris had been eclipsed as a center of the fine-art trade by London and New York. It was still a fashion capital, but British and American designers now seemed to generate the most buzz. In opera and theater, too, Paris had become a relative backwater. French intellectual life was suffering: The country's vaunted university system had sunk into mediocrity. Even the Sorbonne was now second-rate—no match, certainly, for Harvard and Yale.

Nothing in the cultural sphere was spared—not even food. The malaise extended into the kitchens of France, and it wasn't just haute cuisine that was in trouble. France had two hundred thousand cafés in 1960; by 2008, it was down to forty thousand, and hundreds, maybe thousands were being lost every year. Bistros and brasseries were also dying at an alarming clip. Prized cheeses were going extinct because there was no one with the knowledge or desire to continue making them; even Camembert, France's most celebrated cheese, was now threatened. The country's wine industry was in a cataclysmic state: Declining sales had left thousands of producers facing financial ruin. Destitute vintners were turning to violence to draw attention to their plight; others had committed suicide. Many blamed foreign competition for their woes, but there was a bigger problem closer to home: Per capita wine consumption in France had dropped by an astonishing 50 percent since the late 1960s and was continuing to tumble.

This wasn't the only way in which the French seemed to be turning their backs on the country's rich culinary heritage. Aspiring chefs were no longer required to know how to truss chickens, open oysters, or whip up a béarnaise sauce in order to earn the *Certificat d'Aptitude Professionnelle*; instead, they were being tested on their ability to use processed, powdered, frozen, and prepared foods. France still had its outdoor markets, but *hypermarchés*—sprawling supermarkets—accounted for 75 percent of all retail food sales. Most ominously, the bedrock of French cuisine—home cooking, or *la cuisine familiale*—was in trouble. The French were doing less cooking than ever at home and spending less time at the dinner table: The average meal in France now sped by in thirty-eight minutes, down from eighty-eight minutes a quarter-century earlier. One organization, at least, stood ready to help the French avoid the kitchen and scarf their food: McDonald's. By 2007, the chain had more than a thousand restaurants in France and was one of the country's largest private-sector employers. France, in turn, had become its second-most-profitable market in the world.

Food had always been a tool of French statecraft; now, though, it was a source of French humiliation. In July 2005, it was reported that French president Jacques Chirac, criticizing the British during a meeting with Russian president Vladimir Putin and German chancellor Gerhard Schroeder, had harrumphed, "One cannot trust people whose cuisine is so bad." In the not-so-distant past, Chirac, simply by virtue of being France's president, would have been seen as eminently qualified to pass judgment on another country's cuisine—and, of course, in disparaging British cooking, he merely would have been stating the obvious. Coming in the summer of 2005, Chirac's comment revealed him to be a man divorced from reality. Was he not aware that London was now a great food city? Just four months earlier, *Gourmet* magazine had declared London to be "the best place to eat in the world right now" and devoted an entire issue to its gustatory pleasures. As the ridicule rained down on Chirac, his faux pas assumed metaphoric significance: Where once the mere mention of food by a French leader would have elicited thoughts of Gallic refinement and achievement, its invocation now served to underscore the depths of France's decline. *They've even lost their edge in the kitchen.*

French cooking had certainly lost its power to seduce. Several days after Chirac's gibe made headlines, members of the International Olympic Committee, despite having been wined and dined for months by French officials, selected London over Paris as host city for the 2012 Summer Games—fish and chips over foie gras.

There were other indignities, less noted but no less telling. In October 2006, New York's French Culinary Institute marked the opening of its new International Culinary Center with a two-day extravaganza featuring panel discussions, cooking demonstrations, and gala meals. The FCI was one of America's foremost cooking schools, but it was also a wellspring of French cultural influence—a culinary consulate of sorts. Its faculty included Jacques Pépin, André Soltner, and Alain Sailhac, three expatriated French chefs who had helped unleash America's food revolution. To assure a suitably splashy debut for its new facilities, the FCI brought ten eminent foreign chefs to New York. Amazingly, though, the list was headed not by a Frenchman but by three Spaniards: Adrià, Juan Mari Arzak, and Martín Berasategui. Not only that: the other seven chefs were Spanish, too. The French Culinary Institute threw itself a party and there wasn't a single chef from France there.

All this was a reflection of what was happening in France. Twenty-five years earlier, it had been virtually impossible to eat poorly there; now, in some towns and villages, it was a struggle to find even a decent loaf of bread. The France memorialized by writers like M. F. K. Fisher, Joseph Wechsberg, Waverley Root, and A. J. Liebling; that inspired the careers of Julia Child, Alice Waters, and Elizabeth David; that promised gustatory delight along every boulevard and byway—that France, it seemed, was dying. Even those epiphanic vegetables were harder to come by. When Waters started regularly visiting France, she would smuggle tomato vine cuttings home to California; now, she smuggled vine cuttings to her friends *in* France.

It saddened me to see this way of eating, and being, disappearing. In France, I didn't just learn how to dine; I learned how to live. It was where my wife and I had fallen in love, a bond formed over plates of choucroute, platters of oysters, and bowls of *fraises des bois* (Ladurée pastries, too). When we began traveling to France as a married couple, great meals there weren't just occasions for pleasure; they were a way of reaffirming our vows. The calendar indicates that our children couldn't have been conceived in France, but from the moment they were able to eat solid foods, they were immersed in our Francophilia. They became acquainted with crème caramel before they ever knew what a Pop-Tart was. But it now appeared that the France I grew up knowing would no longer be there for them.

Were the French really willing to let their culinary tradition just wither away? Did they no longer care to be the world's gastronomic beacon? What did eminent French chefs and restaurateurs such as Alain Ducasse and Jean-Claude Vrinat have to say about all this? And what of the almighty Michelin Guide, long a symbol of Gallic supremacy in matters of food and wine—was it still a force for good in French kitchens, or had it become a drag on progress? Even as France's culinary influence was waning, the country continued to churn out talented young chefs; what did they think needed to be done to get French cooking out of its slump? As signs of France's decline continued to accumulate, these and other questions began to weigh on me, and I eventually decided to seek some answers.

A Potted History of French Cuisine

I N EARLY MARCH 2007, on a day when spring's imminent arrival could be felt in the breeze and in the jauntier pace of the sidewalks, I interviewed Guy Savoy at his eponymous Paris restaurant just off the Avenue de Wagram, one of the big boulevards jutting out like spokes from the Arc de Triomphe. Five years earlier, Savoy had earned a third Michelin star, after inexplicably having been denied a promotion for nearly two decades. In the opinion of many seasoned eaters, Michelin's failure to award its highest rating to the very gifted Savoy had been a travesty, among the worst injustices ever perpetrated by a guide that could be as cruel as it was powerful. Now that the prize was his, the fifty-three-year-old Savoy seemed determined to cash in on long-delayed opportunities. He already operated several very successful bistros in Paris, but now he was moving farther afield. In 2006, he had opened an opulent restaurant at Caesars Palace in Las Vegas, and restaurants in Moscow, Dubai, and even Kiev were apparently in the works. Following in the path of Paul Bocuse and other three-star chefs, Savoy was turning himself into an international brand, a *chef d'entreprise* rather than a *chef de cuisine*. He was in effect hanging a sign in his own kitchen with a message reading: "My work here is done."

In light of this, I figured I'd hear a lot of talk about business, perhaps some bravado and bluster, too (the home page of Savoy's Web site included the extravagant claim, "When art is on the menu"), but probably not much about food. Short and roundish, with a wispy salt-and-pepper beard, dark, bushy eyebrows, and a receding thatch of gray hair, Savoy turned out to be quite a bit more charming than I'd anticipated, and more reflective than many of the chefs that I'd met. Indeed, he was an excellent interlocutor, offering detailed, considered answers to almost every question I posed. Even so, the conversation kept drifting back to the commercial side of haute cuisine—the expense of running a restaurant in France, the globalization of the culinary profession, the free-spending clients in Vegas. It was all very interesting, but I couldn't help but wonder if the heart of a chef—of a *chef de cuisine*—still beat within.

In one last bid to steer the discussion toward the business of actually cooking, I mentioned the apprenticeship Savoy had done with the brothers Pierre and Jean Troisgros at their three-star restaurant in the city of Roanne. I commented that training with such legendary figures must have been magical. Savoy nodded his head vigorously and said that it had indeed been so. Here, I expected him to recall a moment of culinary genius he'd witnessed or a nugget of wisdom that Pierre or Jean had imparted one afternoon over coffee and a smoke. Instead, though, he told me that the real magic of Troisgros had lain in the ordinary, the routine—in the quotidian act of taking impeccable ingredients and swiftly, respectfully turning them into food of the most glorious quality. In Savoy's account, this was not merely cooking; it was a ritual suffused with beauty and spirituality. Consider, he said, a freshly caught turbot that has just arrived in the kitchen. "It is a fat, perfect turbot—magnificent to look at, to smell, to touch. It is maybe twenty or thirty years old, with a story of its own. In a matter of minutes, we entirely change its story. We cut it, we season it, we cook it; we instantly turn something that was completely primordial into something refined and sensual; a thing of pleasure. This transformation—for me, that was the magic."

With that pithy but gorgeously evocative description of a fish's last day, Savoy didn't just answer my doubts about his cardiovascular system; he managed to capture the singular genius of French cuisine. It wasn't just the way the French prepared food that set them apart from the rest of humanity; it was the way they thought and talked about food. More than any other nation, the French elevated cooking to a creative art and eating to an exalted hobby. In their hands, food became a source of gratification, a noble calling, a subject of impassioned debate, a means to political power, and a point of national pride. In time, they taught much of the world how to cook and eat, and the triumph of French cuisine became arguably the most benevolent example of imperialism the world has ever known—an imperialist tradition Savoy was now helping to perpetuate. As I sat there looking at this acclaimed chef, swooning not over something he'd sautéed but something he'd said, I asked myself: How did these people get to be so good at food?

It is a question that scholars have been chewing over—often quite literally—for decades now. For a long time, it was believed that the French owed their mastery of food and wine to the Italians, and specifically the Florentine chefs whom Catherine de Médicis, homesick for her native fare, took with her to France when she married Henri II in 1533. But the prevailing wisdom now is that the Italian connection has been exaggerated. The late French philosopher Jean-François Revel called it "le fantôme des Médicis"; his research found that the Italians did nothing more than add a little refinement to the pre-existing court fare, a claim seconded by others who have investigated the matter. The consensus is that a distinctive, modern French cuisine mainly took shape on its own. *Le Cuisinier François*, a cookbook published in 1651 by Burgundian chef François Pierre de La Varenne, is widely credited with being the first literary work to demonstrate "a clear break with medieval food and the recognizable beginning of the modern French cuisine," as Stephen Mennell puts it in his excellent book *All Manners of Food*.

La Varenne was part of a group of talented chefs who transformed French cuisine—which is to say, French court cuisine—during the seventeenth century. They cut back on exotic spices, long a hallmark of aristocratic fare, in favor of domestic herbs and seasonings, such as thyme, parsley, and shallots. During this period, butter became a staple of French sauces, along with meat and pan juices and the combination of fat and flour. *Le Cuisinier François* included a recipe for bouillon, from which the base sauces of French cuisine would later emerge, and recipes for such future classics as *boeuf à la mode* and asparagus with *sauce hollandaise*. The cuisine that emerged during this period wasn't just a uniquely French one; as Jean-Robert Pitte notes in his book *French Gastronomy*, it was also a triumph of northern France over southern—"of the Capetians, of dairy breeding and dairy products over the south."

By the sixteenth century, the Bourbon dynasty was ruling France, and several of the kings were world-class trenchermen, none more so than Louis XIV, who ascended the throne in 1643 and remained there until his death in 1715. In keeping with tradition, the Sun King usually dined by himself at Versailles, surrounded by scores of courtiers (more than three hundred people were involved in preparing and serving his food). The big extravaganza was his midday meal, which might consist of a soup and an appetizer, followed by multiple chickens, turkeys, partridges, pigeons, capons, and meats, all washed down by bowls of fruit and dried preserves. It was during Louis XIV's reign that France became Europe's leading power—military, diplomatic, and cultural. The European upper classes adopted French as their preferred language, while French art, literature, architecture, and scholarship set the standards of excellence. Thanks in no small part to his majesty's prodigious appetite, this influence extended to the dinner table, and French cuisine came to be acknowledged as the continent's finest.

With the French Revolution (1789–1799) and the fall of the ancien régime, many chefs found themselves out of work, and of necessity they began catering to the general public by opening restaurants, which proliferated in Paris in the wake of the political and social upheaval. The same period saw the emergence of France's first truly major chef and the first codifier of French cuisine: Marie-Antoine Carême, known as the cook of kings and the king of cooks. Born in 1783 and trained as a pâtissier, Carême defied the prevailing trend and spent his career working exclusively for wealthy patrons. He cooked for the famed diplomat Talleyrand, and he later did stints in London, as chef for the Prince Regent, and in Saint Petersburg, where he fed Tsar Alexander I.

But though employed as a private chef, Carême, a man of uncommon talent, ambition, and ego, aspired to both modernize and popularize haute cuisine. In the kitchen, his chief aim was to simplify food: He emphasized the use of seasonal ingredients, continued the trend started by La Varenne and his peers of substituting fresh herbs for aggressive spices, and produced lighter sauces intended to complement meats rather than overwhelm them. It was in the realm of sauces that he left his most enduring mark. Sauce-making was already seen as the essential art of French cooking, but it was very much a free-form art, with few if any organizing principles. Carême devised a classification of sauces, breaking them up into four broad categories, each based on a so-called mother sauce: allemande (egg yolks and lemon juice), béchamel (flour and milk), espagnole (meat stock, brown roux, and mirepoix), and velouté (light fish or meat stock and a white roux). These four sauces were not only the foundation of all other sauces, but of modern French cuisine.

Carême died at the age of forty-eight; the poet Laurent Tailhade would later write that he had been felled "by the flame of his genius and the charcoal of the roasting ovens." (In death as in life, he was a trailblazer: the twentieth century would see several leading French chefs die young, done in by the strain.) But he left behind an enormous body of work, not least his magnum opus, *L'Art de la cuisine française au dix-neuvième siècle*. Published in five volumes between 1833 and 1847, it is one of the most ambitious and comprehensive cookbooks ever written, consisting of hundreds of recipes. Within each section of the work, there was a linear progression, each recipe building on the ones that preceded it and setting the table for those that followed. When one thinks of French cuisine, one thinks of order—orderly kitchens, dining rooms, and meals. It was Carême, more than anyone else, who imposed this order.

Carême also invested French cuisine with a powerful chauvinism. His writings were unabashedly nationalistic manifestos that, collectively, amounted to a cultural imperialist's call to arms. Carême believed that French cuisine was superior to all others and didn't hesitate to say so. "O France! My beautiful homeland," he wrote.

"You alone unite in your breast the delights of gastronomy." And it wasn't just that French cuisine was better; Carême bluntly asserted that dishes invented elsewhere were inevitably *made better* by French chefs. His cookbooks contained recipes for a handful of foreign sauces and soups, all of which were given Gallic makeovers and emerged so vastly improved, in Carême's judgment, that they were no longer foreign and had effectively become French.

Carême's literary efforts put him at the vanguard of another important development: food as intellectual fodder. Indeed, his career intersected with those of Jean-Anthèlme Brillat-Savarin and Alexandre Grimod de la Reynière, men of aristocratic backgrounds for whom dining was as much a cerebral pursuit as a restorative one. As Priscilla Parkhurst Ferguson observes in *Accounting for Taste: The Triumph of French Cuisine*, more than any recipe or chef, it was the gastronomic discourse fostered by the writings of Brillat-Savarin and Grimod that cemented "the iconic status of the culinary in French culture."

Born in Paris in 1758, Grimod was the world's first food critic. From 1803 to 1812, Grimod published an annual dining guide called *L'Almanach des Gourmands*. It proved immensely popular; so much so that in 1806, he started a monthly gastronomic newsletter, *Journal des Gourmands and des Belles*, which also attracted a wide audience. A man whose sensibilities were firmly anchored in the pre-Bastille era, Grimod intuited that new money loved nothing more than to parade as old money, and he transmitted "the good taste of the defunct regime" to "the *nouveaux riches* of the Directory, the *parvenus* of the Consultat, and the *arrivistes* of the Empire," as French historian Pascal Ory dryly puts it. In both *L'Almanach* and a later book he authored, *Manuel des amphitryons*, Grimod instructed his bourgeois readers in the art of the table—in things like organizing menus, arranging place settings, and carving meats. In offering such guidance, he was both democratizing haute cuisine and ensuring that this particular vestige of the royal court survived the revolution.

While Grimod focused on the practical, Brillat-Savarin, a lawyer by training, took a philosophical approach to food and wine. *The Physiology of Taste*, which he published in 1825, is the most celebrated gastronomic treatise ever written. The compendious book was a meditation on fine dining, exploring how history, biology, and culture influenced how and what we ate. It was full of now-famous aphorisms ("Tell me what you eat, and I shall tell you what you are") and included a number of charmingly quirky detours, such as a look at the aphrodisiacal properties of truffles. The point of the book was to establish fine dining as a thinking man's activity, as much a mark of cultural refinement as was a love of literature, art, and music. In one of his more sweeping pronouncements, Brillat-Savarin declared, "Animals fill themselves; people eat; the intelligent person alone knows how to eat." With *The Physiology of Taste*, gastronomy was given a highbrow gloss, and gourmandism—defined by Brillat-Savarin as "the passionate, reasoned and habitual preference for objects that flatter taste"—acquired the status of a noble avocation.

But a culture of gourmandism could not have flourished in France without the acquiescence of the church. According to Jean-Robert Pitte, there was, from the early Middle Ages on, a religious divide in France on the question of dining. On one hand, there were clerics who believed that eating and drinking well was an integral, even divinely sanctioned, part of Christian life; they didn't live to eat, but they believed it was acceptable to find enjoyment in food. Arrayed against them were those peddling an ascetic brand of Christianity that made little distinction between the pleasures of the flesh and the pleasures of the table. In their view, food was nothing more than a source of sustenance, and to treat it as more was indeed a sin.

These opposing views had their decisive clash during the Protestant Reformation. French Protestants, known as Huguenots, represented the abstemious school; they decried luxury dining, denounced alcohol consumption, and otherwise tried to stamp out gourmandism. The most famous of their number was the philosopher Jean-Jacques Rousseau; he had no use even for the sense of taste and would just as soon have done without. But a majority of French preferred a sunnier Christianity, one in which the faithful could find sensual pleasure at mealtime and still have their tickets punched to the next world—and, of course, there were well-fed clerics ready to provide theological justification for having one's cake and eating it. "Gourmandism indicates a willing resignation to the orders of the Creator who, having commanded us to eat in order to live, invites us to do so through appetite, sustains us through taste, and rewards us through pleasure," wrote Abbot Migne in 1848.

A century earlier, Cardinal de Bernis, Louis XV's ambassador to the Vatican, had made the same point, albeit rather more amusingly. Asked why he used a good Meursault while saying Mass, he explained that "I would not wish my creator to see me grimace at the moment of communion." The cardinal's choice of a Meursault was symbolically resonant in another way: It was in the village of Meursault, early in the twelfth century, that Cistercian monks were given their first vineyard, by the Duke of Burgundy. As more vineyards came into their possession, they experimented with a number of grapes and ultimately settled on Chardonnay and Pinot Noir, which remain Burgundy's signature varieties. In addition, the monks exhaustively studied variations in soil and exposure among the plots of land they farmed and noted differences in the character and caliber of the wines these plots yielded. In time, they expertly carved up the vineyards so as to match grapes to land. In recognizing that certain parcels produced better wines than others, the Cistercians arrived at an insight that would come to serve as the central organizing principle of French viticulture: *terroir*, which can be loosely translated as "location, location, location." Not only did the ecclesiastical authorities sanction a culture of gourmandism in France; they helped foster it.

By the 1870s, four decades after Carême's death, his new cooking had grown old and it was felt that French cuisine needed an overhaul. It was at this moment that another transformative figure emerged. Georges Auguste Escoffier's reputation would eventually eclipse Carême's, and more than seventy years after his death, he remains France's most celebrated chef. The irony is that he spent most of his career outside of France. Born in 1846 in a village near Nice, he began his culinary training at the age of thirteen, working in a restaurant owned by his uncle. While serving as chef at the Hôtel National in Lucerne, he met a young Swiss entrepreneur, César Ritz, with whom he formed a business partnership that would revolutionize not just the hotel industry, but also (again) haute cuisine.

In the late nineteenth and early twentieth centuries, the first luxury hotels appeared in European cities. It was a period of relative calm and prosperity, and with the proliferation of rail connections on the Continent, it became easy for the affluent to travel to distant cities on business and for pleasure. Accustomed to being pampered at home, they wanted to be no less comfortable on the road, and suitably lavish hotels were established to cater to their whims. Escoffier and Ritz were at the forefront of this development. In 1890, they teamed up at the newly opened Savoy Hotel in London. Nine years later they started their own posh London property, the Carlton, where Escoffier would spend the rest of his career. The two men also collaborated on the Hôtel Ritz in Paris, which welcomed its first guests in 1898.

Cooking for large numbers of people, most of whom now had neither the time nor the desire to spend countless hours at the table, confronted chefs with some unique challenges. It was Escoffier who updated haute cuisine to meet these demands, and in the process he radically altered its preparation and service, and the manner in which it was eaten. For one thing, he completely revamped the organization of professional kitchens. Until this point, kitchen stations essentially functioned as autonomous fiefdoms; each station was responsible for certain dishes and there was generally little interaction between stations. Whatever its virtues, this arrangement was completely unsuited to the high-volume, high-speed cooking required of hotel kitchens. Escoffier kept the stations in place, but instead of assigning them specific preparations, he divided them by specific functions. Thus, the *garde-manger* was responsible for cold dishes, the *saucier* was in charge of sauces, the *rôtisseur* oversaw grilling, roasting, and frying, and on down the line. Indeed, it was an assembly-line approach to cooking, in which several stations typically contributed to a dish. As Stephen Mennell observes in *All Manners of Food*, this emphasis on specialization and interconnectedness was a reflection of the times: Escoffier had brought the industrial revolution into the kitchen, and the function-based division of labor that he introduced has remained standard procedure.

So, too, the changes he introduced to menus and presentation—changes that were also imposed by circumstance, as Escoffier himself acknowledged. "The complicated and sometimes heavy menus," he wrote, "would be unwelcome to the hypercritical appetites so common nowadays; hence the need of a radical change not only in the culinary preparations themselves, but in the arrangements of the menus and the service." Traditional French service, in which all the dishes were delivered simultaneously, had largely given way to *service à la russe*, in which dishes were brought to the table and consumed one at a time. Escoffier took the logical next step and organized his menus by courses: Grouped at the top were appetizers, below which were listed fish and meat dishes, which then gave way to desserts. He also invented the à la carte menu, another concession to the times: It allowed busy diners to construct meals as they wished rather than having to submit to endless banquets.

Escoffier was not just a managerial genius; he was also a gifted and inventive cook who conceived more canonical dishes than had perhaps any chef in history. Although he bemoaned the dining public's preoccupation with novelty and complained of the physical and mental burdens of having to satisfy its seemingly endless appetite for new taste sensations, his imagination was equal to the task. *Tournedos Rossini* and *Peach Melba*, his most famous creations, were just two of many influential preparations that emanated from the kitchens of the Savoy and the Carlton. As Stephen Mennell notes, some of Escoffier's signature dishes, such as Peach Melba, were truly unique; others were twists on classics; and still others were regional peasant dishes given haute-cuisine makeovers. The dishes in this last category spoke to the symbiotic relationship that now existed between haute cuisine and bourgeois fare. The former provided the latter with recipes and instruction; the latter furnished the former with talent (then, as now, top French chefs generally came from the countryside, having received their early tutelage from their mothers and grandmothers) and inspiration (the kind of inspiration that would lead Émile Jung, many years later, to create the aforementioned, marriage-challenging *baeckeofe*).

Like Carême, Escoffier was anxious to simplify haute cuisine— to make preparations less complicated, to achieve greater harmony among ingredients, and to produce more subtle, elegant flavors. "Keep it simple" was his famous dictum. (Of course, in embracing Carême's philosophy, Escoffier was also implicitly critiquing the old master's cooking: The fare that he derided as unbearably heavy and hopelessly antiquated had its origins in Carême's kitchen.) Escoffier built on Carême's legacy in other ways. To Carême's four mother sauces, for instance, he added a fifth: tomato sauce. His five-thousand-recipe doorstop, *Le Guide Culinaire*, published in 1903, supplanted *L'Art de la cuisine française* as the definitive text on French cooking and established Escoffier as the "great codifier" in the words of Julia Child. Thereafter, it was Escoffier's cuisine that was the dominant form, a position it would retain late into the twentieth century. Even now, *Le Guide Culinaire* remains an indispensable reference for young chefs.

During his career, Escoffier trained numerous chefs (and one future revolutionary: Ho Chi Minh is said to have done a pastry *stage* at the Carlton in 1911). Like Carême, he saw food as a means of transmitting Gallic values and influence, and the French chef as a kind of ambassador. "The art of cooking may be one of the more useful forms of diplomacy," he wrote. "Called to every part of the world to organize the restaurant services of the most lavish hotels, I have always been careful to provide French materials, French products, and above all, French personnel. Because the development of French cooking is largely due to thousands of cooks who work in all four corners of the world. They have expatriated to make known, even in the most remote countries, French products and the art of preparing them. It is a great satisfaction for me to have contributed to this development. Throughout my entire career, I have 'sown' some two thousand cooks all over the world. Most of them have founded lines in these countries, and you could say that they are so many grains of wheat sown in uncultivated territories. Today, France harvests the bounty."

And as was true of Carême, Escoffier was convinced that France was uniquely blessed in the quality of its foodstuffs and uniquely disposed to culinary greatness. "I am often asked for reasons why French cooks are superior to those of other countries," he wrote. "The answer, it seems to me, is simple: you only have to realize that the French soil has the privilege of producing, naturally and in abundance, the best vegetables, the best fruits, and the best wines in the world. France also possesses the finest poultry, the most tender meat, and the most delicate and varied game. Its sea coasts provide it with the most beautiful fish and crustaceans. Thus, it is completely natural for the French to become both gourmands and great cooks." By this logic, French mastery in the kitchen wasn't primarily a function of training or traditions; it was mainly the result of superior *terroir*. Those who advanced this notion were explicitly claiming that France, insofar as gastronomy was concerned, was the Chosen Land—God's Pantry. The implications were clear: In the realm of cuisine, France had certain insurmountable advantages. This conviction fostered immense pride; later, it would encourage complacency.

After three decades in London, Escoffier retired to Monte Carlo, where he died in 1935. By then, another revolutionary influence had arrived on the French food scene: the Michelin Guide. The tire company, founded in 1888, had begun publishing a traveler's guide to France in 1900. In 1926, Michelin introduced its now-famous star system, awarding individual *étoiles* to restaurants whose food merited recommendation. In 1931, the Guide added a more complex system of ratings for food. A single star now denoted "a very good restaurant in its class"; two stars were bestowed for "excellent cooking, worth a detour"; and three stars were given to restaurants with "exceptional cuisine, worth a special journey."

Although Michelin's timing was not ideal—France, like the United States, was then in the throes of the Great Depression, and another war loomed just over the horizon—the union of motoring and meals proved to be a masterstroke, not only for Michelin (the publicity generated by the Guide was a boon for tire sales) but also for French gastronomy. The advent of the automobile during the 1920s gave city dwellers easy access to the French countryside, and all the urbanites now hitting the roads needed places to eat and the skinny on the best local food. The rural hospitality industry flourished, especially along the main north-south route between Paris and the Riviera. The Guide became an invaluable resource for the just-passing-through tourist, calling his attention to the finest tables in Burgundy, Lyon, the Rhône Valley, Provence, and the Côte d'Azur.

In 1933, Michelin awarded three stars to Fernand Point's La Pyramide, a restaurant in the town of Vienne, south of Lyon. Point, born in 1897, was a brilliant chef, and on the back of those stars, La Pyramide became perhaps the most celebrated restaurant in French history. Joseph Wechsberg, in his classic book *Blue Trout and Black Truffles*, wrote of making numerous pilgrimages to Vienne "undaunted by distances, borders, and custom guards. Each meal has been a memorable event—one of those rare moments when you know that it couldn't be any better ... Point is incontestably the greatest chef on earth. His perfection, like the perfection of Toscanini, is a blend of hard thinking, much work, and a dash of genius." Point was revered for such dishes as *queues d'écrevisses en gratin, turbot au champagne, volaille de Bresse truffées en vessie*, and his famous *gâteau marjolaine* (read it and drool: ganache, vanilla cream, and hazelnut cream set atop layers of almond meringue). He was also cherished for his hospitality, playfulness, and wit. It was Point who offered possibly the sagest advice on how to choose a restaurant: "Go to the kitchen to shake the chef's hand. If he is thin, have second thoughts about eating there; if he is thin and sad, flee." For the record, the six-foot four-inch Point tipped the scales at a jolly 365 pounds. It was not his corpulence, however, that earned him the nickname "Magnum"; credit for that belongs instead to the magnum of Champagne that he drank every day.

Point, who died in 1955 at age fifty-eight (it was the girth that did him in), didn't produce a compendious cookbook à la Carême and Escoffier; a posthumous collection of his recipes stands as his only contribution to the literature. His contribution to French cuisine's human capital, however, remains unrivaled. In the decade between the end of the Second World War and his death, Point trained the most glittering collection of talent ever assembled at one stove, a roster that included future three-star chefs Louis Outhier, François Bise, Claude Peyrot, Jean and Pierre Troisgros (who would mentor not only Guy Savoy, but also another future three-star recipient, Bernard Loiseau), and Paul Bocuse, who came to be considered Point's greatest student, his surrogate son, and his heir. So coveted was a spot in Point's atelier that even the reject pile included future legends. A young Alsatian cook named André Soltner, having heard that La Pyramide was the place to work, once wrote a letter to Point requesting a job. He was turned down, and he eventually ended up migrating to New York and opening an establishment there called Lutèce, which became America's most lauded French restaurant.

Like all chefs of his generation, Point was strongly influenced by Escoffier, and in keeping with the prevailing style, his food was unabashedly rich (he famously said, "Butter! Give me butter! Always butter!"). However, Point departed from convention in several important ways. For one thing, he served rustic local specialties alongside his more elaborate, Escoffian creations. He was also fanatical about freshness, which might sound unremarkable now but was a major innovation at the time. In the 1930s, top restaurants generally didn't change their menus to reflect what was available in the market, nor did they hesitate to serve dishes that had been prepared the day before. Point would have none of that; he did much of his own shopping, bought whatever looked best and adjusted his menu accordingly, and insisted on making everything from scratch each morning. This emphasis on freshness would later serve as the cornerstone of the nouvelle cuisine revolution, which was led by some of La Pyramide's most famous alumni.

Aux Armes, Cuisiniers!

Fᴿᴏᴍ ᴘʜᴏᴛᴏꜱ, ɪ ᴋɴᴇᴡ that the exterior of Paul Bocuse's eponymous restaurant in the village of Collonges au Mont d'Or, near Lyon, was painted in flamboyant shades of red, yellow, and orange and that it was adorned with decals of roosters, cakes, and roast chickens. But seeing it for the first time in person, on a sunny November morning in 2006, I decided it wasn't quite as hideous as the pictures had led me to believe; it just looked like a particularly colorful music box. Nor, contrary to my expectations, was the restaurant purely a monument to Bocuse. The courtyard was enclosed by a long wall decorated with murals of Antoine Carême, Fernand Point, the Troisgros brothers, and—funnily enough—Julia Child.

The restaurant's bar was a shrine, but it was a shrine to Point; photos of Bocuse's mentor filled the room. Bocuse hadn't entirely cut himself out of the scene: Numerous pictures of him were scattered around the restaurant. One framed image stood out: Entitled "The Last Supper," it showed Bocuse and a dozen other prominent French chefs, all dressed in tan sackcloth and seated at a long table bearing glasses of wine and loaves of bread. Bocuse, cast in the role of Jesus, was at the center of the shot, surrounded by the twelve "apostles" and gazing benevolently at the camera with his hands resting on the table and open to the sky. For all its cheesiness, the photo perfectly captured Bocuse's place in the gastronomic firmament. He was France's most famous chef and was widely regarded as the chief custodian of a culinary tradition stretching back hundreds of years.

The elderly man with puffy raccoon eyes who shuffled into the lounge that morning bore only a passing resemblance to the dashing figure in the picture. But despite his frail appearance, the eighty-year-old chef maintained a schedule that would have exhausted people half his age; just hours after meeting with me, he would be off on a four-day trip to Japan, where he was considered to be a virtual deity. Dressed in black trousers and a black sweater, Bocuse greeted me warmly and directed me to a table in the middle of the room. I had been told that he liked to put on a show for visiting journalists, and it didn't take long for the extravaganza to begin. About five minutes into the interview, a reporter and a photographer from the newspaper *Le Figaro* arrived and were ushered into the kitchen. (Evidently, Bocuse had been double-booked for the morning.) A few minutes later, "Monsieur Paul," as he was called, was summoned to join them. After another ten minutes, the kitchen doors swung open and I was beckoned inside. There, I found Bocuse standing behind an island counter in his chef's whites and toque, meticulously arranging a half-dozen or so fully feathered dead birds and rabbits. In this garb, he looked like another major religious figure: The creaseless, full-length white apron and the way that it clung to his body called to mind papal vestments.

It turned out the *Figaro* team was there to shoot a holiday spread featuring the great man. For about fifteen minutes, the kitchen came to a halt as Bocuse's crew gathered around him to pose. The veteran chef needed no coaching: As soon as the camera started clicking, he tilted his head slightly upward and, suddenly, he was no longer the pope but the famous *coq gaulois*, the rooster whose imperious manner symbolized French pride and hauteur. The kitchen scene finished, Bocuse led me and the *Figaro* pair back to the bar, where he instructed a waiter to bring a bottle of wine. I assumed we were going to have a mid-morning aperitif, and we did. But the wine was also intended as a prop for the next set of photos, this one of Bocuse *à table*, raising a glass in celebration. After snapping those pictures, the photographer asked me to sit next to Bocuse and to clink glasses with him. I did as told. "No, look each other in the eyes, like lovers," he commanded with a laugh. I lifted my glass again and cast a sheepish glance at Bocuse. I was stunned by what greeted me—a facial expression so amorous that for a moment I feared he was going to try to lock lips. The man knew how to play the camera.

By the time the photo session wrapped up, it was past noon. Bocuse suggested that we head to the dining room and chat over lunch. He ordered for me but decided not to have anything himself, which turned out to be a wise choice (but then, he was trading on inside information): The food was awful. It was no secret that the restaurant, first awarded three stars in 1965, had slipped, and it was generally assumed that Michelin continued to bestow its highest rating on it only out of respect for Bocuse. Even so, I was dumbstruck by how bad my lunch was. Every dish was overwrought and plodding, none more so than Bocuse's homage to his mentor, the *filets de sole aux nouilles Fernand Point*, which consisted of a piece of tasteless fish submerged in a cream sauce thicker than plaster of Paris and flanked by a small pile of gummy noodles. Forget Point; this was a parody of Escoffian cuisine. No one served food like this in France anymore, and it was especially strange to find it in the restaurant of the most celebrated figure of the nouvelle cuisine revolution. Wasn't this the sort of gut-busting, artery-clogging fare that Bocuse and his fellow rebels had sought to extirpate? Indeed it was, and they had succeeded—but their success had had little to do with Bocuse. Although he made himself synonymous with nouvelle cuisine, Bocuse's creative input had been slight. His real contribution had been to redefine what it meant to be a chef, an innovation that did not necessarily redound to the benefit of French cuisine.

These days, the nouvelle cuisine era, which began in the late 1960s and reached its apogee in the mid-1970s, tends to be depicted as an embarrassing chapter for French gastronomy, a period marked by comically small portions and absurd flavor combinations—food that is as cringe-inducing now as bell-bottoms, disco, and other emblems of that regrettable time. But nouvelle cuisine has been unjustly maligned. For one thing, it liberated a generation of French chefs from having to spend their lives replicating the greatest hits of yesteryear; they were Escoffier's progeny, but they were no longer his prisoners. Escaping Escoffier was the driving motive behind nouvelle cuisine. The

American Journal of Sociology is not the most obvious place to look for an exegesis of France's food revolution, but in 2003 it published an insightful look at the movement's intellectual foundation. The authors, Hayagreeva Rao, Philippe Monin, and Rodolphe Durand, explained that Escoffier's towering influence had shackled several generations of French chefs and denied them creative independence. A chef might own his restaurant, but he couldn't be his own man at the stove; his role was simply to "translate the intentions or prescriptions of Escoffier's guide into products. Chefs under classical cuisine lacked the freedom to create and invent dishes, and the nouvelle cuisine movement sought to make chefs into innovators rather than mere technicians." It helped that French diners were also in the mood for something different. The public was becoming increasingly health-conscious, and haute cuisine was now perceived as oppressively heavy (a recurring theme in French culinary history).

But these developments in themselves would only have produced incremental changes; what turned the mood in France's kitchens rebellious was the upheaval that swept the country in 1968. The student riots in May of that year, and the nationwide strike that followed, drove President Charles de Gaulle from office and nearly sparked a second French Revolution. The churning political environment triggered an uprising in the cultural realm. Like the student protesters, writers, critics, artists, and filmmakers rebelled against what they saw as a crushing authoritarianism at the heart of French society, and the result was an outpouring of avant-gardism. The guiding impulse was a desire to be unshackled from tradition, to no longer be bound by the Old Way of Doing Things, to have freedom to create.

To young chefs, stuck making tired dishes handed down by long-dead masters, this talk of liberation was seductive, and they soon began a joyous insurrection of their own. What distinguished nouvelle cuisine from some of the other cultural irruptions of the period, the *American Journal of Sociology* article went on to point out, was that it was led by insiders—by French cuisine's most promising talents, men with impeccable pedigrees who were already assuming leadership roles within the fraternity of French chefs. The desire for change among figures like Michel Guérard, Alain Chapel, Jean Delaveyne, Roger Vergé, Alain Senderens, and Jean and Pierre Troisgros gave nouvelle cuisine instant legitimacy.

What also set nouvelle cuisine apart was the central role that food journalists played in defining and popularizing it. Indeed, it was as much a journalistic movement as a culinary one, and its foremost chroniclers, Henri Gault and Christian Millau, became nearly as famous as the chefs they wrote about. Gault and Millau were Parisian journalists who had worked together from the early 1960s. In 1969, they started a monthly magazine called *Le Nouveau Guide Gault-Millau*, which in addition to reviewing restaurants and calling attention to the chefs doing the most interesting New Cooking also provided the ideological underpinnings to France's gastronomic revolution. For Gault and Millau, nouvelle cuisine was a revolt against the conservatism that had settled over France's kitchens—a conservatism that they blamed in large part on the Michelin Guide, which they viewed as a reactionary influence that had turned high-end cooking into a congealed bore. With their distinctive brand of restaurant criticism—punchy, open-minded, iconoclastic—they sought to knock Michelin from its plinth; to wean chefs and diners of their habit of "slouching toward Bibendum," as they put it.

But Gault and Millau were not above a little imperiousness of their own, especially as their prominence grew. In 1973, the same year they issued their first restaurant guide for France, they published the Ten Commandments of nouvelle cuisine:

1. Thou shall not overcook
2. Thou shall use fresh, quality products
3. Thou shall lighten thy menu
4. Thou shall not be systematically modernistic
5. Thou shall seek out what the new techniques can bring you
6. Thou shall eliminate brown and white sauces
7. Thou shall not ignore dietetics
8. Thou shall not cheat on thy presentation

9. Thou shall be inventive
10. Thou shall not be prejudiced

It was a manifesto that invited mockery, and mockery gleefully accepted. It was widely noted, for instance, that nouvelle cuisine was hardly an original concept—that many of these same "revolutionary" dicta had also characterized earlier outbreaks of New Cooking in France. As the British food writer Elizabeth David archly put it, "Nouvelle cuisine then, as now, meant lighter food, less of it, costing more." The skimpy portions (which were made to appear even smaller by the fashion of using oversized plates and bowls) and the hefty checks rankled many critics and customers. Nouvelle cuisine also gave rise to some truly hideous cooking. Lesser talents attempted to mimic the nouvelle stylings of Guérard, Chapel, and company, and the results were often uproariously bad. Meats and fish were found floating in raspberry sauces, with kiwis inevitably garnishing the plate. Atrocities like these were what gave nouvelle cuisine a bad name.

But every revolution generates excesses; the real test is what they produce of lasting value, and on that score, nouvelle cuisine yielded quite a lot. It was, firstly, a technological revolution. French chefs began using blenders, food processors, microwave and steam ovens, and other devices that allowed for more precise, less labor-intensive cooking. These new tools were complemented by new ideas about what and how to cook. Reflecting the movement's roots in the kitchen of La Pyramide, freshness and seasonality were the mantras of nouvelle cuisine: This was market-driven cooking in a way that traditional haute cuisine (Fernand Point excepted) had not been. With leading chefs regularly traveling abroad now and eager to demonstrate the inquisitiveness that Gault and Millau had prescribed, exotic spices came back into vogue after being shunned for two centuries, and there was greater receptiveness to foreign ingredients and influences in general. Japanese cuisine was a particular source of inspiration; many chefs were struck by the simplicity of the presentations and the emphasis on freshness and returned to France eager to apply these ideas to their own efforts. At the same time, new uses were found for more familiar ingredients. Nouvelle cuisine popularized duck breasts, for instance, and the now-ubiquitous *magret de canard* is one of its more obvious (and delicious) legacies. High-end cooking became crunchier and healthier: Chefs eased up on the butter, flour, and cream, made more use of natural juices, stopped cooking fish and vegetables to death, and sought to produce dishes that would send diners home feeling sated but with their belts still buckled tight.

The most dramatic expression of this new health-consciousness, and the most famous innovation of the nouvelle-cuisine epoch, was Michel Guérard's *cuisine minceur* (loosely, "slimming cuisine"). Guérard, a prodigiously talented chef who first achieved renown in Paris in the mid-1960s, had moved to the spa town of Eugénie-les-Bains, in the Pyrenees foothills, in 1974. Inspired by the setting and by the growing demand for lighter fare, Guérard conceived an entirely new idiom: low-cal haute cuisine. It included original creations—mousseline of crayfish with watercress sauce—but also featured classics such as *blanquette de veau*, which Guérard retooled into what was essentially an upscale Weight Watcher's entrée. The genius of *cuisine minceur* was in finding ways to strip the calories out but keep the flavors in: Instead of flour, butter, and cream, sauces were assembled from vegetables, herbs, and olive oil, yet they were made to taste as rich and substantial as the real stuff.

Word of Guérard's alchemy traveled widely, and his cookbook *La Grande Cuisine Minceur*, was an international sensation. In 1977, a French chef named Michel Richard opened a pastry shop in Los Angeles and was besieged by foodies who mistakenly thought he was Michel Guérard. They would show up with copies of *La Grande Cuisine Minceur* and ask Richard to sign it; he told them that they had the wrong guy, but many of them wouldn't be deterred, and he ended up autographing a number of books. Writing in the *New York Review of Books*, Alexander Cockburn boiled the dietetic message of *cuisine minceur*, and by extension nouvelle cuisine, down to its crude but joyous essence: "Eat like a hog and stay healthy."

But this period also produced some landmark dishes. Probably the most famous was the Troisgros brothers' *l'escalope de saumon à l'oseille*, or salmon in sorrel cream sauce, which departed from custom in several important ways: The fish was cut scaloppine-style, it was flash-cooked and left rare on the inside, and the sauce contained not a drop of flour or butter (there was, however, a little cream—nouvelle cuisine didn't entirely dispense with the good stuff). The quick dip in the pan left the salmon tasting as if it had just been plucked from the stream, and the light sauce had a garden-fresh tanginess to match. In keeping with the spirit of the times, nouvelle cuisine also yielded some truly subversive twists. Guérard and Alain Chapel both put salads on their menus, which was unheard of then for Michelin-starred restaurants. More provocative still, Guérard dared to mix his humble greens with foie gras, while Chapel studded his with lobster. Thus was the revolution sliced, diced, tossed, and served.

Conspicuously absent from discussions of nouvelle cuisine's culinary legacy is Paul Bocuse. This is no accident: As cooking goes, he was not a central figure. Christian Millau, interviewed three decades after the nouvelle cuisine starburst, insisted that Bocuse was "never included" in the movement and was just a reasonably good classical chef. This might seem uncharitable of Millau (and a bit of revisionist history, too; after all, the Gault Millau guide named Bocuse to its Chef of the Century list in 1989), had not Bocuse himself provided a wealth of evidence to support this claim. On a visit to New York at the peak of the nouvelle cuisine craze, Bocuse confided to the expatriated French chef Jacques Pépin that he didn't understand what the whole thing was about, and in the years since the revolution fizzled, he has missed few opportunities to disparage it. When I asked Bocuse, over my distinctly un-nouvelle lunch, what he thought had been the big, animating idea behind nouvelle cuisine, he immediately quipped, "Nothing on the plate, everything on the check," and burst out laughing. Something told me I wasn't the first journalist to hear that line. So how did Bocuse become the most acclaimed chef of the nouvelle cuisine era—the one who graced the cover of *Time* and was personally awarded the Légion d'Honneur by the president of France?

It was mainly a triumph of showmanship. Bocuse was an accomplished chef, but he was an even better entertainer and self-promoter. Millau, who years later would write a satirical novel featuring a chef named Paul Baratin (*baratin* translates roughly as "carnival barker"), once traveled to Florida with Bocuse and spent an evening at a garish themed restaurant near Disney World. Bocuse was so smitten with the scene—the big steaks, the cowboys, the dancing girls—that Millau finally piped up, "Paul, I'm afraid you missed your calling in life." Bocuse nodded in agreement and seemed to really mean it. According to Millau, Bocuse made himself the face of nouvelle cuisine because he was the most *médiatique* of his contemporaries and wherever the spotlight went, he followed and made sure that it shined brightest on him. "He always wanted to be number one," says Millau.

Bocuse used the hype surrounding nouvelle cuisine to turn himself into a global brand. Over the years he would establish frozen food lines in France and Japan, a chain of brasseries in the Lyon area, and restaurants in Tokyo, Hong Kong, Melbourne, and, yes, Disney World. To be sure, his empire-building didn't only benefit him; French cuisine also profited from it. The hospitality school that he founded, L'Institut Paul Bocuse, became an important incubator of culinary aptitude. In 1987, he started the Bocuse d'Or competition, in which teams of chefs representing countries from around the world battle each other in a multiple-day cook-off, and this event is now considered the Olympics of food and haute cuisine's biggest international stage. Above all, his bonhomie and bravado made Bocuse an outstanding ambassador for France and French cooking, a point vividly illustrated in the photos that line the walls at Collonges au Mont d'Or.

However, in pursuing these far-flung interests, he ceased to have a direct hand in the food that went out under his name and thereby helped create a new template for the culinary profession: the chef manqué, discharging the financial affairs of his restaurant and providing "editorial" guidance but leaving the cooking entirely to underlings. This took the idea of liberation far beyond what the nouvelle cuisine revolution had set out to achieve. Nouvelle cuisine was about creative freedom, but with Bocuse, it became freedom to not create—to abandon the kitchen. His absenteeism was a source of controversy and, on at least one occasion, hilarity. In a joint appearance with Bocuse on French television, Mimi Sheraton of the *New York Times* facetiously suggested that, like the flag that flies over Buckingham Palace when the Queen is at home, a flag should fly above Bocuse's restaurant when he was in residence. Bocuse was so incensed that as soon as the show ended, he lurched at Sheraton and tried to tear off her wig and mask (this was back in the day when major food critics made an effort to conceal their identities). He missed, and she ended up pushing him to the ground.

Within the culinary fraternity, however, Bocuse set an alluring example. He demonstrated that not only could chefs escape the grimy, grinding business of making food; they could become wealthy and famous in the process. They could act and be paid like captains of industry and treated like rock stars. For men who had spent decades hunched over hot stoves, often at great cost to their health and happiness, this was an enticing prospect. In time, economic necessity would oblige many French chefs to pursue outside interests—to take on consulting gigs, to open additional restaurants, and to otherwise stray from their kitchens. Initially, though, it was a lifestyle choice, and it was Bocuse who showed the way. Whether out of need, desire, or both, truant chefs became increasingly prevalent in the 1980s and '90s, and this was undoubtedly a factor in the diminished creativity, and perhaps also quality, of French cuisine by the turn of the century. French chefs would deny that the ancillary activities had any such effect, and they would scoff at the suggestion that Bocuse somehow led the profession astray; to them, he is a hero. But Pierre Gagnaire, one of the few truly innovative French chefs of recent vintage, revealed more than he perhaps intended when I asked him about Bocuse's legacy. He lauded Bocuse's panache and his fidelity to the métier. But about his food, Gagnaire admitted, "I'm not impressed so much."

A few months after my visit to Bocuse, I had lunch at Restaurant Alain Chapel. Like Bocuse's flagship, it was located just north of Lyon, in the village of Mionnay, and likewise on a heavily traveled thoroughfare. But that's where the similarities ended. In contrast to Bocuse's gaudy palace, Chapel was painted a quiet shade of yellow with green awnings, and a simple outdoor garden led to a sparsely elegant dining room. The décor reflected Chapel's personality, the antithesis of Bocuse's. He was a quiet, cerebral man (his favorite recreation was taking long walks in the nearby woods with his beloved dog) with a poetic spirit. That spirit manifested itself in his cookbook *La cuisine, c'est beaucoup plus que des recettes*. Recalling the foods that he ate in his youth, he wrote,

Rye bread, broad bean soup, sautéed apples (delicious dumplings), butter and cheeses from the high mountain pastures, they all testified to an impoverished cuisine, resolutely lacking in all disguise, all artifice, all magic. Something resolutely material ... at a table without crystal or table manners, I learned that cooking is much more than recipes. It is the products, first and above all, and the feelings that are no doubt rooted in the landscape, the faces, a familiar everyday life, a happiness more ample than the table. The sincerity of beings falling somewhere on this side of economic constraints and the game of appearances. The sincerity of beings like that of things, of broad beans or of rye.

Chapel trained at La Pyramide (but following Point's death) and returned to Mionnay in 1967 to take over the bistro, La Mère Charles, that his parents had opened when he was a child. (He would rename it Restaurant Alain Chapel in 1976.) At the time, the restaurant had one Michelin star; it was awarded a second in 1969 and a third in 1973. The speed with which Chapel was promoted spoke to his talent: He was a brilliant chef whose gifts were perhaps matched only by Guérard. Gault Millau said that a meal at Chapel was like "a symphony." Craig Claiborne, the restaurant critic of the *New York Times*, described Chapel's *gâteau de foies blondes*, a blend of puréed chicken liver and beef marrow in a lobster and cream sauce, as "one of the absolute cooking glories of this generation." In keeping with the experimental ethos of nouvelle cuisine,

Chapel's food was innovative, even audacious (lobster in a salad was ballsy indeed), but there were also earthy, humble dishes—stuffed calves' ears with fried parsley, for instance—that evinced the same rootedness that he had experienced in the foods of his childhood. Above all, he was guided by Curnonsky's deceptively simple maxim: Good cooking is when things taste of what they are. Chapel was fanatical about the quality of ingredients—"the products." Nouvelle cuisine stressed freshness, but he took it to an extreme, even cultivating his own fruits and vegetables. A few vivid flavors in complete harmony with one another—that was what he endeavored to put on the plate.

Mionnay became an essential destination for young cooks looking to hone their talent. When Pierre Troisgros sent his son Michel off to acquire some additional seasoning, he had him work for Guérard; for the great Swiss chef Frédy Girardet, another lion of nouvelle cuisine; and for Chapel. In the late 1970s, a ferociously ambitious cook from the French southwest named Alain Ducasse spent two years at Chapel's side; he would go on to earn three stars himself and become the most recognized chef of his generation, success that he would attribute in large measure to his stint with Chapel. When I asked Gagnaire, after he had dismissed Bocuse's food, which older chefs had influenced him, he immediately said Chapel. The acclaimed American chef Thomas Keller has also cited him as a source of inspiration.

For Chapel, the nouvelle cuisine movement may have been liberating in a creative sense, but the artistic freedom did nothing to alleviate the stress of the job. In 1990, while visiting friends in the city of Avignon on a day that the restaurant was closed, Chapel suffered a heart attack and died. He was fifty-three and left behind his wife, Suzanne, and two young sons, David and Romain. He thus became the second major figure of the nouvelle cuisine revolution to go to a premature grave; seven years earlier, Jean Troisgros had died of a heart attack at the age of fifty-six. Suzanne Chapel decided to keep the restaurant open; she took charge of the dining room and installed Chapel's longtime protégé, Philippe Jousse, as chef. On word of Chapel's passing, Michelin demoted the restaurant to two stars. Bernard Naegellen, the

Guide's director at the time, later told journalist Rudolph Chelminski that this was a mark of respect for the deceased chef, that to have left the third star would have been tantamount to saying that "he had counted for nothing in the excellence of his restaurant." Seventeen years later, the third star had still not been restored.

Before lunch, I spoke with Jousse. A lean, boyish forty-seven-year-old whose age was betrayed only by the dark circles under his eyes, Jousse was known to be a great talent who had sacrificed his own aspirations in order to keep his mentor's restaurant and memory alive. He insisted he wouldn't have had it any other way. "I've stayed here because this is where I learned everything," he said. "When Madame Chapel asked me to stay, I couldn't say no, because I couldn't bear to see this restaurant disappear." He admitted he was frustrated by the lack of a third star, and wondered if perhaps Michelin regarded the restaurant as a shrine to Chapel. "We don't know what the reason is; we go to see Michelin regularly—nothing." But more distressing, he said, was the lack of interest in the French press; no one wrote about Chapel anymore. He said he and Madame Chapel were partly to blame for this. "We don't know how to communicate," he said quietly.

Suzanne Chapel was a woman still in mourning. She was rail-thin, with willowy blonde hair that was turning gray, and the lines of her face were etched in sorrow. She'd had a previous career, as a nurse, and even now, many years later, she moved uneasily through the restaurant, clearly uncomfortable in the role of *patronne*. She admitted as much. "No, I can't say there is a pleasure in doing this; I had another *métier*," she told me. "But we had people who depended on us, people we were responsible for, so it was important that the restaurant stay open." She, too, expressed frustration with Michelin and chalked up the restaurant's inability to recapture the third star to "political influence," though she didn't elaborate.

It was all pretty sobering, and the melancholy followed me to the table. But the airy dining room, with its pretty, floral-patterned wallpaper, lifted my spirits, and by the time I'd finished my glass of Champagne, I was ready to eat. Jousse had promised to serve me some of Chapel's specialties, and the first course was straight from the master's book. It consisted of three plump, bright-green asparagus spears, served alongside a poached egg, its yolk flaming orange, and surrounded by morels and chunks of crayfish. It was a simple, early-spring dish, but the flavors were as vibrant as the colors, and they exuded an overwhelming sense of place—of the soils and waters that nurtured them, but also of the restaurant itself. Maybe I was projecting, but it really felt as if Chapel was on the plate.

Daniel Boulud, a native of the Lyon area who had gone on to become an enormously successful chef in New York, once told me that Chapel was the John F. Kennedy of French cuisine—an iconic figure struck down at the zenith of his career. And as with Kennedy's death, Chapel's passing seemed to represent not only lost promise, but lost possibilities. Chapel was a businessman, as attentive to the bottom line as other chefs. Like Bocuse, he went to Japan, opening a restaurant in the city of Kobe in 1981, and it is conceivable that had he lived, he would have pursued additional projects. It was said that he hoped to one day have a restaurant in the United States, maybe in Florida.

But up until his death, and apart from the restaurant in Japan, Chapel remained anchored to Mionnay and dedicated to his craft. Guy Gâteau, who worked for Chapel from 1973 to 1980 and rose to be the number one in the kitchen, told me that as the years went by, Chapel stepped away from the stove, but he remained close to the flame—closer, certainly, than Bocuse. He could be found at the expediting station, exhorting his *brigade*, and the creative spark never went out. Working with Gâteau and Ducasse and other gifted lieutenants, Chapel never stopped trying to push his cuisine, and, by extension, French cuisine, to new heights of refinement, ingenuity, and pleasure. For French gastronomy, said Gâteau, Chapel and Bocuse "were the two faces of Janus." The great Rhône winemaker Jean-Louis Chave, whose father, Gérard, was one of Chapel's closest friends, put it somewhat more directly: "There were two ways things could have gone, the Chapel way or the Bocuse way. Chapel died, and Bocuse won."

*   *   *

The mid-1970s also proved to be a turning point in the world of French wine. In 1970, Steven Spurrier, a twenty-nine-year-old Englishman, purchased a wine shop on the Place de la Madeleine in Paris and soon expanded it to include a wine school. One of the first people he hired was Patricia Gallagher, an American expatriate working in Paris as a freelance journalist. Over the next few years, Spurrier and Gallagher traveled widely to source the most interesting wines and worked tirelessly to promote both the shop and the school. Hoping to tap into the excitement over America's bicentennial celebration, they decided to organize a tasting pitting some top Burgundies and Bordeaux against a handful of California Cabernet Sauvignons and Chardonnays. Spurrier and Gallagher assembled a distinguished group of participants—all of them French—that included Aubert de Villaine, the owner of Domaine de la Romanée-Conti, Burgundy's preeminent estate; Odette Kahn, the editor of France's leading wine publication, *La Revue du Vin de France*; and Jean-Claude Vrinat, the owner of Taillevent, a three-star restaurant in Paris.

The tasting was held on the afternoon of May 24, 1976, at the InterContinental Hotel in Paris. Twenty wines were poured—ten reds, ten whites—and all were served blind, with the judges unaware of the identities of the wines in their glasses. The white wines were tasted first, and when Spurrier announced the results, the sound of jaws hitting tables echoed across Paris: The 1973 Chateau Montelena Chardonnay, from Napa Valley, had finished first, ahead of one *grand cru* white Burgundy and three other venerable French whites. The reds were tasted next, and shortly before six P.M. Spurrier dropped another bombshell: The 1973 Stag's Leap Wine Cellars Cabernet Sauvignon had come out on top, besting a group that included two Bordeaux first growths, the 1970 Château Mouton Rothschild and the 1970 Château Haut-Brion.

The so-called Judgment of Paris made headlines around the world: The United States beats France *at wine!* (Three decades after the fact, the tasting remained a source of fascination; in 2005, former *Time* magazine correspondent George Taber, who was the only reporter at the InterContinental that afternoon, published a book about the tasting, titled *Judgment of Paris: California vs. France and the Historic 1976 Paris Tasting That Revolutionized Wine*, which quickly yielded a pair of Hollywood scripts.) Overlooked amid all the panting were a few salient facts: Blind tastings often produced surprising results, and California wines tended to show better in their youth than did French wines. To proclaim, as some did, that the tasting had revealed French wines to be overrated was silly. Nonetheless, the Judgment of Paris showed that other places were capable of making good wine and that French superiority could no longer simply be assumed.

France in Crisis

I T WAS A BRIGHT, warm early May morning, and Marc Sibard was seated on a bench outside his Paris wine store, Les Caves Augé, a glass of Alsatian Muscat in one hand and a lit cigarette in the other. Les Caves Augé, located on the Boulevard Haussmann, was said to be the city's oldest wine shop; with its comically narrow aisles and chockablock displays, it was undoubtedly the city's most cluttered one, but also probably its finest. Augé had a sensational selection, with all the most sought-after names from all the major wine regions of France. Dauvissat, d'Angerville, Lafon, Joguet, Selosse—they were all here; you just had to find them. The forty-four-year-old Sibard, Augé's proprietor for nearly two decades, was short, bald, and stocky, with a graying soul patch on his chin and a pugnacious personality to match his bulldog aspect. He and I got along well, but some Americans apparently found him difficult. Part of the problem, it seemed, was that he was unwilling to allow rich tourists to cherry-pick Augé's choicest bottles—things like Jean-Louis Chave's Hermitage, a much-sought wine from the northern Rhône Valley. It was a stand I personally admired but that had, unsurprisingly, sent more than a few frustrated New York collectors skulking away and muttering darkly about the Second World War and ungrateful frogs.

On this morning, Sibard was talking not about troublesome clients but about the problems of doing business in France. He had a thriving enterprise in the heart of Paris, but the French government seemed determined to throw up as many barriers to success as it could. "In France," he said, "the better you do, the more they try to fuck you,

43

the more they want you to die." Business owners had to contend with exorbitant taxes, inflexible labor laws, and a morass of burdensome regulations. He gave me an example that he considered particularly outrageous. "A few years ago," Sibard said, "they put in place a law that says wine shops cannot display AOC wines next to *vins de pays*." In the official hierarchy of French wines, AOCs were considered premium offerings, *vins de pays* were one level of quality down, and *vins de table* occupied the lowest rung. In reality, the classifications were not quite so well delineated: There were lots of awful AOC wines, and there were many excellent *vins de pays* and even some first-rate *vins de table*. Indeed, some of the best wines being made in places like the Loire Valley were classified as *vins de pays* or *vins de table*. Augé stocked a number of these, and both as a practical matter and as a sales strategy, it made no sense to segregate them from the AOC bottles.

But to resist doing so was now a punishable offense. "If customs finds you keeping the wines next to each other, you pay a fine," Sibard said. The idea that some bureaucrat, working in the bowels of a French ministry, had decided that it was the government's role to dictate how Les Caves Augé displayed its wines was unfathomable to him. "Can you imagine this bullshit?" he asked, his voice rising in exasperation. Pointing at the open wooden crates splayed about the inside of his shop, he said, "If they come here, I'm dead; it's such a mess in there." In his view, everything about the way France now operated was designed to stifle ambition and thwart initiative. "We don't motivate people to excel," he said. "It is all about the lowest common denominator now, and what we get is mediocrity instead." He paused briefly to admire an attractive female passerby, asked an assistant to fetch the bottle of Muscat so that we could top ourselves up, and resumed his peroration. "But if you say the system is fucked too loudly, customs will be visiting you the next morning," he said, shaking his head. "Do you want to know something? France is the last Communist country on earth."

Sibard was exaggerating; surely he knew that Vietnam and Cuba still swore allegiance to Marx and Lenin, and had I pressed him, he probably would have admitted that, no, France was not truly Communist. But his was the sort of remark that one heard frequently now in France, and it contained at least a kernel of truth: France's government seemed determined to take a hammer and sickle to free enterprise, to punish the striver rather than the slacker, and to micromanage the economic life of the nation down to the last cream puff, and the results, if not as catastrophic as what befell the Soviet Union, were pretty dire all the same. Since the early 1980s, France had been one of the industrial world's perennial laggards, with unremittingly sluggish growth and high unemployment. The failure of the French political establishment to reverse the country's slide had created an increasingly embittered and cynical electorate—one that took its revenge in 2002 by choosing not a Communist but a fascist, Jean-Marie Le Pen, as one of the two candidates to face off in the final round of that year's presidential election. On top of all this, many of France's cities were now gripped by ethnic unrest, its once-vaunted university system was in shambles, and the rot had spread to the cultural sphere—even to the holy sanctum of the French table.

By the mid-2000s, many people had concluded that France's malaise was irreversible. An entire school of literature emerged declaring France *fini*. These polemics bore uniformly apocalyptic titles— *Doomed France, Bankrupt France, Scared France, Gallic Illusions, France in Freefall*—and their authors were known, collectively, as *les déclinologues*. Although they wrote from different perspectives and zeroed in on different aspects of France's struggles, they delivered the same basic message: France had become a profoundly dysfunctional nation.

Indeed it had: After nearly three decades of dreadful governance, it was a country mired in economic, political, social, and spiritual crisis. The presidencies of François Mitterrand and Jacques Chirac, which together spanned from 1981 until 2007, were disastrous for France. Although the men were ideological opposites—Mitterrand was a Socialist, Chirac a conservative—there was, in the words of Nicolas

Baverez, one of the chief *déclinologues*, a "sinister continuity" between them. They were united, said Baverez, by "their talent for winning elections and ruining France."

In fairness, France's woes did not originate with Mitterrand. In the wake of the OPEC oil embargo in 1973, France's economy, like those of all the major industrialized countries, plunged into recession, ending *les trente glorieuses*, the thirty fat years that had followed the Second World War. The same toxic stew that choked the economies of Britain and the United States—weak growth combined with rising inflation and unemployment—left France ailing. A second energy crisis, in 1979, deepened the pain for all three countries. That same year, frustrated British voters swept the Conservative Party to power, and its leader, Margaret Thatcher, who campaigned on a promise to revive the British economy, became prime minister. In 1980, Ronald Reagan, who also ran on a platform of economic renewal, was elected president of the United States in a landslide. A year later, French voters elected Mitterrand, who came to office pledging to institute an ambitious program of left-wing reforms. Which voters you think made the smarter choices depends on your politics, but insofar as the restaurant business was concerned, the United States and Britain unquestionably took the better route. What was true in the eighteenth century was no less true at the end of the twentieth: Chefs need prosperous patrons. Notwithstanding their other effects, the Reagan and Thatcher eras made the rich richer and spawned vast new wealth, money that bankrolled gastronomic revolutions in the United States and Britain. The French economy stagnated and French cuisine did likewise.

The irony, at least as far as the food part goes, is that Mitterrand was one of the most enthusiastic feeders ever to hold the French presidency. When he took office, there was fear that his ideology would seep into the kitchen of the Élysée Palace, France's White House, and that all pomp and extravagance would be taken off the menu. An enthusiastic and discerning palate had long been seen as not merely a desirable quality in the man at the top, but an obligatory one. Plying his guests with luxurious food and fine wine—"governing from the table," in the words of Jean-Robert Pitte—was a way for the president to advance his political interests and, more importantly, the interests of France. The worry was that the Socialist Mitterrand would forsake this tradition in favor of a more proletarian diet.

The concerns were unfounded. Mitterrand proved to be one of the all-time great Champagne Socialists and an ardent champion of the culinary arts. In fact, his gourmandism would yield arguably history's most famous last supper since the Last Supper. In December 1995, seven months after leaving office, the seventy-nine-year-old Mitterrand lay dying of the prostate cancer he had secretly battled for the duration of his presidency. Given to dramatic gestures, Mitterrand asked some thirty friends and relatives to gather at his home near Bordeaux to share in a farewell repast. As Mitterrand was helped to the dinner table and swaddled in blankets, all the color and vigor drained from his body, it seemed doubtful that he would be able to remain upright, let alone eat. But then came the raw oysters, harvested from the nearby Atlantic. The sight appeared to revive him; by the time the last shells were removed, he had slurped down nearly three dozen.

He ate the two courses that followed, foie gras and capon, with equal gusto, although the effort required caused him to doze off several times. But he was completely awake when the meal reached its scandalous denouement. For his last morsel of earthly fare, Mitterrand had requested France's forbidden fowl: ortolan, a tiny songbird considered a delicacy by gastronomes but now an endangered species and therefore off-limits to hunters, chefs, and diners. Imperious to the end, Mitterrand had decided to flout the law in order to satisfy his appetite one more time. The ortolans had been prepared in the traditional way—drowned in Armagnac, de-feathered, and roasted—and Mitterrand and his guests consumed them as tradition dictated: They draped napkins over their heads and ate the birds in their entirety—bones, organs, veins, everything.

Mitterrand swallowed two ortolans and apparently never put another piece of food in his mouth.

But while Mitterrand's gustatory exploits were impressive, his leadership was not. He inherited an ailing economy and turned what might have been temporary weakness into a chronic condition. Most of the damage was done during his first two years in office. Convinced that France could spend its way to recovery, Mitterrand cast aside any semblance of budgetary restraint. Government spending increased 25 percent (12 percent in inflation-adjusted terms) in 1981 and surged 27 percent the following year. Among the many added expenditures, social security spending went up by 20 percent, the minimum wage was raised by 40 percent, government-provided housing subsidies were increased by 25 percent, and hundreds of thousands of civil-service positions were created, all of which came with lavish benefits and pensions.

The vastly increased spending was just one part of the equation. Mitterrand had run for office promising "a rupture with capitalism," and from the point of view of French business, he delivered. In addition to the sharp increase in the minimum wage, the workweek was cut to thirty-nine hours (and later reduced to thirty-five) with no corresponding loss of pay; revised labor laws made it more difficult to fire employees, and severance pay was increased for those who did get canned; French workers were given a fifth week of paid vacation; the retirement age was lowered to sixty; and generous government-funded early retirement schemes were vastly expanded. In addition, banking and several other key industries were nationalized.

By 1982, it was clear that Mitterrand's medicine was lethal: Inflation was at 12 percent, unemployment had increased by nearly one third and stood at 9 percent, and the French franc had plummeted in value. In response, the president did a volte-face and imposed draconian austerity measures. Spending growth was cut sharply, wages were frozen, and prices for electricity and other government-provided services were increased. Later, a number of banks and other nationalized companies were returned to private hands. But many entitlements had been conferred during Mitterrand's first two years, and entitlements, once granted, are notoriously difficult to rescind. Most of the ones that Mitterrand introduced remained in place, and notwithstanding the new emphasis on fiscal discipline, the general thrust of French economic policy—massive state intervention, a neutered private sector, and a strong pro-labor tilt but at the expense of job creation—went unchanged. As Timothy B. Smith, a historian at Canada's Queen's University, observes in his excellent book *France in Crisis: Welfare, Inequality, and Globalization Since 1980*, Mitterrand, like Thatcher and Reagan, implemented such a radical and far-reaching agenda during his first years as president that long after he was gone, French politicians still had their "hands tied by the … nature of the social programs introduced and expanded during the early 1980s."

That was certainly the case for Chirac, who succeeded Mitterrand in 1995. He inherited a hamstrung economy in dire need of reform, but reform required political courage that Chirac did not have, and as a result, his presidency served mainly to perpetuate and deepen the problems that Mitterrand had bequeathed him. Economic growth remained anemic. France's GDP grew 2 percent on average during Mitterrand's two terms in office; it averaged 2.2 percent under Chirac. During that same twenty-six-year period, the U.S. economy averaged 3 percent annual growth while Britain's averaged 2.5 percent. A one-percent growth differential in a single year is significant; multiplied twenty-six times, it is staggeringly large. Among other things, economic activity creates jobs. During Ronald Reagan's eight years as president, the U.S. economy spawned 17 million jobs and under Bill Clinton, it created another 22 million. France, by contrast, spent these years amassing a standing army of idle workers. When Mitterrand was elected, the country had 1.6 million jobless and an unemployment rate of 7 percent. By the end of his second term, 3 million were without work and unemployment stood at 12 percent. The numbers improved marginally with Chirac, but unemployment never dipped below the high single digits, and when he left the Élysée, France still had nearly 3 million jobless. And those were just the official figures; it was widely believed that the true unemployment rate was somewhere between 15 and 20 percent.

To a foreign tourist sipping an overpriced kir royale at the Café de Flore on the Boulevard Saint-Germain, none of this would necessarily have been apparent. Indeed, from that vantage point, France might have appeared to be just about the most agreeable place on earth. And certainly, some of the changes enacted by Mitterrand and Chirac seemed very appealing. Less work for more benefits—what was not to like? But many of these initiatives proved over time to have devastating side effects. For instance, in the decade after the workweek was cut from thirty-nine hours to thirty-five in 1998, wages completely stagnated, badly eroding the living standards of many French. And they were the lucky ones—they at least had jobs.

But there was one sector of the economy that flourished during the Mitterrand and Chirac years: the public sector. While France had never been short on *fonctionnaires*, the size of the bureaucracy exploded after 1981. When Mitterrand was first elected, the country had 3.8 million civil servants; when Sarkozy was sworn in twenty-seven years later, that figure had swelled by nearly 40 percent and the state now employed 5.2 million people—one jobholder out of every five. By then, it was estimated that France had between five hundred thousand and one million more civil servants than it needed.

Public-sector jobs had also become the cushiest around. On average, they paid 20 to 30 percent more than private-sector jobs, were essentially tenured positions (it was virtually impossible to be fired), and offered an astonishing array of perks. Civil servants worked fewer hours than their private-sector peers and enjoyed more vacation and sick days. Employees of the French national railroad were permitted eighteen free rail trips in Europe annually; while employees of the French national electricity company were eligible for reductions of up to 95 percent for their electricity bills. But the best part of working for the government was retiring. The retirement age for French bureaucrats was fifty-seven, and many of them were able to call it a career even sooner than that—some as young as fifty. They were also entitled to pensions that were equivalent to 85 percent of their best six months' salaries. Not surprisingly, in a survey published in 2005, three quarters of French ages fifteen to thirty said that they wanted to join the civil service.

Nor was it surprising that public sector employees were the most resistant to reform—the merest hint of it would send them into the streets in protest. In 2000, there were 710 total strike days per 1,000 civil servants, versus just 52 for private-sector workers. Employees of the state railroad were particularly prone to walking off the job; in 2000, they were responsible for 40 percent of all work stoppages, even though they accounted for just one percent of all French workers. "It's always the most privileged people who strike," Serge Levaton, a seventy-year-old retired doctor, told the *New York Times* while marooned in Paris during a massive transit strike in 2002. "I would like the public service to cease to exist. They only have privileges but no obligations."

But it wasn't just civil servants who were unwilling to make concessions. French workers in general were resolutely opposed to seeing their perks cut so that jobs could be created and the economy might recover, and rather than risking confrontation, the government left the status quo largely unchallenged and tried to keep the unemployed quiescent by extending fairly lavish benefits to them, as well. An unemployed worker could expect to receive benefits up to 75 percent of his last salary, for a period of three years or even longer. He could also obtain generous housing subsidies and other forms of assistance. People were able to maintain decent lives on the dole and lost any incentive to seek work. (One honest soul even wrote a book about the more than twenty years he spent living off government checks.) In addition to making unemployment a palatable option, French politicians also took care to absolve themselves of any blame for the country's economic woes. Rather than admitting that France's problems were mostly homegrown, they claimed that international trade and American turbo-capitalism were the culprits, and they fed the public a steady diet of antiglobalization rhetoric—what Timothy Smith calls the "Big Excuse." The constant refrain was that France was a victim of forces beyond her control.

Amid all the stagnation and sloth, many French who did have ambition and drive went abroad in search of opportunity and a better life. By 2007, more than two million were residing overseas. Some four hundred thousand were in the Greater London area alone—an expatriate community so large that Sarkozy went to London, which he described as "one of the great French cities," to fish for votes in 2007 and to urge his compatriots to return. "France is still your country even if you are disappointed by it," he implored. "To all the expatriates who are unhappy about the situation in France ... come home, because together we will make France a great country where everything will be possible, where fathers won't fear for the future of their children, and where everyone will be able to make their plans come true and be responsible for their own destiny." But a survey of French expats found that 93 percent were happy with their new lives and that 25 percent had no intention of ever going back to France.

Chefs were among the economic refugees. The Mitterrand and Chirac years were particularly tough on France's culinary industry. Thanks to rigid employment laws, the hospitality sector was left with an enormous labor shortage—by the mid-2000s, some 80,000 positions were unfilled, mostly because the cost of filling them was too high. But even when employers were willing to bear those costs, they often struggled to find takers. For bakers, pâtissiers, and other artisans, it became increasingly difficult to find young people interested in the hard work of apprenticing. "We've lost that spirit of sacrificing," said Gérard Mulot, an eminent Parisian pâtissier; like many of his peers, he was deeply pessimistic about the future of his profession.

Persistently sluggish growth and the thinning wallets of many French likewise made it difficult for restaurants to fill seats. Compounding the problem was France's value-added tax (VAT). A quick snack at a café, a *steak frites* at a corner bistro, or a three-star feast automatically incurred a 19.6 percent VAT surcharge to the bill (along with the built-in 15 percent gratuity). The VAT became an obsession among French chefs, who were adamant that it was killing their businesses. Adding to their frustration, fast-food restaurants had a lower VAT rate, just 5.5 percent, since they were classified as takeaway establishments. In 1999, hundreds of chefs, wearing toques and banging on pots and pans, held a demonstration outside the parliament building in Paris. They came armed with eggs and flour, which they proceeded to throw at the riot police; the cops responded with tear gas. But the chefs felt they had no choice but to unleash the full force of their pantries. "If the VAT remains this high," André Daguin, the head of the hospitality industry association and a former two-star chef, told the *Boston Globe*, "the haute cuisine restaurants will survive. The fast-food places will thrive. But everything in between will eventually disappear."

Nor were onerous tax rates and crippling labor laws the only problems facing the culinary industry. Under Mitterrand and Chirac, the government truly became a leviathan; with so many bureaucrats now on the public payroll, the red tape grew accordingly. Timothy Smith cites the example of French tax administration. Rather than putting assessment and collection under one roof, France had different departments for each, and the result was that tax collection in France, as a percentage of GDP, cost six times what it did in the United States. Starting a business required nightmarish amounts of paperwork and haggling. Establishing a new company in the United States took only seven business days; in France, it required sixty-six.

For aspiring restaurateurs who succeeded in navigating, pleading, or bribing their way past the authorities, throwing open the doors to customers brought no relief. In 1998, a representative of the Office of Competition, Consumption, and Repression of Fraud showed up at Jean Bardet's eponymous two-star restaurant in the city of Tours, in the Loire Valley, and began looking for signs of fraud. The inspector found that some of the asparagus in the kitchen that day was not local, as the menu promised, but was from another part of France;

that some of the fish being served might not have been line-caught, as advertised; that the veal chops came from a different source than the one listed on the menu; and that the wine list, though said to contain only AOC wines, in fact had a pair of non-AOC offerings. Elsewhere, these discoveries would have been recognized for what they were: minor inconsistencies resulting from hiccups in the restaurant's supply chain, or simple oversights. In France, they were crimes. A local court found Bardet guilty of fraud and fined him $4,600. Headlines across the country reported his conviction with high moral censure and little respect for the facts; one paper claimed that he had sold supermarket wines, another that the asparagus had come from (gasp!) Spain. Michelin decided that the charges were serious enough to merit removing the restaurant from the Guide until the matter was resolved. A spokesman icily told *Business Week*, "We cannot include a restaurant involved in such legal proceedings, and which could close at any moment." Eventually, another judge reduced Bardet's fine to $3,700, and Michelin took the restaurant out of purgatory. But it was a wonder Bardet didn't take after his tormentors with a meat cleaver.

He surely would have had Mark Williamson's support. Williamson, the owner of the popular Willi's Wine Bar and another Paris restaurant, Macéo, moved to France from the United Kingdom in 1975 to work as a chef. At the time, England was still in the throes of an economic crisis that had started in the late 1960s and that was punctuated by rolling power outages; prior to leaving for France, Williamson had cooked at a restaurant in London, and he and his colleagues frequently found themselves toiling in the dark. France, by comparison, was in reasonably ruddy health, and during his first months there, he heard expressions of sympathy for the state Britain was in. "When I arrived here," he recalls, "everyone said they were so sorry about England, that it was a pity what was happening to such a great country. I knew the French didn't really mean it, but that's what they said." In France, Williamson found a vastly superior place to be a chef and restaurateur. "It was a much livelier restaurant scene, with a better quality workforce," he said. "In the 1970s, people probably worked too much. But they took pride in the profession, and it gave them a good standard of living."

Thirty years later, Williamson was back where he started: in a country with a broken economy and a broken spirit. "It's absolutely horrendous what's happened," he said. Had he thought about closing down his restaurants? "Yes, on a regular basis," he said. But at fifty-four years old, he was close enough to retirement that he would just stick it out for a while longer. The only kind of business that was really possible in France now, he said, was one in which you did all the work yourself; otherwise, it was too much hassle and aggravation.

It wasn't the taxes and fees that troubled him as much as it was the blizzard of paperwork. Since the 1980s, the number of government agencies that he had to answer to, and the amount of documentation required of him, had grown exponentially. "You are literally sending documents to the government every single day," he said. "Tax forms, employment forms, questionnaires." Between the two restaurants, Williamson employed twenty-six people, and the dossier for every member of the staff bulged with official forms. He set aside one day a month exclusively for paperwork, but it usually ended up requiring several days of his time. Different government agencies often demanded the same information, yet nothing was ever done to streamline the process. At this point, Williamson said, he really needed a full-time assistant to handle all the correspondence with the government, but that kind of nonessential hiring was out of the question; besides, it simply would have created more paperwork.

Williamson told me of his most recent run-in with the bureaucracy. The agency in charge of tax collection had decided that it wanted business owners to submit their monthly VAT payments electronically and had sent out a downloadable program that would enable them to do so. For some reason, the program was not usable on a Mac, which was the type of computer that Williamson owned. Because he was unable to file the VAT payments electronically, he started getting fined 120 euros per month. To resolve the problem, he called the official help line, but trying to get even a simple question answered was next to impossible. "No one is ever at their desk, and if they are, they are always watching the clock or stepping away," said Williamson. "They are almost never there physically; you speak to someone, and the next thing you know she's off on maternity leave, or away for training, or on vacation. It has slowed the flow of things incredibly." It took several days of back-and-forth before he was finally told that a decision had been made some time earlier to exempt Mac users from having to file electronically and that he could continue to submit his payments via bank transfers. "It's mind-blowing; I should have filed a complaint with the European Court of Justice," he said. Unaccountable, capricious bureaucrats siphoning off huge amounts of the country's wealth in order to take care of themselves; in Williamson's view, there was something profoundly sinister about this state of affairs, and here he made the same provocative claim as Sibard. "It is a Communist system, and these people are just apparatchiks," he said. "I mean, really, what's the difference between Cuba and France?"

Williamson now regularly sent his two children, aged twenty-two and seventeen, overseas so that they could get a taste of the can-do spirit that no longer existed in France. The older one had done an internship with a venture capital firm in Sydney, the younger one had worked as a *stagier* at a restaurant in New York. "When you are brought up surrounded by a passive work ethic, by this belief that work is owed to you and that you don't have to invest yourself in your work, it's really bad," said Williamson.

What he found particularly insidious was the oft-repeated claim that the policies of the Mitterrand and Chirac years had helped sustain the French way of life. To Williamson, there was no doubt that the standard of living for most French had declined since the 1970s. "It's great to have all this free time," he said, "but you need money to enjoy it. So many people in France are now living on the minimum wage. You walk into the big supermarkets and you see what people are buying—the standard of living is way below what it was in the seventies." He said the story was written in the faces of the people he encountered on the Paris subway. "The thing that always strikes me when I take the Métro is that everyone looks so fucking miserable," he said. "You can't really blame them. They've had their lives taken away from them; everything is programmed. All they want is to get a job as a *fonctionnaire* and to wait until retirement."

The Pain from Spain

FROM THE OUTSIDE, MOST Michelin three-star restaurants exude grandeur. Strangely, Restaurante Arzak evoked thoughts of Little Italy. Located a mile or so from the center of San Sebastián, a city on the northern coast of Spain, hard up against the Pyrenees Mountains and just minutes from the French border, Arzak occupied a building with an exterior aspect—red brick and salmon-colored stucco, white awnings emblazoned with the restaurant's name— more suggestive of a Bay Ridge spaghetti house than a gastronomic Lourdes. Entering through the small, Spartan bar area, I half-expected to see a TV set tuned to ESPN mounted on the wall. It was only when I arrived in the dining room and spotted the white linen tablecloths and the elegant cutlery and stemware that I was assured that, yes, this really was a three-star establishment. And even then, there was a sense of the unusual. The contours of the walls made it appear as if Arzak had been shoehorned into someone's house, which it was: It was the house in which Juan Mari Arzak grew up. He had converted it into a restaurant and from this unlikeliest of launching pads, Spain's food revolution, the most important culinary movement since nouvelle cuisine, had taken off.

In the opinion of many observers, *la nueva cocina*, as the New Spanish Cooking was known, wasn't just *nouvelle cuisine* by another name; it was a continuation of France's gastronomic insurrection. In 1976, Paul Bocuse, in his self-appointed role as French cooking's roving ambassador, took part in a food conference in Madrid, during which he shared some of the central tenets of nouvelle cuisine (this despite having told Jacques Pépin that he didn't really understand what the movement was about). At the time, Spain was just beginning its transition to democratic rule after four decades of stifling right-wing dictatorship under Francisco Franco. Franco's death in late 1975 opened the door to political, economic, and cultural renewal, and this sense of liberation and opportunity reached into the kitchens of Spain. In the audience that day in Madrid were two young chefs from San Sebastián, Juan Mari Arzak and Pedro Subijana. They were intrigued by what they saw and heard and made their curiosity known to Bocuse, who invited them to visit him in Lyon to learn more about what he and other French chefs were up to. Arzak and Subijana spent ten days in France—hanging out in Bocuse's kitchen, visiting the Troisgros brothers—and returned to San Sebastián determined to give their native Basque cuisine a similar facelift. With several like-minded colleagues and a group of freethinking diners happy to be lab rats in exchange for complimentary meals, they began holding get-togethers during which updated versions of Basque classics and entirely original creations were presented. Thus was born contemporary Basque cuisine; the experimental spirit that guided it quickly spread to other parts of Spain, notably Catalonia, and what began as a regional phenomenon became a national one known as *la nueva cocina*.

Thirty years on, with Paul Bocuse now cracking jokes about nouvelle cuisine, its spirit still animated Spain's gastronomic discourse, as I learned when I interviewed Arzak at the French Culinary Institute's gala event in New York in October 2006. I had asked him about his experience in France in 1976, and just as he began to reply, Ferran Adrià walked into the room. He overheard our conversation, and within moments, he and Arzak were vigorously debating whether Alain Chapel or Michel Guérard had been the most important figure of that era. They spoke Spanish, firing back and forth at such a pace that my translator finally gave up and just listened. After about ten minutes, Adrià announced that he had to get ready for his cooking demonstration, but as he left, he told me (as if I didn't now realize it) that this question was one of great consequence; indeed, he was spending much of his free time these days studying the nouvelle cuisine movement.

Whether *la nueva cocina* was an extension of nouvelle cuisine or simply a by-product, it was driven by the same hunger for innovation, openness to new ideas, and desire for creative freedom. It drew heavily on the principles of molecular gastronomy, a culinary approach founded on a self-evident proposition—cooking is a form of chemistry—that had given rise to some of the most intricate and controversial food ever created. It introduced all sorts of laboratory equipment to professional kitchens, an array of test tubes, syringes, pH meters, and lasers that poured forth a riot of strange powders, foams, jellies, flash-frozen dishes, and unusual flavor combinations. In Spanish hands, at least, the results were often playful (melon caviar served in a real caviar tin, pistachio truffles frozen with liquid nitrogen) but also sometimes gratuitously provocative (coconut ravioli in soy sauce, Parmesan ice cream sandwiches).

La nueva cocina has its roots in San Sebastián, and the city now boasted more Michelin-starred restaurants per capita—eighteen as of 2008, with three three-stars—than any other in the world (an achievement that caused some in France to regard it as a hemorrhoid on the bottom of France). Arzak was awarded three stars in 1989, one of the first Spanish chefs to be so honored ("it was like winning the Nobel Prize"). His daughter Elena now ran the kitchen, but he was at the restaurant most days, and the two appeared to work as a team. While their food was not as outré as Adrià's, the Arzaks also had their hands firmly planted in the molecular gastronomy tool kit and were not above pyrotechnics; Juan Mari had made headlines at a culinary conference a few years earlier when he prepared an exploding strawberry milkshake using dry ice. I was somewhat dubious of this newfangled cooking, so it was with anticipation but also with a certain ambivalence that I sat down for lunch at Arzak on a warm afternoon in September 2007. The kitchen wasted no time getting to the funky stuff. My first course was a dish of roasted figs served with kefir that had been infused with foie gras oil. I eyed it suspiciously, then reminded myself that an open mind sometimes required an open mouth, and I took a bite. It was delicious. The next course was a sweet, buttery lobster claw in a vermouth and onion sauce and topped with freeze-dried olive oil—also great. After that came an outrageously good white tuna with blackened skin and pickled cucumber sauce, followed by a roast pigeon seasoned with rosemary and served with a side of shaved blue potatoes and blue potato crisps arranged like masts on a ship. For dessert, I was served chocolate grapes in a thoroughly fetching tomato and raspberry soup. Having arrived a skeptic, I staggered away from the table a believer. The food was fascinating, and, more important, it was a pleasure to eat.

The atmospherics also made an impression. Unlike most French chefs, who would sweep into the dining room maybe once per service (and then mostly for the purpose of having their rings kissed), Juan Mari and Elena spent much of the lunch hour tableside—suggesting dishes, fielding questions about the food, hamming it up with regulars. And in striking contrast to high-end establishments in France, which were usually half-empty at lunch and dependent now almost entirely on tourists, every seat at Arzak was filled on a Thursday afternoon, and by a mainly local crowd. Even the most successful French three-stars now seemed like relics of a bygone era. Arzak felt *alive*. And it wasn't just Arzak: Almost every restaurant one encountered in San Sebastián felt that way. There was a similar exuberance to the dining scenes in New York and London, and the contrast between these places and what one found now in Paris and Lyon told the story better than any newspaper or magazine article could: Spain was ascendant, other countries were on the rise, and France had ceased to be the undisputed First Nation of Food.

For this, much of the credit belonged to France. It had set in motion Spain's gastronomic awakening, and a steady influx of gifted French chefs helped do the same in the United States and Britain. André Soltner, Alain Sailhac, and Roger Fessaguet in New York, and the Roux brothers and Pierre Koffman in London, created food the likes of which those cities had never experienced, encouraged the development of artisanal food movements, and nurtured homegrown culinary talent. In the case of Michel and Albert Roux, not only did their restaurants, Le Gavroche and the Waterside Inn, earn three Michelin stars; two of their protégés, Marco Pierre White and Gordon Ramsay, became the first British-born chefs to win the Guide's highest rating. The culinary vitality on display in New York and London by the mid-2000s quite literally grew out of the kitchens of those transplanted French chefs.

But there was also no denying that France had slipped. "French restaurants had been the kings of the world, but in the 1990s, they lost their greatness," the long-expatriated Michel Richard (last seen signing autographs on Michel Guérard's behalf) said over coffee one afternoon at Citronelle, his restaurant in the Georgetown section of Washington, D.C. The shifting gastronomic fortunes were, at heart, a reflection of shifting economies. While France stalled, Spain flourished. From the late 1980s on, its GDP grew more than 3 percent per year on average. Between the mid-1990s and 2007, the economy doubled in size, becoming the world's eighth-largest, just behind France and ahead of Russia, India, and South Korea. During this same period, unemployment declined from 25 percent to less than 9. All this progress naturally accrued to the benefit of Spain's restaurant industry, which had another thing in its favor: Spain's VAT was only 7 percent, almost a third less than the rate in France.

Likewise, the vast wealth created in New York and London during the 1980s and the 1990s fueled vibrant restaurant scenes there. Scores of ambitious new establishments opened, their owners confident that if they put good food on the plate and offered a winning ambiance, their investments would be rewarded. Robust economic growth didn't just promote spending at the table; it also encouraged exploration. As *New York Times* restaurant critic Ruth Reichl observed in 1998, "The fate of restaurants ... is tied to the economy. It's not just because people spend more in times of prosperity. Diners also become more adventurous when they are flush; it is no coincidence that the great advances in American dining have all occurred during bull markets. Remember the early 80's? It was an exhilarating time when restaurants reinvented themselves to give us New American cooking, open kitchens and casual chic. But then came the recession of the early 90's, and a spate of the safe and the dull ... When times turn tough, customers turn conservative. In response, restaurateurs get frightened; many close their doors, and those who stay open stick to the tried and true, producing copycat cuisine that is the edible equivalent of Hollywood studios churning out Jaws 3, 4 and 5."

Booming economies did indeed yield innovative chefs and intrepid diners; Spain was the obvious example, but this was also true in Britain and the United States. In 1995, a young, self-taught chef named Heston Blumenthal opened a restaurant called the Fat Duck in the village of Bray, near London, offering wildly inventive dishes (oyster with passion fruit jelly and lavender, for instance, and bacon-and-egg ice cream) that incorporated elements of molecular gastronomy. Londoners quickly embraced the restaurant, and Michelin did, too, awarding Blumenthal's restaurant three stars in 2004. Exactly ten years after Blumenthal started the Fat Duck, *Gourmet* magazine named London the best food city in the world. The magazine's editor? Ruth Reichl. (To appreciate how far British cooking had come, consider what Michel Roux had to say in his memoir, *Life is a Menu*, about the food he encountered in London in the 1960s. "One of the most chilling experiences of my life was discovering the British pea," he wrote. "I happened on this fluorescent green object, almost the size of a quail's egg, when I passed a Lyons Corner House near Marble Arch soon after arriving in London. Through a steaming window, I saw plates with these peas, a dollop of tomato ketchup and bleached-white Mother's Pride bread smeared with deep yellow salted butter. I was appalled not only by this sight, but also by the fact that people seemed to be tucking in with such gusto. It bothered me that millions in the British Isles were eating in such a way. Like a witness of an atrocity, I told myself I had to put this out of my mind as quickly as possible.")

The U.S. dining scene of the 1990s didn't yield anything quite as audacious as Blumenthal's cooking, but it did bring to the fore some hugely talented and original chefs, notably Thomas Keller, who combined an almost monastic reverence for classic French techniques with an ingenuity that saw him give haute-cuisine makeovers to such down-market American staples as macaroni and cheese, surf and turf, and coffee and donuts. His Yountville, California, restaurant, which opened in 1994, was called the French Laundry, and it had the unmistakable look and feel of a Michelin three-star. In 2006, Michelin introduced a guide to the San Francisco Bay area and gave the French Laundry three stars, to go along with the three that Keller's New York restaurant, Per Se, had earned the year before when he became the first American-born chef to achieve that distinction.

If the rise of Spain, Britain, and the United States underscored the financial problems facing French chefs, it also posed them an artistic challenge. By the early 2000s, San Sebastián, Bray, and Yountville were the foodie destinations; France, by contrast, was increasingly seen as a culinary museum, a place with a bright past but not very promising future. One could still eat well there, but it seemed to no longer generate the big ideas and the breakthrough flavors. (The Spaniards, on the other hand, were all about big ideas and breakthrough flavors; Ferran Adrià closed El Bulli for six months every year in order to travel the world looking for inspiration and to come up with new creations in his Barcelona test kitchen.) In treating France as passé, said New York chef Daniel Boulud, gastronomes were merely falling in line with the French themselves. "In Spain, nobody is nostalgic about anything," he says. "In France, it's all nostalgia. They are caught between tradition and globalization."

In 1996, a dozen top French chefs, among them Alain Ducasse and Joël Robuchon, issued a manifesto denouncing the "globalization of cuisine" and the notion of "innovation at any price" as affronts to the French culinary tradition. They wrote that "a great dish is not a juxtaposition, it is a blend ... a great dish doesn't abuse either herbs or spices. A great dish is a model of simplicity, harmony, and tastes ... French cuisine owes its reputation to the reputation of [France's] regions, the region owes its reputation to the products of its *terroir*. Our knowledge and our traditions are a benchmark." Eighteen months later, some of their more iconoclastic peers, among them Pierre Gagnaire, Michel Troisgros, and Michel Bras, fired back. The "Group of Eight" declared themselves the heirs to the nouvelle cuisine movement and averred that the way forward for French cuisine was not to wallow in history but to embrace globalization and encourage experimentation in the kitchen.

While the acrimonious debate over sauces and syringes raged on, many of the chefs had a more pressing concern: staying in business. By the 1990s, it had become exceptionally hard to make money on a three-star restaurant. This was especially true outside the major cities; as more people traveled by air and rail, there were fewer potential clients who could be persuaded by the Michelin Guide to take a detour. Top chefs now needed financial backers and other sources of revenue. Many of them started smaller, more casual restaurants to help support the flagships. In 1990, Georges Blanc opened one across the street from his eponymous three-star in the village of Vonnas. Eight years later, he founded bistros in the nearby cities of Mâcon and Bourg-en-Bresse, and in 2001, he opened a 110-seat restaurant in Lyon. He also operated several boutiques and hotels. "The three-star is not profitable," Blanc flatly told me when I interviewed him in April 2007. "Three stars used to be profitable; twenty-five years ago, there were more customers, and our costs were lower. But now, because of the thirty-five-hour workweek and other laws, we have to pay a lot for good staff. Staff costs make up forty to fifty percent of the bill. My business today is profitable, but only because of the other restaurants and the hotels."

A few weeks earlier, I had driven from Paris to Vézelay, a picturesque village at the northern tip of Burgundy, to meet Marc Meneau, its most famous and now most embattled citizen. Meneau was the chef and owner of L'Espérance, a celebrated restaurant just down the hill from the town center. I'd eaten a mediocre lunch there several years earlier. The food hadn't troubled me as much as the wine list: It was obscenely expensive, which was all the more difficult to swallow just a short drive from some of France's greatest vineyards. I had briefly contemplated insulting the kitchen by ordering a Coke, but a young Japanese sommelier, doing a *stage* with the restaurant, had guided me to a decent half-bottle. Ultimately, though, the extortionate wine prices weren't enough: Meneau's company was now in liquidation proceedings, and with L'Espérance's survival in doubt, Michelin had suspended its three-star rating and omitted it from the 2007 Guide.

I arrived in Vézelay at around noon and waited for Meneau in the restaurant's lounge, a bright, airy space overlooking the garden and opening directly into the dining room, which was empty. The bar area wasn't seeing much action, either: Only two of its tables were occupied. Still, it was early, and the briskness with which members of the large waitstaff moved about suggested that more guests were due imminently. Oddly, though, amid all this purposeful scurrying, no one seemed to notice that a large framed poster had somehow ended up on the floor of the lounge, resting against the wall.

After perhaps fifteen minutes, Meneau, dressed in his chef's whites, came ambling into the room and greeted me with a perfunctory nod and handshake. Lean and tall, he had always cut a dashing figure, but not now: His hair was white and unruly, his face was covered in gray stubble, and his skin had a sickly pallor. Meneau led me through the kitchen, mindlessly grabbing a piece of candied fruit from a baking sheet en route, and then up a rickety staircase to his glass-enclosed second-floor office. I began by asking where things stood with his company, but before I could finish the question, he cut me off. "Are you here to talk food or business?" he demanded, his tone defiant. "Because I am only interested in talking about food."

So we talked food and the state of French cuisine. Meneau insisted that France was still the gastronomic world's pacesetter: "Food that nourishes the spirit, that shows *terroir*; France is certainly the richest country when it comes to this." But having just chastised me for bringing up his financial situation, he suddenly wanted to discuss it. He said that the restaurant business was in bad shape at the moment; France's economic problems made it very difficult to run an enterprise of any kind, especially a restaurant, and most especially one in the countryside. "Here, we have to attract people; we need to give them a reason to travel down from Paris, or to get off the highway," he said. "We need to provide luxury—rooms where they can spend the night, a pool, flowers everywhere. In the city, you don't have to do all these things."

To support L'Espérance, he had opened four casual restaurants in the area, and he had also taken out some loans, which he now found himself struggling to repay. But he was surprisingly upbeat about his prospects. His case would be heard by the court soon, and he was optimistic a solution would be found allowing him to remain open. "This is not like the United States, where they just shut you down," he explained. "Here, they take into account the social cost. Many people in this area depend on my restaurant. If I close, it's not just a problem for me." I asked how business was holding up; the French press had reported his difficulties, and with L'Espérance absent from the 2007 Michelin, I imagined turnover had suffered. The restaurant was doing extremely well, he claimed; clients were coming to show their support and to help him pull through.

We finished up, and his secretary walked me back through the kitchen and to the lounge so I could have a quick cup of coffee. Meneau's twenty-one-year-old son, Pierre, was there, and we chatted about the restaurant's plight. A roundish young man with a Prince Valiant haircut, he said his parents had options if L'Espérance went under; in fact, his father had already received several job offers. Obviously, though, they were hoping to survive this crisis and remain in Vézelay. His father had been born there and had devoted his life to the village. From where I stood talking to Pierre, I had an unobstructed view of the dining room. Only two tables were occupied, six diners in total. If restaurant-goers were rallying to Meneau in his moment of need, it was not apparent on this afternoon. Waiters and busboys continued to circle the room, but they were like nightshift employees, just trying to make the hours pass. By then, it was clear that no one else would be coming for lunch. But the fallen poster was gone.

While Meneau's surly mood made for a challenging interview, it was at least reassuring to find him combative rather than despondent. L'Espérance was located just thirty miles up the road from Saulieu, the village that was home to Bernard Loiseau's three-star, La Côte d'Or. The restaurant's renown predated Loiseau's presence there. Back in the 1940s and '50s, La Côte d'Or's reputation had been second only to La Pyramide's, and its chef at the time, Alexandre Dumaine, had been nearly as influential as Fernand Point. Loiseau, who had apprenticed for three years with the Troisgros brothers and then worked in Paris, took charge of the restaurant in 1975. La Côte d'Or's landmark status appealed to his vanity: He wanted to be among the giants, and working in Dumaine's old kitchen was a powerful statement of intent.

Two years after arriving in Saulieu, Loiseau was awarded his first Michelin star; the second came in 1981, and he reached the pinnacle a decade later. In the years between his second and third stars, Loiseau remodeled the restaurant's kitchen and public rooms and also added luxury guest quarters. Almost all of the work was financed with bank loans, and by the late 1980s, Loiseau was five million dollars in debt and paying forty thousand dollars a month to his creditors. Even after winning the third star, he continued borrowing and spending. And the outlays were no longer confined to La Côte d'Or and Saulieu: Between 1998 and 2000, Loiseau acquired three properties in Paris and turned them into bistros. By 2000, he had gone through ten million dollars.

Much of the spending was warranted. The restaurant had needed renovating, and like L'Espérance, La Côte d'Or now required more than just good food to attract clients. Loiseau outfitted it with the kinds of amenities—a spa, a fitness center, a heated pool—that could tempt wealthy Parisians to journey down for a night or a weekend. But there was another factor, too: The manic spending was also inspired by his desire to be the next Paul Bocuse. It was an ambition that the older chef seemed to encourage. When Loiseau was awarded his third star, Bocuse hosted a celebration in his honor at Collonges au Mont d'Or. Bocuse rented a pair of elephants for the occasion, and he and Loiseau each climbed aboard one of the pachyderms, magnums of Champagne in hand, to pose for the assembled journalists. He and Bocuse spoke often by phone, and though there was always an undercurrent of competition, Bocuse plainly regarded Loiseau as his culinary offspring, the next ambassador of French cuisine.

Like Bocuse, Loiseau loved the camera, and his high-energy persona earned him the nickname "Monsieur 100,000 Volts." Following Bocuse's lead, he opened a restaurant in Japan and started a line of frozen foods. In 1995, he was awarded the Légion d'Honneur by François Mitterrand, joining Bocuse as the only chefs to have the prestigious medallions personally affixed to their lapels by a French president. Three years later, he made headlines by becoming the first chef to get a listing on the Paris Stock Exchange. He took his company public mainly because he needed to raise money to pay off his debts. But there was also a healthy dollop of gimmickry and showmanship: He told one interviewer that he was "the Hermès of food" and that "we're in the era of marketing. You have to create a brand name with concepts. Today I have a brand. It took me twenty years to do it. That's why I am going public now. Because it will explode."

That last word has a grim, premonitory ring. I had dinner with my wife at La Côte d'Or in September 2000. It was said that the quality had declined; never having been before, we couldn't say whether the kitchen was struggling, but the food wasn't impressive. Even the Loiseau classics—frogs' legs with garlic purée and parsley juice, chicken poached with truffles under its skin—were lackluster, with flavors that seemed washed-out. It was a Sunday night and a popular time of year for tourists, but the dining room was almost empty. (Loiseau's wife, Dominique, would later tell us that business was suffering; Americans, in particular, weren't coming as much anymore, and they were desperate to get them back.) Loiseau was around, dressed in his chef's jacket. He appeared to be in a good mood despite the slow turnover; he could be seen joking with the staff, and he was delightful when we chatted with him for a few minutes. He was a picture of fatigue, though—drawn, with dark circles under his eyes. He looked like he needed a month at the beach.

In the fall of 2002, there were whispers that Loiseau's third star was in jeopardy, and he and Dominique traveled to Paris in November to meet with Derek Brown, Michelin's editorial director. Several months later, on January 18, FranÇois Simon, the influential restaurant critic for *Le Figaro*, published an article previewing the 2003 Michelin Guide. Evidently tapping an inside source, Simon reported that Loiseau, after "a big scare," would be keeping his third star for at least another year but would fall two points, from 19/20 to 17/20, in the forthcoming Gault Millau guide. In mid-February, the 2003 Gault Millau was released and La CÔte d'Or had indeed been downgraded. Loiseau had once told fellow chef Jacques Lameloise, "If I lose a star, I will kill myself." Now, faced with that possibility and having been sanctioned by Gault Millau, Loiseau fell into a deep funk. The gloom didn't lift even after he learned that La CÔte d'Or had retained its third star in the 2003 Michelin. On Monday, February 24, he went home after lunch service, grabbed a gun, and took his own life, leaving behind his wife and three young children.

In the judgment of Bocuse and other chefs, Loiseau had been the victim of malicious rumors. They blamed Simon (this despite the fact that he was right about the Gault Millau demotion and had said that Loiseau would keep his third star), but they also lashed out at the two major guides, which were accused of placing hellish demands on chefs and of treating them callously. The *New York Times* quoted Loiseau's assistant as saying that her boss, during his visit with Michelin the previous autumn, had been urged to "be careful, stay in your kitchen and don't do too much business." However, Derek Brown denied issuing any sort of warning. "We didn't and never would threaten to take away a star, and we didn't advise him what to do," he told the *New Yorker* three months after Loiseau's death. "We are not a consultancy, after all."

It was subsequently learned that the fifty-two-year-old chef had suffered from bipolar disorder. We also know, thanks to Rudolph Chelminski's excellent book, *The Perfectionist*, that Loiseau was haunted in his last years by a sense that culinary fashion had passed him by. (He was one of the chefs who had signed the letter condemning the globalization of haute cuisine.) He was already in a fragile state when the speculation about his third star began, and the prospect of losing it ultimately drove him to reach for his rifle. But although his suicide, in hindsight, looked preordained, it is fair to wonder if things might have turned out differently had he not run himself senseless pursuing the kind of glory that Bocuse had achieved. While it would be absurd to suggest that Bocuse was in any way responsible for what befell Loiseau, the example that he set clearly propelled the younger chef along his tragic arc. Had Loiseau not been led astray by his determination to emulate Bocuse, the food coming out of his kitchen perhaps wouldn't have suffered, and critics would have had no reason to reconsider La Côte d'Or's standing. His death, at any rate, was a tragedy for French cuisine, and one that would have seismic consequences.

Star-Crossed

"WE HAVE TO CUT it. We have to kill it. We have to burn it." It was nine o'clock on a warm, hazy morning in May 2007. Paris was still half-asleep, the café was a picture of tranquility, and Luc Dubanchet was issuing a battle cry. The bellicose talk was directed not at another nation, nor at international terrorists, but at an enemy that he seemed to believe was nearly as dangerous: the Michelin Guide. A former editor of the Gault Millau guide, Dubanchet had left four years earlier to launch his own insurrectionary publication, *Omnivore*. Like the Gault Millau of old, *Omnivore* sought to call attention to innovative chefs trying to shake French cuisine out of the slumber into which it was thought to have fallen. The magazine quickly won an ardent following, and its popularity had spawned an annual restaurant guide celebrating "young cuisine" and a yearly food festival that attracted top chefs from around the world.

But as with Gault Millau, *Omnivore* was defined as much by what it was against as by what it was for, and what it was against was the tyranny of the Michelin Guide. To hear Dubanchet tell it, the Michelin Guide was a dead weight for French cuisine. It discouraged creativity, demanded a level of opulence that made fine dining appealing and accessible only to rich fogeys, and was unacceptably opaque about its reviewing methods. Dubanchet said that he had started *Omnivore* in part to combat "the Michelin way of thinking about food, and the Michelin way of building restaurants, and the Michelin way of not explaining." It wouldn't be easy, he acknowledged; he and his colleagues were up against a pillar of French cultural life. But as the slight, bespectacled thirty-five-year-old sipped his coffee and looked out across the Place de la Bastille, cradle of an earlier revolution, he expressed steely confidence in the uprising he was leading. "I want war," he said. "I want to tear down the Michelin system."

Even for an American well versed in the passions and peculiarities of French food culture, it was hard not to burst out laughing as Dubanchet enumerated the reasons why Fortress Michelin needed to be stormed. This was, after all, a restaurant guide he was talking about—a powerful one, to be sure, but a restaurant guide all the same. But while Dubanchet's martial language may have been overwrought, he wasn't exaggerating Michelin's clout, nor was he alone in believing that the Guide had become a malignant influence. Indeed, Michelin was now facing perhaps its most serious backlash ever, one that involved not just journalists but also some of the world's most esteemed chefs—a few of whom had even taken the radical step of handing back their Michelin stars. At the same time, several scandals had so tarnished the Guide's once-unassailable reputation that by 2007 it was fair to wonder if a revolt was even necessary: Michelin seemed to be destroying itself. If one accepted Dubanchet's critique of the Guide, this was a salutary development. But for nearly a century, Michelin had been France's culinary bible, and while the Guide's diminished stature could be seen as an opportunity for French cooking to reinvigorate itself, it could just as easily be taken as a sign of France's gastronomic decline.

Almost from the moment it began dishing out stars, in 1926, Michelin had been regarded as the Holy Writ of French gastronomy. This didn't please everyone; A. J. Liebling was no fan of the Guide, decrying its influence as "a depressing example of the subordination of art to business." But he was the rare heretic (and an American, besides); most French restaurant-goers happily submitted to its dictates. In time, it became rare to set foot in a French car that didn't have a well-worn copy of the famous red book in its glove compartment or side pocket, and in a country in which dining truly was a national pastime, the annual publication of the Guide, with its promotions and demotions, was the Oscars of the eating class.

Likewise, since the days of Fernand Point and his contemporaries, chefs had been obsessed with satisfying one guest above all others: the anonymous Michelin inspector. If they could send him home happy, success was assured. For French chefs, Michelin wasn't merely a source of approbation; it defined what it meant to eat well in France. In this sense, it was as much a beacon for haute cuisine's practitioners as it was for its consumers. Years after Point's death, one of his disciples, Alain Chapel, would describe the *Guide Rouge* as "a light to guide us."

By outward appearances, the Guide was a dim, almost imperceptible, light, especially to modern diners accustomed to having exhaustive restaurant reviews available at the click of a mouse. In more than two thousand tissue-thin pages, it contained no actual descriptions of meals or settings. It provided only restaurant details—locations, contact information, prices, specialties of the house, amenities, days closed—some of which were conveyed via symbols rather than words. (It also included separate listings for hotels.) Alongside these were the main attraction, the ratings, expressed through the Guide's most important symbol of all: a small star. It would be hard to think of a more potent emblem in any realm of human activity. A single star could validate a career and put an entire village on the map. Two stars brought regional fame, sometimes even national recognition. Three stars, the highest and rarest classification (the most restaurants in France ever to hold three stars at any one time was twenty-seven), conferred admission into the pantheon of France's greatest chefs. With a third Michelin star, a chef not only became a gastronomic colossus; he became a cultural icon, as esteemed as any novelist, poet, musician, or artist.

But how to win Michelin's benediction was far from clear. What distinguished a three-star restaurant from a two-star? Chefs were always welcome to visit the Guide's offices on the Avenue de Breteuil in Paris (the Michelin company was based in Clermont-Ferrand) to discuss their status, and many availed themselves of the opportunity. However, the answers they received were as vague as those dispensed to inquiring journalists. Michelin said its ratings were based solely on the quality of the food and had nothing to do with the setting; that three- and two-star restaurants received more scrutiny than other establishments; and that its inspectors dined incognito and paid on the company tab. But Michelin wouldn't reveal the number of inspectors it employed, never explained its decisions, and appeared to take pleasure in being evasive.

So chefs were left to draft their own road maps to the Promised Land, and many ultimately concluded that, contrary to Michelin's mantra, the difference between a two-star rating and a three-star rating had little to do with the cooking and a lot to do with the ambience. The Michelin Man, they came to believe, had a yen for luxury and wanted his surroundings to be as sumptuous as his food. Paul Bocuse won his third star supposedly after prettifying his bathrooms, and the lesson drawn by other chefs and restaurateurs was that a baronial atmosphere was a prerequisite to earning Michelin's ultimate accolade. In 2007 a trio of European economists—Olivier Gergaud, Linett Montaño Guzmán, and Vincenzo Verardi—published a study showing that Michelin was indeed influenced by the décor and even by the quality of the neighborhoods in which restaurants were located. Their regression analysis led them to conclude that the Guide "overcompensates chefs who invest heavily in their setting (and location) and undercompensates those who strictly focus on cuisine quality." Several generations of French chefs could have told them that, without having to resort to the fancy math.

Over the years, Michelin's primacy did not go unchallenged. The Guide Kléber, put out by another tire company, was its main rival for several decades. Gault Millau came along in the 1970s and briefly threatened Michelin's reign. During its heyday, Gault Millau generated more buzz than the *Guide Rouge*, and in championing nouvelle cuisine, it also influenced culinary fashion in a way that Michelin had never done. However, it didn't succeed in dethroning Michelin; nor, apparently, did it give the venerable Guide much of a fright. Even as it was being pursued in its own backyard, Michelin had turned its critical eye to restaurants and hotels outside of France, and, by the mid-2000s, it would be publishing guides to twenty European countries. In moving into these other markets, Michelin was not just spreading its reach; it was reinforcing the centuries-old notion that in matters of food and wine, France knew best. For a time at least, chefs and diners in the countries that fell within Michelin's expanded purview welcomed its arrival and generally treated its verdicts as sacrosanct. As in Paris, Lyon, and Marseille, a three-star rating in London, Munich, or Madrid was headline news and invariably turned a restaurant into a magnet for locals and tourists alike.

But in 1999, the unthinkable happened: A pair of three-star recipients in London, Marco Pierre White and Nico Ladenis, announced (separately) that they were handing back their *étoiles* and taking their restaurants in new directions. If it wasn't Michelin's Waterloo, it was at the very least a warning of trouble ahead. Explaining his decision, Ladenis suggested that Michelin had fallen out of step with what diners wanted. "I have now reached the age of sixty-five and like an old elephant with its nose in the air, my sense of smell tells me that fashion, people, expectations, and restaurants are undergoing convulsive changes," he said. In his view, traditional three-star dining had become passé, and so had Michelin. "Restaurant prices are simply too high," Ladenis said. "I wish to remedy this, and to exit Michelin was my only way out." Michelin, clearly stung, responded by insisting that chefs could not actually give back their stars; only the Guide itself had the power to withdraw them. But the legalistic face-saving did nothing to change the story line.

A three-star rating had always been considered tantamount to a winning lottery ticket, but it was now increasingly seen as both a creative and financial burden. In 1996, three years before Ladenis and White told the Guide to go jump in the Thames, Pierre Gagnaire's three-star restaurant in Saint-Étienne went bankrupt, a first in the annals of Michelin. For Gagnaire, the problem was location: The restaurant was situated in an industrial city that didn't attract many tourists and where the locals didn't much appreciate his eclectic cooking—or the exorbitant prices. As far as Saint-Étienne's mayor was concerned, it was good riddance: He said there was no place for a restaurant charging hundreds of dollars per head in a city in which people "cannot find [money] for their children's school lunches." Gagnaire's demise might have been dismissed as a product of uniquely bad circumstances had it not been for the financial woes that struck another three-star chef, Marc Veyrat, that same year. Nine million dollars in debt after extensive renovations (including gold-plated bathroom fixtures), Veyrat was forced to close his restaurant for a month when he couldn't repay the loans. The banks gave him a reprieve that allowed the restaurant, located in the Alps, to reopen, but Veyrat's near-death experience underscored the point: Outside of Paris, at least, a three-star rating had become as much a millstone as a money spinner.

That was certainly true for Bernard Loiseau, and when he committed suicide in 2003, even chefs who had profited mightily from those little stars turned on Michelin, which they accused of demanding too much ostentation and of putting unbearable pressure on them. Paul Bocuse, who had arguably prospered more than any chef in history from his three-star rating, sounded a mutinous note, warning in the days after Loiseau's death that "the profession is going to react."

It did eventually react, but not before Michelin inflicted several wounds on itself. A year after Loiseau's death, a former inspector, Pascal Remy, violated Michelin's Omertà and published a tell-all book, *L'inspecteur se met à table* ("The Inspector Sits Down to Eat"), based on the secret diary he had kept during his sixteen years with the company. Remy claimed that Michelin had just five inspectors for all of France, many fewer than was assumed. Puncturing another myth, Remy said that lots of restaurants were not visited annually; indeed, several years sometimes passed between reviews. He also asserted that some three-star establishments were considered untouchables and were sliding by on their reputations and that chefs were able to beg and cajole their way to higher ratings.

Michelin's reputation suffered another blow the following year when it was forced to pulp copies of its 2005 Guide for the Benelux countries because it included a restaurant in Belgium that hadn't yet opened. The restaurant's owner told reporters that his establishment had been given an entry because of his "good relations" with Michelin and that the premature listing was the result of an "agreement" that he had reached with the Guide. Surveying all this damage, the great chef Joël Robuchon delivered a quietly stinging rebuke. "Today, after all these mix-ups, it saddens me that we are beginning to question the impartiality of [Michelin's] judgment," he told a French television audience. "I hope that Michelin will get back on its feet. It was brilliantly led in the past."

It was another heavyweight French chef, Alain Senderens, who administered the coup de grâce: In May 2005, he announced that he was handing back his three stars, which he'd held for twenty-eight years, and converting Lucas Carton, his restaurant on the Place de la Madeleine in Paris, into an upscale brasserie. Although he insisted that his decision was not an indictment of Michelin, he said the cost of maintaining a three-star rating had become too burdensome, a comment that certainly had the ring of an indictment. He repeated those sentiments when I had lunch with him a year later. Echoing Nico Ladenis, the sixty-seven-year-old Senderens said that haute cuisine had entered "a new age" in which diners wanted good food for less money and chefs wanted to serve impeccable fare without having to also provide lots of bells and whistles. But didn't Michelin insist that stars were based purely on the quality of the cooking? Senderens smiled. "They like luxurious restaurants," he diplomatically replied. But to continue catering to Michelin's predilections no longer made sense financially or strategically. "I was spending hundreds of thousands of euros a year on the dining room— on flowers, on glasses," he said. "But it didn't make the food taste any better." It sounded like the epitaph for an era.

The Michelin era had begun in 1900, with the publication of the inaugural Guide. Its first editor was André Michelin, who with his brother Édouard had founded the tire company in 1888. After his death in 1931, he was succeeded by a nephew, Pierre Bourdon-Michelin, who oversaw the Guide through the Second World War. Thereafter, a trio of outsiders—René Pauchet, André Tichot, and Bernard Naegellen, the last two former inspectors—held the job. Naegellen, who served as director from 1985 until 2000, was the embodiment of the Michelin Man—charmingly evasive, wearing his authority lightly but wielding it unsparingly. When Naegellen retired, Michelin shocked the culinary establishment by appointing a British inspector, Derek Brown, to succeed him. "It's a scandal," Paris-based restaurant critic Gilles Pudlowski told the *Times* of London. "England is the European country where you eat least well. An Englishman will bring nothing good."

On that last score, at least, Pudlowski was prescient; little good did come from Brown's editorship, though how much of the blame should fall on him is debatable. The low point of his tenure was Loiseau's suicide. Brown naturally sought to absolve Michelin of any culpability and denied ever having warned the late chef that his third star was at risk. But for good measure, he opted to break with precedent and not strip La Côte d'Or of its third star, as had been brusquely done to Restaurant Alain Chapel after its namesake passed away. The Remy tell-all also appeared on Brown's watch, and by the time the Briton stepped down in the summer of 2004, having reached the mandatory retirement age of sixty, Michelin's brand looked to be in serious trouble.

Michelin decided to shake things up by appointing an outsider, Jean-Luc Naret, to succeed Brown. Naret, a forty-three-year-old Frenchman, was a hotel industry veteran with no prior Michelin experience and no particular gastronomic credentials. But the company now wanted a charismatic front man who could help restore the Guide's reputation, and the youthful and urbane (not to mention perpetually tanned) Naret fit that description. Michelin also needed someone who could smooth the Guide's passage into new markets. In early 2005, the company announced plans to venture beyond Europe for the first time by publishing a Guide to New York. There, it would be going up against the very popular and democratic Zagat guide in a city accustomed to detailed, transparent restaurant criticism. To win over American diners, Michelin would have to be far more communicative than it had been back home, and it was with this, too, in mind that Naret had been hired.

The New York Guide was published in the fall of 2005, and the reaction was a collective yawn: The three-star picks (Le Bernardin, Jean Georges, Per Se, and Alain Ducasse New York) didn't cause much controversy, and while there was considerable quibbling over the one- and two-star choices, most food-savvy New Yorkers seemed proudly indifferent to Michelin's arrival. Undeterred, Michelin hailed its American debut as a success and not long thereafter unveiled plans to publish Guides to San Francisco, Los Angeles, and Las Vegas. And in early 2007, Naret announced that Michelin would be coming out that year with a Guide for Tokyo. Haute cuisine was now a global phenomenon, and Michelin intended to be the universal arbiter.

All of this made Naret a busy man. After several months of trying, I finally managed to catch up with him in New York in July 2007. We met for a drink at the boutique Midtown hotel where he was staying. The bar area was filled with what the locals tended to refer to as Eurotrash, and Naret, who had just flown in and would soon be leaving for San Diego and Tokyo, seemed very much at home. He was wearing a stylish dark blue suit, a white dress shirt (*sans cravate*) with a flamboyantly large collar, and a white pocket square. He suggested that we take a seat in the small lobby so that we could "watch all the very nice women coming and going." Naret had his usual George Hamilton tan, and I joked about airplanes now coming equipped with sunning salons, which elicited a wan smile from him.

He suggested we drink beer; I ordered a Belgian lager, and he went with a Heineken. Naret confirmed that he had indeed been hired to bring greater transparency to the Guide's operations and to lead its expansion. "We need to protect the anonymity of the inspectors, but we also need to explain what we are looking for," he said. "Michelin had never communicated its values. We shouldn't be afraid to go in front of the public. I've done twelve hundred interviews with journalists around the world, and I always say they are welcome to ask any question." I took that as an invitation and asked him how many inspectors Michelin currently employed in France. "About fifteen," he said. Okay; maybe glasnost really had come to the Avenue de Breteuil. Naret went on to tell me that he dined in multiple restaurants himself each week but was not an inspector and did not personally decide on the allocation of stars. And how often were the three-star establishments visited? He said it was six to twelve times a year for three-stars and four to six times for two-stars. When I pointed out that a lot of people were under the impression that the difference between a three-star and two-star was mainly a function of the décor, Naret smiled and shook his head. "What matters is what's on the plate," he said. But Alain Senderens, who knew something about winning three stars, had said that the sumptuousness of the setting mattered, and ever since Bocuse renovated his bathrooms, chefs had believed this to be the case. "Everyone always brings up the loo," Naret said, laughing. "We never tell chefs that they have to invest in all these other things." So for forty years, the great chefs of France had been laboring under an enormous misconception and spending millions of dollars they didn't need to spend? "Yes."

By now, we were on to a second round of beers, and I'd come to like Naret. He seemed like an oily character, and I found much of what he said unconvincing, but he was very friendly and forthcoming. The conversation had turned to specific chefs, and whether it was the Heineken talking or the new voice of the Michelin Guide, Naret was remarkably candid. I mentioned a recent visit to Georges Blanc and how empty the dining room had been; Naret told me the Guide had lately received a slew of reader letters regarding Blanc. As he said it, he arched his eyebrow as if to indicate that the mail was not running in Blanc's favor and that his third star might be at risk. Talking about Ferran Adrià's influence, I brought up a meal I'd had a few weeks earlier at the two-star Cordeillan-Bages in Bordeaux, whose chef, Thierry Marx, was keen on Adrià-like foams and flourishes. I told Naret that I found Marx's food disappointing—the kitchen seemed too focused on pyrotechnics and not sufficiently attentive to basics. The lamb I'd had was overcooked and tasteless. He nodded in emphatic agreement, said he'd had a similar experience, and confided that the bullet-headed Marx, once touted as a sure bet for three stars, would now probably never get promoted. I asked if he really thought that the food at Bocuse still merited a third star. "Sometimes it's good, sometimes it's not, but overall, as an experience, he maintains his level." Not exactly a resounding endorsement. I also broached another sensitive subject: Why, I wondered, hadn't La Côte d'Or been demoted to two stars following Loiseau's death, as had been the case with Alain Chapel's restaurant? Bernard Naegellen had explained, in regard to Chapel, that to leave the third star in place would have suggested that the deceased chef had had nothing to do with his restaurant's success. Naret, completely contradicting his predecessor, said that "stars are not as attached to the man; they are attached to the team of the restaurant, and if they continue to do the same job, there is no point to take stars away." In Michelin's judgment, La Côte d'Or had not faltered in the wake of Loiseau's suicide and therefore it had kept its third star. Four years later, it still had it.

I told Naret that I would be in Paris in September and asked if I could join him for a meal so that I could see how the Michelin Man went about appraising a restaurant. To my surprise, he agreed, and two months later, we met up for lunch. His choice of restaurants was intriguing: Carré des Feuillants, located off the Place Vendôme, was a perennial two-star that many people felt had been unjustly denied a promotion. Guy Savoy had been made to sweat for seventeen years before finally earning his third star, and now it was Alain Dutournier, the chef and owner of Carré des Feuillants, who seemed to be the un-chosen one. In picking Carré des Feuillants, was Naret subtly indicating that a third star was at last in Dutournier's grasp? I walked into the restaurant at twelve-thirty precisely. The receptionist greeted me and asked for the name of the reservation. I suddenly recalled with some alarm that Naret's assistant hadn't told me the alias he'd be using. I wasn't quite sure of the name, I told her. She asked if I knew the company that had booked the table. I pretended to draw a blank on that, too. Wearing a look of polite bafflement, she invited me to take a seat in the lobby. A few moments later, one of the captains came in from the dining room, exchanged a few whispered comments with the receptionist, and cast a suspicious glance my way.

I figured I was probably just minutes from being asked to leave (or being hauled off by the gendarmes) when Naret came breezing through the front door. Although it was a sunny, mid-September afternoon with temperatures well into the sixties, he had a bright purple scarf wrapped rather dramatically around his neck—not exactly the look of a man moving about town incognito. In fact, he wasn't seeking anonymity at all: He had booked under his own name. As we were shown to our table, Naret reminded me that he was not an inspector and thus had no need for pseudonyms. It was better if he reserved as Jean-Luc Naret, he said. Michelin took a dim view of restaurants that lavished preferential treatment on certain guests, and what better way of finding that out than having the Guide's editorial director in the dining room? He sometimes had inspectors visit restaurants at the same time he was there so that he could compare notes with them later and determine if favors had been dispensed. "So there might be an inspector here right now?" I asked. "Possibly," he said with a cagey grin.

The Carré des Feuillants staff didn't fawn over Naret. They were obsequious, of course (it came with the territory), but no more so than they were with the other diners. Dutournier also played it cool: Rather than rushing out to greet Naret, he waited perhaps half an hour to come into the dining room, and he stopped to exchange pleasantries with a few other guests before sauntering over to see us. But once at our table, the stocky, gray-haired chef was a picture of timidity: He seemed to bow as he shook Naret's hand, meekly said "Hello," and then stood there wearing a nervous, expectant smile. His demeanor was almost supplicatory, which was jarring to see in this normally cocksure chef, a frequent and animated presence on French television. Michelin's influence might have been waning, but it evidently still had the power to make famous French chefs quake in their clogs. For his part, Naret was curt: He thanked Dutournier for the greeting, said he looked well, and then flashed him a look that seemed to say "dismissed." Dutournier quickly wished us a *bon appétit* and retreated to the kitchen. I couldn't decide if Naret was being scrupulously professional and avoiding small talk or smelled weakness and was being gratuitously cruel.

Naret ordered oysters in seawater gelée, a specialty of the house, for his first course and roasted turbot for his main. Although he wasn't an inspector, he obviously knew the criteria that Michelin used to assess the quality of meals, and I was hoping he would provide a running commentary on the food. But despite my gentle entreaties, Naret didn't say anything about it: He just ate—and fast. So instead, we talked some more about Michelin's methodology (as much as he would reveal, anyway); discussed the imminent debut of the Michelin Guide to Tokyo (reaching into his jacket pocket, he pulled out an inspector's report for one restaurant in Tokyo and joked about losing it on the street; I got enough of a look to determine that it was a report on Beige, Alain Ducasse's restaurant on the Ginza); and traded gossip. Apropos of our earlier discussion, I decided to test his familiarity with the New York food scene by asking if he knew which Manhattan restaurant was notorious for serving markedly superior food to regulars and VIPs. Before I could finish the question, Naret gave the chef's initials, an impressive display of insider knowledge. (He went on to confide that this practice had cost the restaurant a star.) As our desserts were being cleared, I made a last attempt to get Naret to cough up some insights into what we'd eaten. I asked if he thought the quality of the lunch was consistent with the restaurant's two-star rating, to which I received a one-word reply: "Yes." He then told me that he would not be returning to Carré des Feuillants for a while: This had been his fifth visit to the restaurant in 2007, and he was worried that perhaps the long-suffering Dutournier was getting the wrong idea. "You mean he might think you're considering him for a third star?" I asked. "Exactly."

Several months later, back in Paris, I decided to get another perspective on the Guide from someone else who could speak about it with authority: Pascal Remy. He had suggested a drink at a hotel on the rue de Rivoli, across from the Louvre. I went there expecting to meet a short, bald man (weren't all inspectors short and bald?) with a hunted look about him. Instead, Remy turned out to be tall, handsome, and quite jocular (with a full head of hair, too). Over a glass of Champagne, Remy told me that while he was officially *persona non grata* within the French culinary establishment, he was doing consulting work for some restaurants and even heard periodically from former colleagues at Michelin. He was hoping his notoriety might yield a television project: He envisioned a series in which he and various guest stars would travel to top restaurants around the world and critique the meals they were served. The idea didn't sound very promising, and I had the impression that the people he'd shopped it to hadn't thought so, either.

When we turned to the book, Remy insisted that everything he had written was true. He said the number of inspectors had declined sharply, and that by 2003 there indeed had been just five for all of France, down from a dozen in the late 1980s. He said that inspectors typically spent three of every four weeks on the road. Each day consisted of a lunch and dinner, with both meals taken anonymously. The rest of the time was spent making non-anonymous inspections of hotels and restaurants to see if any information needed updating. He said restaurants weren't visited nearly as frequently as Michelin claimed; one-stars, for instance, would be visited perhaps every second year. "There is one uncontestable point," he said, grinning. "Michelin inspectors always pay their way. After that, everything is contestable."

He reiterated his claim about certain chefs and restaurants being untouchable. Among these, Bocuse was the one with the worst food but also the most secure rating. "The Michelin Guide made Bocuse, and now he is considered sacred," said Remy. "He is more powerful than the Guide." He went on to say that it was silly to even think of the Guide as still being primarily concerned with cuisine; the Guide was now just a vehicle for the Michelin corporation. "Michelin's goal is to get people talking about Michelin," he said. The Tokyo Guide had just been released, and to the astonishment of gastronomes everywhere, all one hundred and fifty restaurants listed in the book had been awarded stars, giving the Japanese capital more *étoiles* than Paris. But Remy said he wasn't surprised: "The goal was to infiltrate the Japanese market for Michelin tires, so the inspectors were there to give lots of stars."

I asked him what he thought of Naret. "Berlusconi?" he replied, a twinkle in his eye. It took me a second to figure out what he meant, then I recalled Naret's dark, receding hair and perma-tan and got the joke. He said Naret was a salesman, selling books in order to sell tires. "He was recruited for publicity, to make people talk about the Michelin brand," he said. "He is the super ambassador." Remy said that he'd heard from insiders that Naret was not a very popular figure at the Avenue de Breteuil office, in part because he was apparently earning three times the salary that Naegellen—"a real inspector"—had pulled down. I told him that I'd met several times with Naret and that he'd insisted that the power to give or take away stars rested not with him but with the inspectors. Remy shook his head. "The inspectors are marionettes," he said; if the director wanted the Guide to make a statement by either promoting or demoting a restaurant, the statement would be made.

Listening to Remy, I was struck by how completely at ease he looked and sounded. He was either an astonishingly persuasive fabulist or he was telling the truth (at least as he saw it). I asked him about the Loiseau affair and what role, if any, he thought that Michelin had played. He claimed that, contrary to its denials, Michelin had indicated to Loiseau that his third star was in jeopardy. There was a written report about the visit that Loiseau had paid to the Guide's offices in November 2002, in which it was stated that he had been told there were concerns about the quality of his food and that he needed to improve things. Not only that: After the meeting, Dominique Loiseau had written a letter to Michelin saying that its warning had been heard and that her husband would henceforth be tethered to his kitchen; according to Remy, she even underlined the word *warning*. The fact that Michelin had not removed La CÔte d'Or's third star after Loiseau's death, Remy said, suggested that the Guide may have felt that it bore some responsibility for what had happened. He also told me that the day after Loiseau's suicide, the chef's file, containing the account of his visit and the follow-up letter from his wife, had mysteriously vanished. So the written evidence was gone? Not entirely, said Remy. "Copies exist."

A few days later, I had lunch with Gilles Pudlowski at Benoit, a venerable Paris bistro now owned by Alain Ducasse. Pudlowksi was a French phenomenon. Trained as a literary critic, he had turned to restaurant writing in the 1970s as one of the provocateurs at Gault Millau. He was now the food critic for the newsweekly *Le Point* and also published two annual restaurant guides, *Pudlo Paris* and *Pudlo France*. Pudlowski had spent most of his career challenging Michelin's hegemony in one way or another. Yet when I brought up Michelin's travails over lunch, he seemed genuinely pained by the Guide's diminished stature. "For us, Michelin was the grand old lady," he said. "It was a defender of France's cultural patrimony. Now, it makes scandal and provocation. It's unfortunate."

The Last Gentleman of Europe

TAILLEVENT IS LOCATED ON a small, strangely nondescript street a few blocks in from the Champs-Élysées. Its name is on the awning, but the restaurant's entrance is so understated that you almost expect to be asked for a password before you step inside. After checking your coat, you are led down a hallway toward the dining room, and as you approach its threshold, you feel hungry, but you may also feel a twinge of nerves. There are thousands of restaurants in France, but only around two dozen of them hold three Michelin stars. These select few are supposed to represent French cuisine in all its refinement and splendor; they are considered the standard-bearers, and none more so than Taillevent. As you are shown to your table, the normal calculus is inverted. At other restaurants, you wonder if they'll prove to be worthy of you; sliding into your seat at Taillevent, you wonder if you'll prove to be worthy of it.

A waiter appears—discreet and courteous, of course, but with a friendliness to his smile that you didn't expect. He suggests a glass of Champagne and returns a few minutes later with the aperitif and a small plate of *gougères*. Served warm, they are the airiest, most delectable cheese puffs imaginable, and their golden-brown color, set against the deep yellow of the Champagne, the wood paneling of the walls, and the soft lighting of the room, has an oddly sedative effect; it seems like a cue to relax, and so you do. The head captain approaches the table, and although he is dressed in a tuxedo, he exudes geniality. Whether or not you are a familiar face, he greets you like one, tells you how delighted he and his colleagues are to see you, and makes small talk for a few minutes—about Paris, or his recent visit to New York, or the French soccer team. He has a playful demeanor and cracks a joke or two; you notice later that gentle waves of laughter ripple across the room from wherever he happens to be standing.

As you continue chatting with him, a man holding a menu hovers into view a few feet from the table. He is in his sixties, with a trim frame and a heavily receded gray hairline. Dressed in an elegant business suit, he looks like a bank executive, an impression reinforced by his large tortoiseshell glasses. Although the maître d's eyes never leave yours, he seems instantly aware that his boss is nearby and gracefully brings the conversation to a close. As he steps away, you sit up in your seat and cast a quick glance down to make sure your tie is where it should be. Taillevent's formidable reputation rests largely on the shoulders of Jean-Claude Vrinat, and now that this legendary restaurateur is standing before you, that edgy feeling returns. Surely, this is the moment you are going to be sized up, deemed unworthy, and condemned to an evening of quiet misery.

However, Vrinat turns out to be just as hospitable as everyone else. Indeed, after several minutes of his undivided attention, a bizarre thought occurs: Although there is nothing the least bit obsequious about his demeanor, Vrinat seems almost flattered by your presence. Sometime later, perhaps as you're sipping a perfectly aged Bordeaux and savoring the last bite of the gloriously turned out venison or sweetbreads, another, even more disorientating realization sets in: Taillevent is the most exalted of all France's three-star restaurants, yet you're not just being made to feel welcome—you are being made to feel as if you belong here. Patricia Wells summed up the experience perfectly. "If Taillevent did not exist," she wrote, "someone would have to invent it: the pillar of French cuisine, the ideal of what can and should be done in running a restaurant, in treating each guest with honor and dignity."

Wells wrote those words in 1984. Two decades later, she still held to that view, as did many other people. In 2006, Taillevent celebrated its sixtieth anniversary and Jean-Claude Vrinat turned seventy.

Neither showed its age. At the time, the restaurant had been recently renovated and the food, though still traditional, exuded the panache of the restaurant's talented, self-effacing young chef, Alain Solivérès. As for Vrinat, he was as driven and indefatigable as ever, presiding over the dining room every lunch and dinner and constantly seeking new ways of keeping Taillevent vibrant without sacrificing its essential classicism. The fact that it was always full seemed to indicate that he was succeeding. But on February 21, 2007, after thirty-four years at the top, Taillevent was stripped of its third star by Michelin. It was a decision that left Vrinat perplexed and angry, and he wasn't alone.

In demoting Taillevent, Michelin wasn't just punishing a revered institution; it was closing the book on a particular style of three-star restaurant. Vrinat was the ringmaster at Taillevent, but he wasn't its chef; he presided in the dining room and left the cooking to someone else (always a supremely capable someone else, of course). Postwar Paris had a trio of legendary three-star restaurants with this allocation of labor and limelight: La Tour d'Argent, Lasserre, and Taillevent. Lasserre, its dining room under the direction of René Lasserre, was awarded its third star in 1962 and lost it in 1984. La Tour d'Argent's non-cooking owner, Claude Terrail, captured three stars in 1951 and was downgraded by Michelin in 1996. In an age of celebrity chefs, Vrinat's approach to the running of his restaurant was nothing short of antediluvian, and now, in February 2007, with his third star gone, it was officially passé.

It was a form of hospitality that Vrinat had learned at the side of his father, André, but only after an unsettled childhood. Born in 1936, Vrinat was just a year old when his mother died. At the time, the family was residing in the town of Saint-Quentin, in northern France, where André, a sybaritic engineer who had long aspired to a life of food and wine, had opened a hotel and restaurant. Success came quickly; the restaurant earned a Michelin star after just a year in business. But hopes for a second star were dashed by the onset of the Second World War. Fiercely anti-Nazi, André put his son in the care of his grandmother in 1939 and took up arms, first for the French Army, later for the

Resistance. Over the ensuing seven years, Jean-Claude saw his father only sporadically.

At war's end, André returned to Saint-Quentin to find the auberge in ruins. He sold what remained of the property, moved to Paris, and in late 1946 opened Taillevent—named for the fourteenth-century chef believed to have penned France's first cookbook. Two years later, he recaptured his Michelin star. In 1950, Taillevent took up residence in its present location, a townhouse on the rue Lamennais. With chef Lucien Leheu in the kitchen, Taillevent earned a second Michelin star in 1954.

Despite having grown up around food and wine, Jean-Claude had little interest in the restaurant trade. After graduating from lycée in 1954, he studied law and business in Paris. In 1959, he interned with several multinationals in Brazil. He returned home to perform his military service, which threw him into the last spasms of France's withdrawal from Algeria, and then decided to take a job in Brazil with the J. Walter Thompson advertising agency. One of his father's friends talked him out of it. "He said Brazil had a bright future, but that it was unclear when exactly that bright future would arrive," Vrinat recounted with a laugh. "He suggested that I instead go to work at Taillevent. I thought about it, realized he was right, and so that's what I did."

Over the next decade, André groomed his son to succeed him, and it was during this period that Vrinat's interest in *restauration* finally blossomed. His personal life also flourished: He was married to Sabine Delame Lelièvre and had two children—a daughter, Valérie, and a son, Charles-Édouard. In 1970, Claude Deligne took over Taillevent's kitchen. In 1972, André retired; the next year, the restaurant was awarded a third star. "The timing was unfortunate," said Vrinat. "The third star belonged to my father." In the years that followed, Taillevent not only cemented its hold on that star; it came to be considered the iconic three-star. It was a favorite canteen of French politicians and business leaders, and lunch service would invariably see tables full of gray eminences huddling over digestifs and Cuban cigars late into the afternoon. But the clubby atmosphere was deceiving; whether you were a president or a rube from Peoria, you were accorded the same exemplary treatment. (Among Vrinat's most cherished clients: the two factory workers who played hooky from the assembly line once a year to splurge on lunch at Taillevent.)

Vrinat and his staff went about their work with a serene perfectionism; no detail escaped their notice, but they made flawlessness look easy and fun, and they made it fun for their guests. One left Taillevent feeling not just satiated, but happy. If you couldn't decide between two dishes, the maître d' would choose for you and give you a half portion of each (which invariably ended up being more like a full portion of both). If you were eyeing your wife's turbot, chances were there was already another fork on the table, awaiting your grasping fingers. Names were recalled without fail, and personal predilections, too. A glass of complimentary Champagne was sometimes offered at the start of the meal, and a glass of the house Cognac, also gratis, was frequently offered at the end of it. Vrinat would often pour the Cognac himself and leave the bottle on the table, an implicit invitation to help yourself to more if the mood struck. It was a shrewd way of earning goodwill, but it also bespoke a generosity of spirit.

A paragon of graciousness—the last gentleman of Europe, you might say—Vrinat also had a knack for defusing even the most challenging situations. There was the day, for instance, that Salvador Dalí, a frequent guest, arrived for lunch accompanied by an ocelot on a leash. Vrinat quietly asked why he had brought the cat; Dalí explained it was his birthday and he wanted to celebrate with someone. The ocelot was permitted to stay, and the meal passed without incident. As Dalí was settling up, Vrinat gently told the artist, "Perhaps next time it would be best if your friend didn't come; I had the sense he didn't especially enjoy himself." Dalí took the hint, and the ocelot never returned to Taillevent.

Vrinat was a charming and erudite man, as conversant in politics and business as he was in food and wine (with three hundred thousand bottles, Taillevent had one of the finest cellars of any three-star, and Vrinat, who participated in the 1976 Judgment of Paris, was considered among France's foremost authorities on wine). But he was not a backslapper; he was always "correct" and radiated a quiet but firm authority. There was also something just slightly inscrutable about his expression. If a waiter or busboy made a mistake, it wasn't hard to read Vrinat's face—the frown could burn a hole in the tablecloth. However, apart from these (extremely rare) instances, he gave little away. Over time, I came to realize that this was probably just as he wanted it. Perhaps he needed a mask of sorts.

In 1975, Charles-Édouard, then three, was diagnosed with leukemia; he died two years later. It was not something Vrinat talked about, and I only learned of it while interviewing him in November 2001. I knew that his daughter helped run Les Caves Taillevent, the wine shop he owned around the corner from the restaurant, and I'd assumed she was an only child. Vrinat corrected me, saying he'd also had a son but "we lost him." As the words left his mouth, his voice cracked and his chest heaved as if he were sucking back tears. "I wanted a son," he said, gazing out his office window, "to take care of him, to be able to do for him the things that my father, because of the war and what happened to my mother, was unable to do for me." Aware that I was a new father, he then offered me some advice: Make sure to have three children, he said, because if you have two and lose one, the other child will grow up lonely.

The following June, I went to Taillevent for lunch with my wife and ten-month-old son. Halfway through the meal, I took James out into the front foyer to give him a change of scenery while my wife finished her main course. To my surprise, Vrinat joined us and spent five minutes crouching down and playing with James. As he gently clutched James's hand and quietly talked to him, his manner wasn't so much grandfatherly as it was paternal. During subsequent visits to Taillevent, I would show Vrinat photos of James, and I noticed he would linger over the pictures longer than politeness required. It wasn't hard to imagine what he was thinking. What was difficult to fathom was how this man who had known so much turmoil and grief became so single-mindedly determined to give tranquility and pleasure to others.

That attitude didn't necessarily extend to the people he employed. He was a difficult boss—liberal with criticism, niggardly with his praise, and punctilious to an extreme (he was even known to personally scrub the toilets if he felt his staff needed a refresher course). He typically descended from his apartment above the restaurant at eight each morning, and apart from an early dinner with Sabine, he was on duty straight through until midnight. It was a job that demanded great sacrifice on his part but even more on hers. (Although, as she cheerfully observed one day over lunch, "In France, all the men have mistresses. His mistress is the restaurant. He comes home late every night, but at least I know where he has been.")

Taillevent was closed on Saturdays and Sundays. Weekends were given over to family—to Sabine, and also to Valérie and her three children—but Vrinat also spent much of his downtime brooding about the restaurant and pinpointing needed improvements. The start of a new week was seldom pleasant for his staff. "Sometimes, I am in a very bad mood." Vrinat admitted. "Monday morning is the worst part of the week for them." He wasn't one to shout his displeasure, though he would if he felt it was needed; rather, he expressed his dissatisfaction through subtle but unmistakable gestures. Working at Taillevent required, among other things, becoming fluent in the boss's body language. One Saturday morning at Les Caves Taillevent, Vrinat found a splintered piece of wood in a display case. He picked it up and began gently tapping it against his leg while chatting with a customer. Within seconds, one of the shop's employees, contrition etched on his face, swooped in to discard the offending spear. Even after nearly three decades at Taillevent, Jean-Marie Ancher, the restaurant's head captain, said that he still feared Vrinat's wrath. "We have a nervousness in our stomachs twice a day, every day," he told me.

Vrinat's imperiousness extended to the kitchen. At Taillevent, the chef's role was to cook, not to be seen or heard. This had been the modus vivendi of his father and Lucien Leheu, and their partnership had prospered for twenty years. But, of course, that was before nouvelle cuisine, and while Claude Deligne, who replaced Leheu and served until his retirement in 1991, was also content to defer to the boss, Vrinat recognized that the culinary profession had changed and that chefs wanted the authority and the attention for themselves now. He knew that his attitude was rooted in a bygone era and he made light of it. "I came along before Paul Bocuse led the chefs out of the kitchens," he jokingly told Frank Prial of the *New York Times*.

But Vrinat had no interest in recalibrating the balance of power at Taillevent, and this had led to a rupture with Deligne's successor, Philippe Legendre. A shy man, Legendre was happy to cede the public relations to Vrinat, but after several years as chef, he began to chafe at the limitations imposed on him in the kitchen. It wasn't that he was prevented from exercising his imagination; he retooled a number of longstanding dishes and also created some new ones, including a stunningly good cream of watercress soup that was fortified with generous dollops of Sevruga caviar and which became an instant classic. But Vrinat's insistence on having the last word about what went on the plate became harder for Legendre to accept, and in 1999 he took his knives and bolted for the Hotel George V.

Vrinat wanted innovation—it just had to be on his terms. While Taillevent served classical cuisine, Vrinat knew that its food had to keep pace with the changing whims of the dining public, and over the years it had: Sauces became progressively lighter, vegetables crunchier. But this wasn't just a matter of submitting to culinary fashion; Vrinat believed it was essential that Taillevent evolve. When Legendre quit, the restaurant was in its sixth decade and had held three stars for more than a quarter-century. Vrinat knew that it now risked being seen as a gastronomic museum, and he was determined not to let this happen.

Nor was he about to allow himself to be labeled a dinosaur. His view of chefs may have been prehistoric, and he certainly understood that he was among the last of a breed of restaurateur, but he bristled at the notion that he was tethered to the past. In 2001, eager to show that he could appeal to a younger, thriftier crowd, he opened a second Paris restaurant, L'Angle du Faubourg, a contemporary bistro one block over from Taillevent. It was done in a chic, minimalist décor and offered updated bistro fare—lamb shoulder with black olives was a typical entrée—punctuated by flights of fancy, such as a dessert of pineapple ravioli. "L'Angle is a *pied à nez*"—thumbing the nose—"at all those who say I am conservative," he said at the time.

This same desire to confound expectations led him to hire Michel del Burgo as Legendre's replacement. Del Burgo, then the chef at the HÔtel Bristol in Paris, had been recommended to Vrinat by his friend and business partner Joël Robuchon, with whom he co-owned a restaurant in Tokyo called Taillevent-Robuchon. Still, del Burgo seemed a strange choice. He was known to be a bit of a culinary daredevil, and the Carcassonne native's food bore a distinctly southern accent. Taillevent's fare, even as it was made lighter, had always been solidly northern French—cream and butter. However, Vrinat not only gave del Burgo the job; he let him apply a few southern touches to Taillevent's cooking (a risotto of cèpes, for instance—so creamy and deliciously earthy it would have made even the most chauvinistic Italian groan with pleasure). But then history repeated itself in cruel fashion: del Burgo lost his infant son to crib death, and not long thereafter, the devastated chef quit.

Alain Solivérès, who had been working at the two-star Les Élysées du Vernet in Paris, took over the kitchen in 2002. He was also from the south, and with him at the stove, Taillevent's food became lighter and sunnier still, with artichokes, tomatoes, and olives turning up in more dishes. However, the additions to the menu were less significant than the subtractions. Two of Taillevent's most celebrated dishes—the *boudin de homard à la nage,* a feathery lobster mousse shaped like a sausage and served in a light fish stock, and the *marquise au chocolat et à la pistache,* a mousse-like chocolate cake served in a glorious puddle of pistachio sauce—were now off the menu. Old-timers and creatures of habit like me were crestfallen, but Vrinat was determined to show that he and Taillevent could evolve.

And it wasn't just the food. Vrinat gave the restaurant a makeover in 2004, putting in new carpeting, upholstery, and lighting. He also redecorated it in a contemporary motif, hanging several abstract paintings and adding some modern ornamental art. The renovations did not suit everyone's taste; head captain Ancher jokingly offered to treat me to dinner if I would use my cutlery to slash a painting he particularly disliked. In truth, though, the new look did make the restaurant seem younger.

Taillevent's appearance was changing in another important way. In the past, men who showed up without jackets and ties were lent them, and if they balked, they ate elsewhere. But the same sartorial rebellion that tore through the workplace in the 1990s—beginning with casual Fridays and eventually resulting in casual Mondays-through-Fridays—quickly spread to restaurants, and Taillevent didn't resist it. The staff stayed tuxedoed, but guests could now leave the jackets and ties at home. Vrinat and his lieutenants didn't necessarily welcome the new look; one night, as I watched an elderly man shuffle through the dining room in jeans, Ancher just shrugged and said, "It's a different world, my friend." But the culture had changed, and Taillevent needed to change with it.

In 2006, as the restaurant turned sixty and he turned seventy, Vrinat continued to look for new ways to project vitality. He now had a blog on Taillevent's Web site, where he posted daily ruminations on food, wine, and other matters. Although the kitchen was functioning well—the reviews for Solivérès were uniformly enthusiastic, and Taillevent was still in possession of its third star—Vrinat felt he needed to pour even more of himself into the restaurant. In 2006, he ended his collaboration with Robuchon in Japan because the two weeks that he was obliged to spend at their Tokyo restaurant each year were two extra weeks that he now preferred to devote to his flagship establishment.

Contentment was an elusive state. "Maybe I can't enjoy today; I'm always worried about tomorrow," he had told me when I interviewed him in 2001. "When I was young, life was not easy. Not knowing if your father will return from war, then seeing him lose everything; it shapes the way you think. It gives you a feeling of insecurity, of anxiety. And then to be in the restaurant business, which is so fickle—this is why I take nothing for granted and am always cautious." But now, though, his anxiety wasn't limited to Taillevent. He was distressed about France, fearful that the country was in terminal decline. "Where is my grandchildren's future?" he said. "Is it in France? I just don't know."

He was worried, too, about the state of French cuisine. Younger chefs, rattled by Spain's emergence, seemed to be forsaking France's culinary heritage in an effort to prove that they could be just as daring and imaginative. Vrinat admired Ferran Adrià and had enjoyed his meals at El Bulli, but he believed that the Spanish chef was sui generis and that his style of cooking was simply not replicable. More importantly, he saw no reason why the French should want to mimic it. "We need to change," said Vrinat, "but is the point of creativity to just be creative?" He thought there was a way of reconciling innovation and tradition and that he and Taillevent could, in some small fashion, help point the way forward. This was now the task he had set himself. "It is my main challenge, and it is a big challenge, and it is the reason why I want to go on as long as I can."

But as 2006 drew to a close, he suddenly found himself with a more urgent concern. In October, he went for his annual appointment with the Michelin Guide. He had expected to see Jean-Luc Naret, but when he arrived at Michelin's headquarters, he was informed that he would instead be meeting with Jean-François Mesplède, the editorial director of the French Guide. Mesplède wasted no time getting to his point: He told Vrinat that he had been to Taillevent recently and thought the quality of the food had slipped. "What did you eat?" Vrinat asked. Mesplède, a former journalist, told him that he had a vegetable starter and a *côte de veau*. And had he liked the *côte de veau*? Mesplède said it had been good but not as good as it needed to be. Vrinat pressed for more details, but Mesplède was vague and just kept returning to the same theme: The cooking had declined. Vrinat left the meeting confused and worried. For reasons that were unclear, he and Taillevent had officially been put on notice.

Three months later, Vrinat learned that Mesplède hadn't been warning him of a demotion; he had been announcing one. On January 18, 2007, *Le Figaro*'s François Simon reported that the 2007 Michelin Guide, due out in February, would bear several surprises, "the most spectacular" of which would be the demotion of "the Parisian institution" Taillevent. Vrinat didn't publicly acknowledge Simon's scoop. He assumed it was true but thought it wiser to wait until the Guide was released before commenting. He also harbored the slender hope that if Michelin heard from enough indignant readers, it might reconsider (though, presumably, the 2007 Guide was already printed). In anticipation of a possible downgrade, Vrinat wrote two messages, one of which would be posted on his blog: a sigh-of-relief statement if Taillevent kept its third star, a concessionary statement if it didn't. Oddly, Vrinat seemed to find more enjoyment in preparing the latter. He decided that it would be accompanied by a photo of a deflated tire, which he thought was a hilarious touch (Michelin being a tire company). As he roared with laughter, his assistant commented, "I think you're secretly praying to lose the third star."

Early on the night of February 20, as Vrinat was greeting some guests, Naret telephoned. It was the first Vrinat had heard from Michelin since the *Figaro* story, and the mere fact of the call was all the confirmation he needed; he had no interest in speaking with Naret. "Tell Monsieur Naret it's seven twenty P.M. and it's time to take care of customers, not to take care of Michelin," he icily instructed the receptionist. The next morning, Michelin announced its 2007 ratings, and for the first time in thirty-five years, Taillevent was not among the three-star recipients. Vrinat wasted no time posting his response, along with the picture of the flat tire. He said he was surprised by Michelin's decision but assured readers that he and the restaurant would "get back in the saddle," and carry on as before. "I've known more painful challenges than this," he wrote.

Shortly after the demotion was made official, Solivérès walked into Vrinat's office and burst into tears, apologizing for having let him down; Vrinat assured him it was not his fault and that there was no need to apologize. The rest of the staff was shaken, too, but as the morning went on, an illusion of normalcy fell over the restaurant. On this of all days, the need for flawless execution and smiling faces was acute; it was imperative that the atmosphere in the dining room be festive, not funereal. As for those closest to Vrinat, Valérie was sad but displayed her father's stoicism. Not so Sabine, who was devastated by the news and furious at what she saw as a gross injustice against Taillevent and her husband.

And, in truth, Vrinat's feelings were more complicated than he let on. Contrary to his assistant's suggestion, he hadn't been *hoping* to lose the third star, but now that it was gone, there was a feeling of liberation. He had always said that keeping a third star was harder than winning one (which for him was doubly true; he acknowledged that his father deserved most of the credit for Taillevent's promotion in 1973). Now he didn't have to worry about it. From this point on, he could channel all his energy into his guests and customers, not fret about pleasing some "faceless inspector," as he put it. He was heartened, too, by the support he received; hundreds of e-mails and letters poured in from clients dismayed by Michelin's decision and vowing continued loyalty to Taillevent.

But like Sabine, he was also angry. He was angry at the way Michelin had handled the demotion; he thought that thirty-four years at the summit merited a degree of respect and that he should have heard from Michelin after the Simon story had appeared. He vowed that any contact with the Guide would henceforth be on his terms and on his turf; there would be no more trips to the Avenue de Breteuil. "I'm not going to go see them. If they want to talk, they can come here; I don't go there." Apart from the issue of poor form, Vrinat was perplexed by Michelin's actions. His October meeting with Mesplède had been bizarre, and Naret's efforts to explain the decision after the Guide was released only added to the confusion. Naret told Bloomberg News that "you need to be perfect every day" to keep a three-star rating, implying that Taillevent had fallen short of this goal. Taillevent could be accused of a few things; inconsistent effort was not one of them.

There was also this. A few days after he broke the news of Taillevent's impending downgrade, François Simon had written a follow-up article that purported to explain Michelin's thinking. He said that there was no problem with either Taillevent's cooking or service but that the restaurant was doing too many covers—one hundred twenty at dinner, he claimed. Although Simon hadn't cited a source, it seemed clear that his information had come from someone inside Michelin, and it was confounding on several levels. For one thing, the figure Simon gave was grossly inflated: As Vrinat jokingly noted, "If we had one hundred twenty people a night, we would have to seat forty of them on the stairs, and it wouldn't be very easy for the service." And why would Michelin, after awarding Taillevent three stars for so many years, suddenly be concerned about how much business it was doing? Moreover, if the restaurant's turnover was indeed the explanation, not only did this contradict Mesplède, who had criticized the food, it also contradicted Michelin's oft-repeated insistence that its ratings were based only on the quality of the meal. If that was really true, and if the cooking at Taillevent was still three-star caliber, the number of diners should have been irrelevant.

Vrinat wasn't the only one mystified. In the *International Herald Tribune*, Patricia Wells fumed that the decision to sanction Taillevent had been "born by a desire to provoke rather than [by] a commitment to Michelin's own customary credibility." That was one possibility. Another one suggested itself. Of all the claims made by Pascal Remy, the easiest to knock down was his assertion that some three-stars were sacrosanct, and because Vrinat was not a legendary chef but only a restaurateur, his third star was the easiest to take. Naret did nothing to discourage this interpretation; when I asked him about Taillevent, he replied with a smile that third stars were "not engraved in stone. They are in crystal, and crystal can break easily."

Although Vrinat recognized that Michelin's decision was laughable and would very likely harm its reputation more than Taillevent's, he couldn't shake a feeling of betrayal. "Michelin represented something," he said over coffee one afternoon. It *had* represented something—not only a certain standard of excellence, but also a certain idea of France. While Vrinat's first concern had always been to satisfy his guests, he had also devoted his life to pleasing those faceless inspectors—to winning their approbation, to affirming that Taillevent itself represented a certain standard of excellence and a certain idea of France. In her anger, Sabine wondered if it had all been a waste—all the hours her husband had worked, all the nights she had sat home alone. "You've given your whole life—to what?" she asked. "We could have gone to exhibitions, or dinners, or the theater, and now you're not any longer three stars. Was it worth it?"

In August 2007, Vrinat was diagnosed with lung cancer. He died on January 7, 2008.

Fast-Food Nation

O N   A   B R I G H T ,   M I L D   Sunday afternoon in March 2007, several hundred people, mostly African and North African émigrés, assembled in Paris's Place de la République. They were ostensibly there for a protest in defense of squatters' rights. But with a presidential election just weeks away, the crowd had broader concerns than just affordable housing, and the gathering quickly turned into a raucous demonstration against the candidacy of Nicolas Sarkozy, a law-and-order conservative reviled by many of France's minority communities. It also became a rally in support of another presidential aspirant, José Bové, who was on hand to help lead the march. Bové was the charismatic French "farmer" (in truth, he was a longtime left-wing militant who lived on a farm in the Massif Central and liked to pose as a man of the soil) who had come to prominence in 1999 after he and some colleagues, outraged by the punitive tariff that the United States, locked in a trade dispute with the European Union, had imposed on Roquefort cheese, bulldozed a McDonald's in the city of Millau. His demolition of the golden arches earned Bové a three-month prison sentence; it also turned him, overnight, into a French folk hero and an icon of the antiglobalization movement.

That same year, Bové took part in angry protests at a meeting of the World Trade Organization in Seattle, and he had since traveled the planet as a self-appointed tribune of the downtrodden and the disenfranchised. He had also kept up his activism in France, championing the cause of small farmers and leading the fight against genetically modified crops and other forms of industrialized agriculture. In February 2007, he had decided to launch a presidential bid, and while no one expected him to win, his exploits—not least the destruction of the McDonald's—had brought him widespread name recognition and support, and it was thought that he might do well enough in a crowded field to at least influence the outcome.

As it happened, the demonstration kicked off directly in front of a McDonald's, which was flanked by a Kentucky Fried Chicken and a restaurant belonging to the Belgian hamburger chain Quick—a murderer's row of *malbouffe* (the French pejorative for fast food). Dressed in corduroys and work boots, with his customary pipe in hand and trademark handlebar mustache, Bové was positioned near the front of the protest and wore a look of serene confidence as it made its way up the Boulevard Saint-Martin. His presence electrified the crowd, which serenaded him with shouts of "Bové! Président!" and "Moustache à l'Élysée." The cries of support continued even as Bové was interviewed by a BBC reporter doing a story on rising anti-American sentiment around the world. Presumably, he had sought out Bové, who had spent part of his childhood in Berkeley, California, in the hope of scoring an incendiary quote. But Bové, perhaps intent on recasting himself as a statesman, offered only boilerplate; from a few feet away, I heard him tell the BBC man that he had no beef with the American people but simply disagreed with the policies of the Bush administration. The interview over, Bové continued marching into the wan late-winter sun, plainly delighted to see how far his celebrated act of vandalism had carried him.

That same afternoon, at a convention center on the other side of Paris, the annual Salon International de l'Agriculture was winding down. Filling several stadium-size exhibition halls, the Salon was a week-long trade show that literally brought the farm to the city. Hundreds of farmers and truckloads of farm animals came to Paris to give urbanites a taste of *la France Profonde*. It was an opportunity for city kids to pet horses, chase chickens, and be flabbergasted by the amount of waste matter that poured out of cows. It was also an occasion to showcase the meats, cheeses, and wines that made the French countryside such a cherished source of sustenance. No less than that, the event was a way for Parisians to express their support of French agriculture—in a sense, to reaffirm their own Frenchness. The patriotic overtones were catnip for politicians: President Jacques Chirac had kicked off the Salon the previous Sunday, and the floor traffic throughout the week included a steady flow of ministers and members of parliament.

Encouraged by the nice weather, an enormous crowd had turned out for the Salon's closing day. Most of the visitors were families with young children. They formed a striking portrait of the new, multicultural France: Many of them were white, but many others were of African, Caribbean, and Middle Eastern descent. Hijabs were nearly as ubiquitous as baseball caps and sneakers. By now, a full week into this jamboree, animal droppings and strands of hay were everywhere and the place reeked of the barnyard; judging by your nose and the bottom of your shoes, you really might have thought you were down on the farm—that is, until the big, splashy McDonald's exhibit, located toward the back of the livestock hall, came into view. What the hell was that doing here, and why was it crawling with people?

As I moved closer, I discovered that no food was being sold; instead, McDonald's was feeding its guests corporate propaganda. Large, colorful placards ringed the display, documenting the amount of French beef, poultry, and vegetables that McDonald's used, detailing the nutritional value of the food it served, and describing the company's eco-friendly practices. The words were accompanied by lots of pastoral imagery—cows, potatoes, sheaves of wheat. Children weren't spared the charm offensive. At an activity table, a sign reading *D'où vient ton McDo?* (Where does your McDonald's come from?) was adorned with more pictures of chickens and cows. Judging by the display, you would never have guessed that it belonged to an American fast-food chain. That, apparently, was the idea. Cooked down to its essence, the message from McDonald's was that its food was French, it was good for you, and it was good for the environment. I wasn't buying it, but the intended audience clearly was. Didn't these kids realize that McDonald's was the Trojan horse of *mondialisation* and that they were committing cultural treason? Why weren't their parents stopping them? Another question occurred to me: What would José do? The answer was obvious: He would have borrowed the nearest bulldozer and leveled the exhibit.

But it wouldn't have done him much good. In the battle for France, Bové proved to be no match for Le Big Mac. The first round of the presidential election was held on April 22, and Bové finished an embarrassing tenth, garnering barely 1 percent of the total vote. By then, McDonald's had eleven hundred restaurants in France, three hundred more than it had had when Bové gave new meaning to the term "drive-through." Among them was a rebuilt and very popular franchise in Millau. The company was pulling in over a million people per day in France, and annual turnover was growing at twice the rate it was in the United States. Arresting as those numbers were, there was an even more astonishing data point: By 2007, France had become the second-most profitable market in the world for McDonald's, surpassed only by the land that gave the world fast food. Against McDonald's, Bové had lost in a landslide.

As reprehensible as Bové's tactics were, it was difficult for a food-loving Francophile not to feel a *little* solidarity with him. If you believed that McDonald's was a blight on the American landscape, seeing it on French soil was like finding a peep show at the Vatican, and in a contest between Roquefort and Chicken McNuggets, I knew which side I was on. But implicit in this attitude was a belief that McDonald's had somehow been foisted on the French; that slick American marketing had lured them away from the bistro and into the arms of Ronald McDonald. However, that just wasn't true. The French came to McDonald's and *la malbouffe* willingly, and in vast and steadily rising numbers. Indeed, the quarter-pounded conquest of France was not the result of some fiendish American plot to subvert French food culture. It was an inside job, and not merely in the sense that the French public was *lovin' it*—the architects of McDonald's strategy in France *were* French.

The principal architect (or culprit, depending on your point of view) was Denis Hennequin, a forty-nine-year-old Parisian. He had joined McDonald's in 1984, straight out of law school. At the time, McDonald's was relaunching itself in France; an effort in the 1970s to establish a presence there had failed because of the company's dissatisfaction with its French franchisee. After stints as an assistant store manager, a training and recruiting consultant, and the Paris regional director, Hennequin was named president and managing director of McDonald's France in 1996. In the eight years that followed, he steered the company through the Bové controversy and into a period of robust growth and expansion. It was a job so well done that in 2004, Hennequin was promoted to executive vice president of McDonald's Europe, and just a year later he was put in charge of European operations, overseeing more than six thousand restaurants in forty countries and a quarter-million employees. Having done the seemingly impossible and made McDonald's safe for France, he was now thought to be in line to take over the entire Chicago-based company. A Frenchman running McDonald's—it would be a hard thought to swallow on either side of the Atlantic.

Within the organization, it was widely agreed that Hennequin had exhibited audacious leadership in France, notably in his handling of the Bové crisis. Rather than doing the prudent, corporate-minded thing and seeking some form of conciliation with Bové, Hennequin had decided to meet provocation with provocation. In 2001, McDonald's France had launched a promotional campaign using Astérix, the beloved French cartoon character whose thick handlebar mustache was the inspiration for Bové's facial broom. That same year, Hennequin rolled another, bigger grenade under Bové's tractor by opening the McDonald's booth at the Salon International de l'Agriculture. There was deep anxiety among Hennequin's colleagues about the reception that awaited them there. "Everyone said, 'They are going to kill us,' " recalled Eric Gravier, a vice president of McDonald's France and a longtime employee. The fears were so great, he said, that they had all their posters made in triplicate because they expected the booth to be pelted with dung. But Hennequin wouldn't be deterred: McDonald's

France was sourcing 75 percent of its ingredients domestically, and he felt it was imperative from a PR standpoint to force French farmers, hypocritically applauding Bové, to publicly acknowledge the large volume of business that they were doing with *McDo*. While the gambit was undeniably bold, Hennequin clearly understood that he was operating from a position of strength, and not only in regard to the farmers. The French public applauded Bové, too, but in the places that mattered most, the stomach and the wallet, it applauded McDonald's more.

The wallet was no minor consideration. McDonald's appealed to budget-conscious students, of course, but with France's high unemployment and sluggish economy, it attracted people of all ages. Pensioners, for instance, were among the chain's most loyal clients. The food at McDonald's was cheap, and it was made cheaper still because its restaurants were officially designated as takeout joints. The value-added tax on meals at such establishments was just 5.5 percent, versus the 19.6 percent levied at "gastronomic" restaurants. This gave McDonald's an even greater competitive advantage over brasseries, bistros, and cafés. It was odd that French politicians, supposedly committed to keeping globalization at bay and defending France's culinary patrimony, would extend such favorable tax treatment to an American hamburger chain, and the different rates were a source of endless consternation to chefs, restaurant owners, and other purveyors of French cuisine. As André Daguin, a retired two-star chef and now the head of the French Hotel and Restaurant Association, put it, "Either our government wants us to be the country with the best restaurants, or it doesn't."

What especially cheesed off Daguin and other chefs was that McDonald's was being taxed as a carryout establishment even though the overwhelming majority of its customers actually chose to dine *chez McDo*. French diners tended to treat McDonald's as if it were no different than the bistro around the corner: They came, they ate, and they lingered. As Gravier artfully put it, "The French population uses McDonald's in a very French way; it is fast food, but not that fast." The data the company collected bore this out. Americans visited McDonald's more often than the French, at all hours of the day, frequently alone, and opted for takeout 70 percent of the time. The French spent more money per visit, came in groups more often than Americans, and did 70 percent of their eating during regular lunch and dinner hours. "We have a food culture in France; eating is not a feeding moment, it is a social moment," Gravier said.

And the company was very adept at catering to French proclivities, a point brought home to me on a visit to a McDonald's on the Champs-Élysées in June 2007. I was part of a group of journalists being given a guided tour by Jean-Pierre Petit, who had succeeded Hennequin as the chief executive of McDonald's France. We had come to this particular McDonald's because Petit wanted to show us the newest addition to the company's product line in France: McCafé, a stand-alone espresso bar offering lattes, macchiatos, and the like, along with fruit tarts, *macarons*, and other classic French sweets. The company was planning to open McCafés all over France, and the Champs-Élysées location was home to one of the first. Some of the other journalists eagerly ordered espresso drinks and pastries, but I wouldn't be so easily gulled—this was still McDonald's. Petit began making the rounds with a plate of *macarons* and insisted I try one. I took a pistachio. Not bad, I thought, but no Ladurée. As if reading my mind, Petit immediately chimed in, "We get the *macarons* from Holder, the company that owns Ladurée." Touché.

In 2004, Mireille Guiliano, the French-born head of Champagne Veuve Clicquot's American operations, published a book called *French Women Don't Get Fat: The Secret of Eating for Pleasure*. According to Guiliano, French women were able to remain so fashionably lean because they ate high-quality, seasonal products, didn't snack between meals, and took pleasure in food, which supposedly allowed them to reach a feeling of satisfaction and satiation with smaller portions. Guiliano's homespun wisdom, with its promise of pain-free weight control and its oh-so-French tone ("Life is too short to drink bad wine and eat bad food"), proved irresistible to calorie-obsessed American women. *French Women Don't Get Fat* quickly climbed to number one on the *New York Times* bestseller list. Worldwide, more than three million copies were sold.

There was just one problem with Guiliano's self-help tome: The title was untrue. French women *did* get fat, and so did their husbands and children. Indeed, the book was released just as France was beginning to grapple with a national epidemic of love handles and spare tires. By 2005, more than 40 percent of all French were considered overweight or obese, a figure that had doubled in less than a decade and which was rising by more than 10 percent annually. If the trend persisted, France was expected to have, on a per capita basis, a population as supersized as America's by the year 2020. The data for children was particularly alarming: Among the under-eighteen-year-olds, the obesity rate was swelling by nearly 20 percent per year. France, experts agreed, was in the grips of a public health crisis. Of course, crisis for some spelled opportunity for others. "The market in France is growing and we believe it has an excellent future," Michael Mullen, the European product manager for Weight Watchers, told the *International Herald Tribune* in 2005.

Not surprisingly, much of the blame for France's increasing flab was pinned on fast food, and five years after José Bové treated his bulldozer to a Happy Meal, the French media continued to lavish praise on those who stood against McDonald's and its ilk. In 2004, a school chef in the city of Marseille named Dominique Valadier briefly became the toast of the nation for his effort to discourage students from going to the nearby McDonald's for lunch. Valadier served all manner of classic French dishes—there was also wine for the teachers—and proudly told visiting journalists that because of the quality of his food, most of the teenagers were now choosing to dine *chez l'école*, rather than going off-campus to eat.

But Valadier was just one man employed by one school. Moreover, it was in homes, rather than schools, that French food culture was under its most sustained assault. There were various reasons for this.

The most obvious and significant one was that millions of French women were now working and had neither the time nor the inclination to prepare a family meal each night; it was easier to throw a frozen pizza in the microwave. While this was arguably a step forward for French womanhood, it was emphatically not one for French waistlines, nor French cuisine. In the eighty years that Michelin had been rating restaurants, nearly every three-star recipient had had his interest in gastronomy nurtured as a child, in the family kitchen. It was true for Chapel, Bocuse, Ducasse—for virtually all of them. With the decline in home cooking, there was legitimate reason to fear that haute cuisine's umbilical cord was being cut.

To be sure, it was not as if the French had all eaten likes kings and queens in the past. Well into the twentieth century, many French lived hardscrabble existences and had very circumscribed diets, and even with the economic boom that the country experienced after the Second World War, there was never a particularly deep reservoir of gourmandism. Joël Robuchon made this point in an interview with Jean-Robert Pitte for *Gault Millau* in 1989. "Only a small number of French possess refined palates," he said. "The French believe they have innate knowledge in the gastronomic domain ... nothing is further from the truth." The ignorance even extended to his clientele. "If 20 or even 10 percent of the customers in my dining room had truly refined taste, I would be happy." Michel Guérard, quoted in the same article, seconded Robuchon's claim. "The French imagine themselves to have amazing palates, whereas they can very often be found lacking," he said. "If we tried to determine what proportion of the French population were connoisseurs, I would say less than 15 percent. The rest eat, but do not know how to tell if a mackerel is cooked well or badly."

Nevertheless, France had given rise to the most artful and sensual cuisine in the world, had spawned generations of brilliant chefs and impassioned and discerning diners, and had taught much of the rest of the planet how to cook and how to eat, and this heritage was now endangered. In more and more French households, supper consisted of slapdash meals consumed in haste, often with the television blaring.

By the mid-2000s, hundreds of bistros, brasseries, and cafés were going out of business each year, scores of starred restaurants were struggling, and the high-quality ingredients that had long been the backbone of French cuisine—the impeccable meats, poultry, fruits, and vegetables—were increasingly difficult to find because fewer and fewer people were producing them.

The French public seemed largely indifferent to these developments. One measure of that indifference: The Slow Food movement barely had a following in France. Slow Food was, as the name suggested, dedicated to combating the depredations of fast food. The goal was to encourage people to take their time at meals, to take pride in what they cooked and pleasure in what they ate, and to support local cuisines and artisans, and although the organization had its roots in Italy, these principles also lay at the heart of French food culture. And indeed, the manifesto that launched the International Slow Food Movement was signed in Paris in 1989. Yet, it wasn't until 2003 that a French chapter of Slow Food was established, and by 2008, there were just 1,800 members, versus 26,000 in Italy and 17,000 in the United States (and the American chapter was formed only three years prior to France's). Whether this lack of interest was because the French didn't believe that their culinary tradition was threatened or couldn't be bothered to come to its rescue was an open question. Either way, it was mystifying to many people. Rob Kaufelt, the owner of Murray's, a popular New York cheese shop, wasn't even inclined to view the issue through the prism of France's rich gastronomic history; to him, it was baffling that *any* advanced Western nation would fail to embrace Slow Food. "Why a modern European, First World country wouldn't have a serious Slow Food movement, tied in with environmental concerns, is a very strange thing," was how he diplomatically put it.

Overseeing all of Europe, Denis Hennequin was a busy man. After several hastily rescheduled appointments, he and I were finally able to meet on a September afternoon in 2007. The interview took place on the lower floor of a McDonald's in the sixteenth arrondissement.

The lunchtime rush had ended, and the remaining customers formed a tableau that surely warmed Hennequin's heart: There was a young African woman nursing her infant, a Caucasian man seated at a counter and working at his computer, and two high-school-age boys of North African descent eating hamburgers and quietly laughing. Had I not known his identity, I would never have taken Hennequin for a McDonald's executive. For one thing, he was whippet-thin, with a lean, angular face to go with his balding pate; if he ate the food he was peddling, it didn't show. Then there was his hipster attire: He was dressed in a three-piece beige linen suit, with a white button-down shirt and no tie, and he also carried a knapsack in lieu of a briefcase—an ensemble that didn't exactly call to mind a Middle American CEO. (Further burnishing his bohemian credentials, Hennequin rode a Harley, and he and his wife and three children performed as a rock-and-roll band—a French version of the Partridge Family.) Likewise, his speech was largely free of corporate jargon—there was no talk of synergies and economies of scale and vertical integration—and he had none of the swagger of a typical executive. Instead, Hennequin had a cool, understated confidence, a demeanor that had undoubtedly served him well in the more than two decades he had spent helping McDonald's win over the deeply conflicted hearts, minds, and alimentary canals of his compatriots.

We took a seat in a booth. He asked an assistant to bring him a cup of coffee. Unbowed by my *macaron* comeuppance and still determined to do what the French manifestly could not—resist McDonald's—I opted for a bottle of Evian. Exercising a boss's prerogatives, he also instructed the assistant to have the music turned down. Finally settled in, Hennequin told me that there had been considerable anxiety when McDonald's had relaunched in France in the early 1980s, brought on by France's culinary tradition and the lukewarm reception the company had received when it had first opened there. "We felt very insecure in this market," he said. "French cuisine has a very strong identity. But the French are full of paradoxes. There is this reputation for slow food, for early retirement, for the thirty-five-hour workweek. On the other hand, France is one of the highest in Europe for productivity and efficiency and for the quality of the workforce. If it wasn't for the *exception française*, it looked like a very good market. The question for us at the start was whether there was room for an American restaurant offering American products with speed, convenience, quality, and cleanliness. Obviously there was."

The company had succeeded in France, he continued, in part by emphasizing the American angle and downplaying the speed factor. This was a bit surprising to hear in 2007, with memories of freedom fries still fresh. But back in the 1980s, Hennequin explained, fast food had been a much harder thing to sell the French than Americana. "We never positioned ourselves as fast food in France," he said. "From Day One, we positioned ourselves as an alternative for families and people who wanted a fun experience, as opposed to just a fast experience. The foundation was a fun family experience. This was a very new concept in France—something exotic." Indeed it was; traditional French restaurants were many things, but kid-friendly was not one of them. America had a certain exotic appeal, as well. "The U.S. and France have always had a difficult relationship, but it's made of love and hate," he said. "The movies, the music—the jazz and rock; we are defensive of our own culture, but very open to American culture." Surprisingly, too, Hennequin claimed that McDonald's status as a symbol of globalization had also worked in its favor, at least with younger French. "Kids here have a fascination with global culture," he said. "They don't have a problem with globalization; it's attractive to them."

This seemed an opportune moment to mention the enemy, and I'd hardly begun to formulate my question when Hennequin nodded, broke into a knowing smile, and said, "José Bové." The two had never met; for Hennequin, it was a matter of principle. "If he hadn't gone so far," he said, "I would have spoken with him, but he destroyed a restaurant and went to jail." Nonetheless, he claimed that Bové had actually ended up doing McDonald's a big favor. The incident in Millau, and the outpouring of support for Bové, had caused Hennequin and his colleagues to realize that they needed to do a better job of communicating. As he put it, "We had French employees, French suppliers, French franchisees; we had this secret story that shouldn't have been a secret—that we were a French-operated company selling an American product." In the aftermath of the Bové imbroglio, the company played up its French connections, and the public responded. "We came out of this crisis stronger," Hennequin said. "French consumers heard our message and said, 'It's my McDonald's.' Bové helped us at the end of the day."

But there were limits to how far McDonald's would go to ingratiate itself to the natives. Although its restaurants in France sold beer, wine would never be offered; doing so would suggest that it was in competition with traditional French restaurants, and that was not the case. "We've never tried to run the bistros and cafés out of business, we've never tried to copy their products," he said. But they were going out of business, and France's culinary tradition was clearly imperiled. The French weren't cooking anymore, and instead of *pot-au-feu*, children were now being reared on fast food. Wasn't McDonald's at least partly responsible for this, and as a Frenchman, did he ever feel even just a little traitorous? "It's not because of McDonald's that people aren't cooking at home," he brusquely replied. "It's because they decided to stop cooking—they are not interested, or are working, or don't want to get their kitchens dirty. That's not my fault. But when you think about it, steak frites was the number-one-selling menu item for kids in French restaurants. You could say we're just giving it to them a different way."

The American company was doing something else for French youths: It was providing jobs—lots of jobs—in a country that was having a conspicuously difficult time creating them. By 2007, McDonald's had nearly fifty thousand people on its payrolls in France, making it one of the country's largest private sector employers, and the average age of its employees was twenty-five. French kids liked eating at McDonald's, and they liked being on the other side of the counter, too. In 2006, McDonald's was ranked the eighth-best company to work for in France. In a nation beset with persistently high unemployment and frequent labor unrest, these were not figures to be sniffed at.

And the importance of McDonald's went beyond just the number of jobs it was creating; it was also where those opportunities were being generated. The chain had many restaurants in predominately immigrant neighborhoods, where the unemployment rates among youths were often as high as 50 percent. These areas seethed with frustration, which frequently expressed itself in random acts of vandalism and, occasionally, in more sustained violence. In October 2005, the suburbs around Paris and a number of other French cities exploded in riots. Thousands of cars were torched and many local businesses suffered broken windows and worse. However, McDonald's outlets were generally spared. "We were very protected," Hennequin told me. "The kids would say, 'Hey, my sister works there.' We've rarely been hit." McDonald's, in his view, was helping to assimilate a large and rapidly growing immigrant population that generally felt marginalized in French society, and it was promoting diversity and solidarity in a country that badly needed more of both. "We are a strong enabler for integration," Hennequin said. "We mix people of different origins, different levels of income."

Eric Gravier made a similar point when he and I spoke. "We help integrate kids who would never find any activity normally," he said. "We teach them to wake up in the morning, wash their hands, smile at customers, respect their colleagues—it's unbelievable what we do for some of them. In a lot of these neighborhoods, there aren't many options; McDonald's is one of them." He said the company went to lengths to ensure that its restaurants were staffed by people of diverse backgrounds. Often, this meant that employees were sent to restaurants in neighborhoods outside their own in order to ensure a racial or ethnic balance behind the counter—a form of coerced integration, perhaps, but valuable in a country stratified along racial and ethnic lines. "We have to mix," said Gravier. "Sometimes we get kids living fifteen minutes or a half hour away from stores, because it gives a mixture; we are careful about preserving multi-origins." In keeping with this policy, the company had resisted demands in some neighborhoods to tweak its menu to accommodate local customs. "They've asked for halal beef in some places, but we've refused," he said. "We don't want to be seen as connected to one group or another; we want to be connected to everyone." He proudly said that French politicians were no longer inclined to demonize McDonald's and were instead coming to recognize the company's social contributions: "They are starting to see us an important actor in terms of diversity; we could become an interesting model for them to look at."

But that didn't change the fact that McDonald's was peddling cheeseburgers in the land of Carême, Point, and Escoffier. Surely, those responsible for upholding France's culinary tradition took a dim view of the fast-food chain? Not necessarily. During a dinner at Alain Ducasse's three-star restaurant at the Hôtel Plaza Athénée in Paris, I fell into a discussion about McDonald's with Denis Courtiade, the restaurant's maître d', and he could hardly contain his enthusiasm. He said he treated his three children to McDonald's every few months and that it was heaven for all involved. "They can run around and break things and have fun; they can't do that in a bistro," Courtiade said. He also marveled at the fast-food chain's transparency—the effort it made to communicate with customers about product sourcing and nutritional values. "It's brilliant how open they are," he gushed. "They tell you everything. I brought the brochure in for the hotel manager because I wanted him to see it."

His sentiments were echoed by Jean-François Piège, who had served as *chef de cuisine* for Ducasse at the Plaza Athénée and was now head chef at the two-star Les Ambassadeurs in the Hôtel de Crillon (and thought to be a lock for a third star). Piège didn't regard *McDo*'s success as a sign of the cretinization of younger French palates. Quite the opposite: He believed it showed good taste. "Other than the croque monsieur, we don't have a tradition of hot sandwiches here," Piège explained to me. "McDonald's gives you a hot sandwich, with flavorful meat; if the choice is between that and a ham and cheese sandwich out of the refrigerator, people are going to choose the hot sandwich. Also,

McDonald's is very economical. Why has McDonald's succeeded here? Because it allows a certain person to eat well."

His mentor and former boss, Ducasse, wasn't quite as generous in his praise when we talked about McDonald's, but neither was he especially worried about its popularity. "You eat simply, cheaply there—it is attractive for the young," he told me. "The young don't have the time for long lunches. They can't sit there drinking Cognacs and Armagnacs after lunch. They are busy; they have meetings. McDonald's offers speed and a good price; if the café owners offer good sandwiches at a good price, with good bread, good butter, good ham, the young will come. Food has to evolve with changes in society." For Ducasse, McDonald's was a challenge to be met, and he was rising to meet it: In 2002, he started a sandwich shop-cum-bakery in Paris called Be Boulangépicier (roughly translated as "bakerygrocery"), and he had just opened a second outlet in Paris and one in Tokyo, as well. The tagline for the shops was *pratique, rapide et savoureux*: Easy, fast, and tasty.

In the world of French gastronomy, Ducasse cut a singular figure and so did Jacques Puisais. Now in his eighties, he was an oenologist and writer who had devoted his career to promoting discernment at the table. He wanted his compatriots to eat knowledgeably, correctly, and well, and had even established an organization called the Institute of Taste to help spread the gospel of good food. He was France's philosopher of flavor, continuing a tradition of culinary high-mindedness that stretched back to Brillat-Savarin and Grimod de la Reynière. Given that McDonald's now seemed to be undoing his life's work, I expected to receive an earful of Olympian thunderclaps when I phoned Puisais at his home in the Loire Valley to talk about the fast-food colossus. After all, this was a man who had told the *Times* of London, in response to a study showing that the French were forsaking croissants for cold cereals, that corn flakes were "a miserable product, consumed in solitude, lending a depressing inhumanity to the morning meal."

But like Ducasse, Puisais wasn't inclined to view the success of

McDonald's as an indictment of the French or a sign of the apocalypse; it was simply a reflection of the changed circumstances in which people now lived and worked. In his judgment, fast food was an expression of the modern condition, and France was a modern country. "Eating well takes lots of time, but we live very quickly now—that's the way of the world," he said. In fact, he respected what McDonald's had achieved in France, and recognized that it provided a vital service. If office workers were only given fifteen minutes for lunch, they needed to patronize establishments that could get them in and out in a hurry. In bistros, it sometimes took fifteen minutes just to get the menu. But while he understood the appeal of McDonald's, he couldn't accept the notion that a meal there was a dining experience; even if you lingered at the table for an hour and finished up with an espresso and a *macaron*, it was still fast food. "McDonald's is a place one eats, but it is not a restaurant," Puisais said emphatically. "There is no wine, there are no vegetables, there is no gastronomic discourse. One cannot truly eat in fifteen minutes."

The Raw and the Cooked

IN THE MONTHS PRECEDING the American invasion of Iraq in 2003, relations between the United States and France turned testier than at any time since the end of the Second World War. The French refusal to back the overthrow of Saddam Hussein prompted an outpouring of vitriol in the United States. French wines were shunned, French fries were hilariously renamed freedom fries in several congressional cafeterias, and an anti-French epithet, coined several years earlier by that well-known foreign policy wise man, Groundskeeper Willie of *The Simpsons*, entered the global lexicon. In one episode of the show, he had referred to the French as "cheese-eating surrender monkeys," and his colorful phrase was invoked, to equally widespread delight and opprobrium, by right-wing American commentators eager to stoke the public's anger.

Although it expressed an ugly sentiment, the phrase was unquestionably catchy, and it was partly grounded in truth: Historically, the French were a nation of cheese eaters. Roquefort, Brie, Pont-l'Évêque: These were names as synonymous with France as Voltaire, Victor Hugo, and Jerry Lewis. The French ate prodigious quantities of cheese and fabricated a dizzying array of them—enough, it was claimed, so that a person could eat a different cheese every day of the year. Charles de Gaulle's famous quip—"How can you govern a country which has two hundred forty-six varieties of cheese?"— underscored not only the tumultuousness of French politics, but also the importance of cheese to French culture.

But four decades after de Gaulle invoked cheese to express his frustration at trying to lead his recalcitrant compatriots, something peculiar and awful was happening: Many French cheeses were in danger of extinction. In fact, a number of them had already been lost. All were raw-milk, or *lait cru*, cheeses—real cheeses, in the view of connoisseurs, who believed that pasteurization denuded the flavor of cheese. (Pasteurization involves heating freshly drawn milk in order to kill any viruses, bacteria, or other microorganisms—the same microorganisms that are believed to impart character and complexity to cheeses.) Although the United States prohibited the importation of raw-milk cheeses aged for fewer than sixty days (by which point, it was assumed, the pathogens would be dead), *lait cru* had been the tradition in France for centuries, one that was steadfastly maintained even with the advent of pasteurization in the mid-1800s.

But now, these cheeses were threatened. At first, the endangered ones were names generally known only to the most passionate aficionados. There was, for instance, Vacherin d'Abondance, a cow's-milk cheese made in the Alps. In 2005, the last person producing it, a septuagenarian named Célina Gagneux, decided to hang up her ladle and smock, and a two-hundred-year-old cheese quietly disappeared. The same fate had befallen dozens of other cheeses since the 1970s, and more were now said to be in jeopardy. By the mid-2000s raw-milk varieties accounted for barely 10 percent of all the cheese produced in France, down from virtually one hundred percent a half-century earlier. An essential part of France's gastronomic heritage and culinary ecology was at risk, yet most French seemed unaware of or indifferent to the plight of these cheeses. A few people tried to raise public awareness and rally support for the embattled cheeses. In 2006, an organization called the Association Fromages de Terroirs, which aimed to call attention to endangered *lait cru* cheeses, mounted a very Gallic PR campaign: It came out with a calendar of lingerie-clad women called From' Girls, with each month's model named in tribute to a particular cheese. Mademoiselle January, for instance, was Barbara Munster, while October was given over to Estelle Livarot. The brainchild of the association's founder, former journalist Véronique Richez-Lerouge (who posed as Éléanore de Mont d'Or, Mademoiselle December), the calendar generated some amused headlines, but it didn't seem to energize consumers. When the 2008 calendar was released, the From' Girls evidently felt more drastic measures were called for: The new pages were filled with exposed breasts and bottoms.

By 2008, the situation had become desperate, for it was no longer just esoteric cheeses that faced an uncertain future. Now, the most popular *fromage* of all, Camembert, was under threat. In March 2007, Lactalis and Isigny Sainte-Mère, the two companies that together accounted for 90 percent of all the raw-milk Camembert produced in France, announced that they would be dropping out of the Camembert appellation unless the rules were changed to permit them to treat the milk they used. Citing an incident in 2005, in which several schoolchildren fell ill after eating *lait cru* Camembert made by Réaux, a producer in western Normandy, the two firms claimed that health concerns on the part of the French public obliged them to begin thermalizing their milk. Thermalization was a gentler form of pasteurization. There were two ways of pasteurizing milk—the long way and the slow way. The former involved heating it at 150 degrees Fahrenheit for 30 to 40 minutes, the latter required heating it at 161 degrees for 15 to 20 seconds. With thermalization, the milk was heated to 150 degrees and kept there for only about 15 seconds—enough time to destroy many of the pathogens that might be swimming around but not all of them. The U.S. Food and Drug Administration didn't consider this an adequate precaution and categorized cheeses made this way as raw-milk products. The European Union, on the other hand, treated such cheeses as pasteurized. Whether thermalized milk was fertile ground for dangerous microorganisms was a matter of dispute; it was unquestionably fertile ground for controversy.

Lait cru Camembert now accounted for less than 10 percent of the Camembert produced in France. But aficionados like Richez-Lerouge considered it to be the truest representation of Camembert and the only kind worth eating. They also believed that there was much more at stake than the fate of this one, wildly popular cheese; in their view, the future of all raw-milk cheeses was on the line. To lose a delicious but little-known variety like Vacherin d'Abondance was a tragedy, but one with limited fallout; to see raw-milk Camembert disappear would be a catastrophe for French cuisine and the French nation. Camembert was France's national cheese—the most celebrated cheese that she produced, a cheese whose history was said to be intertwined with that of modern France. "Camembert is a subject that unites all of France," François Mitterrand once said. Some two hundred years earlier, Brillat-Savarin had expressed similar sentiments in verse:

> *Camembert, poetry,*
> *Bouquet of our meals,*
> *What would become life,*
> *If you did not exist?*

It now appeared that France was in danger of finding out.

Legend has it that Camembert was invented in 1791 by a woman named Marie Harel, who supposedly lived in the village of Camembert, in the Pays d'Auge area of Normandy, with the help of a refractory priest on the run from the revolutionary authorities. The priest, the story goes, was from the Brie region and was given refuge in the Harel household. During his stay there, he shared his recipe for making Brie with Harel, who placed the Brie in a small mold used to produce another local cheese, Livarot, and thus was born Camembert. That its birth supposedly coincided with the birth of modern France had the effect of draping Camembert in the tricolor flag, and the involvement of a priest fleeing persecution gave the story an added cloak of religiosity—indeed, even suggested a touch of divine intervention.

The legend behind Camembert remained a local, and largely forgotten, one until 1926, when an American doctor named Joseph

Knirim traveled to the village of Vimoutiers, a few kilometers from Camembert, to pay tribute to Marie Harel for inventing the cheese that he believed had saved his life. Knirim was not very adept at speaking French. To make sure his message was understood, he carried a document written in French, which he handed to the town's deputy mayor. It read,

France possesses many cheeses, all of which are excellent, but when it comes to digestibility, Madame Harel's cheese, the "veritable Norman Camembert," is surely the best. Years ago, I suffered for several months from indigestion, and Camembert was practically the sole nourishment that my stomach and intestines were able to tolerate. Since then, I have sung the praises of Camembert. I have introduced it to thousands of gourmets, and I myself eat it two or three times a day … In humble expression of my great admiration for Camembert cheese, which is shared by thousands of friends in the United States, I have brought with me across the waters this wreath of flowers to lay on the monument of our common benefactress. May the French and American flags be forever united in the service of mankind.

Pierre Boisard, author of the book *Camembert: A National Myth*, says that the deputy mayor knew of Harel but had no idea where she was buried; she was a footnote in local history (and, it would later turn out, a dubious one). But he and the mayor recognized the potential PR bonanza that Knirim had dropped in their laps and immediately set about exploiting it. The timing couldn't have been more propitious. Just two months earlier, a French court had ruled that Camembert was now a generic name and that Normandy had no special claim to it; Knirim's fantastical story, and the long journey he had made to tell it, offered a chance for the Normans to reinforce their claim to the now wildly popular cheese. Knirim's pilgrimage made headlines across France, and on April 11, 1928, in a ceremony attended by former French president Alexandre Millerand, a statue of Harel was unveiled in Vimoutiers, enshrining her as the creator of Camembert. "The cheese's official celebration by a former president of the Republic gave birth to a modern national myth in which Camembert was to become intricately associated with France itself," writes Boisard. "Since that day, Camembert has become France's foremost cheese, and France has become the country of Camembert."

There was just one problem: Harel was not Camembert's inventor, and the evidence suggests that she didn't even live in the village of Camembert. In reality, Camembert was being made and consumed nearly a century before Harel supposedly created it. Likewise, while she may well have hidden a recusant priest, there is no reason to believe that a cleric on the lam played any part in Camembert's birth. Based on his own research and the work of other historians, Boisard believes that Harel was simply a Norman housewife who made an especially fetching Camembert, one that acquired local renown both because of its quality and because she was an unusually commercial-minded producer and sold her cheese in several different area markets. She passed along her cheese-making skills and entrepreneurial flair to her five children, all of whom went into the Camembert business. It was through her descendants that the myth of Harel was propagated. Facing increased competition in the mid-1800s, the Harel clan spun the story that its matriarch had been Camembert's creator and that they, as recipients of both her bloodlines and her recipe, were the only producers making true Camembert.

But what was true Camembert? As Boisard notes, for the first century of Camembert's existence, there was no generally accepted method of making it; recipes were personal and private, and every producer gave the cheese his or her own twist. As Camembert's renown grew and its sales soared during the latter half of the nineteenth century, its manufacture spread to other regions of France. In 1909, Camembert producers in Normandy banded together to form an organization called the Syndicat des Fabricants du Véritable Camembert de Normandie, whose objective was to have Camembert officially declared a protected name, applicable only to those Camemberts that originated in Normandy. But because Camembert hadn't been around all that long (Roquefort, for example, dated back to Roman times), and because there was not yet a consensus about how and exactly where it should be made (was only the Pays d'Auge acceptable, or could real Camembert be made elsewhere in Normandy?), the syndicate's claim to exclusivity was repeatedly rebuffed. In January 1926, just two months before Joseph Knirim's pilgrimage to Vimoutiers, a court in the city of Orléans tossed out a lawsuit that the SFVCN had brought against a dairy in the Loire Valley for allegedly producing inauthentic Camembert. In rendering its verdict, the court decreed that Camembert had become a generic name and had no geographical significance. Successive French governments, wary of harming dairy interests elsewhere in the country and unwilling to take measures that might cause Camembert prices to rise, likewise rejected the Norman claims.

In 1968, the syndicate finally made some headway when it was granted the right to place a label saying "Véritable Camembert de Normandie" on Camemberts produced in Normandy. Fifteen years later, the French government reversed policy and agreed to officially recognize Camembert's Norman roots by granting appellation (AOC) status to raw-milk, ladle-molded Camembert produced in the part of the Pays d'Auge that included the town of Camembert. The edict didn't prohibit cheese makers in other regions and other countries from using the name "Camembert"; it merely gave this small zone in and around the town of Camembert exclusive right to the name "Camembert de Normandie" and stipulated that only cheeses fabricated in this area, made from local milk, and molded by ladle were entitled to that designation.

The irony is that raw-milk, ladle-molded Camembert was by then virtually obsolete. Over the previous three decades, surging demand and technological advances had turned the fabled cheese into a factory product, made in mechanized fashion from pasteurized milk. A few artisans continued to churn out the real, old-fashioned stuff, but they were a steadily dwindling minority. So how was it that their outmoded

Camembert was granted AOC status? Surprisingly, much of the credit belonged to Michel Besnier, whose eponymous company did more than any other to industrialize Camembert's production and standardize its taste. Besnier's father, André, had started the firm in 1933. Michel took over in 1955, when the company had 55 employees and was turning out around 4,000 Camemberts per day. At the time of his death, in 2000, it had grown to be the second-largest dairy group in Europe, with 15,000 employees and $6.6 billion in annual turnover. (It is now the largest, with 35,000 employees spread over 125 production facilities in 23 countries.) By then, it was manufacturing 240 million Camemberts annually, most of them under its Président label. Started by Besnier in 1968, Président was one of the first pasteurized Camemberts and among the first brands to be distributed nationally. Besnier took pride in its bland reliability, boasting that Président Camemberts were "uniform and better adapted to wide distribution. In supermarkets, our pasteurized-milk Camemberts stand up better in refrigerator sections. They change less after they have been packaged." But according to Boisard, when the syndicate, after winning approval for the "Véritable Camembert" label, pushed to have raw-milk, hand-ladled Camembert awarded appellation status, Besnier threw his support behind the effort because he had grown up in Normandy and "was still sentimentally attached to the Camembert of his childhood." Later, Besnier would acquire two *lait cru* Camembert producers, Lepetit and Lanquetot, which were still in the company's hands in 2007.

But by then, the company was no longer called Besnier. In 1999, it had been rechristened Lactalis—the same Lactalis that, along with Isigny Sainte-Mère, was now threatening to quit the appellation unless the rules were amended to permit thermalized milk.

On a cold, sunny December morning, I drove out to Normandy to visit the village of Camembert and a local cheese maker, François Durand, who had been featured in newspaper articles around the world as the plucky artisan standing firm against the forces of alimentary industrialization. Camembert was located several hours west of Paris, in an area of lush, gently rolling hills not far from Deauville and the Normandy coastline. It turned out there wasn't actually a village in Camembert, however: The town, such as it was, consisted of a tiny, forlorn city hall, a small museum dedicated to Camembert, and a cluster of farms. Its population was said to be around two hundred, but from the looks of things, that figure was the result of some generous rounding-up.

The real shrine to Camembert (the cheese) was Vimoutiers, a town of five thousand people just a few kilometers down the road. Apparently, the two municipalities had long battled over bragging rights to Camembert. The village of Camembert had the name but Vimoutiers had the numbers; the majority won, and it was now Vimoutiers that was considered the cradle of Camembert. The town had a Camembert museum of its own and also boasted not one but two statues of Marie Harel. The original, located near the cathedral, was headless, having been decapitated in a German bombing raid during the Second World War. The replacement statue, which according to the plaque was given to the town by "400 men and women making cheese in Van Wert, Ohio, USA in cooperation with the committee on aid to Vimoutiers," stood outside a building called the Hall of Butter, across a plaza from city hall.

But while Vimoutiers had the inanimate monuments to the glories of Camembert, the village of Camembert had a living, breathing symbol in François Durand. His two-hundred-acre farm was located a few kilometers beyond the village of Camembert (what passed for it, anyway), down a narrow, tree-lined country lane with an expansive view of the surrounding hillsides, which were dotted with cows, sheep, horses, and ramshackle houses sending plumes of chimney smoke into the steely blue sky. It was scenery that could be found in a million different places in rural France, but familiarity made it no less breathtaking. Durand's spread had a hardscrabble look about it, mostly owing to the farm equipment that was strewn about. Behind the main building was a cattle shed, in which several dozen cows were gathered. The presence of these cows, I shortly learned, was what set Durand apart from other Camembert producers and made him an heroic figure in the eyes of Camembert purists—and now, possibly, a martyr for the cause of true Camembert.

Two men were waiting for me in the office: Gérard Roger and Francis Rouchaud. They were leaders of the Comité de Défense du Véritable Camembert, a local organization dedicated to preserving traditional Camembert, by which they meant artisanally produced, *lait cru* Camembert from Normandy. Neither was in the food business— Roger worked in communications, Rouchaud was a marketing consultant—but both were passionate cheese lovers who had thrust themselves to the front lines of the battle to save raw-milk Camembert. They were small fry going up against a pair of industrial giants, but it wasn't until Roger and Rouchaud filled me in on some of the nuances of the Camembert situation that I fully understood just how difficult an undertaking theirs was.

They explained to me that there were only seven raw-milk Camembert producers left in Normandy, two of whom were Lactalis and Isigny Sainte-Mère. Of the five others, they said, four were "small industrial" producers—that is, they bought the milk that they used to make their cheese. Durand was the only real farmer of the bunch, because he had his own cows and gathered his own milk. But what difference did it make, so long as the milk was untreated? In their view, it was the transport that was the problem: Milk that was shipped, no matter how short the distance, invariably lost some of its character in transition. As far as they were concerned, even machine-milking the cows compromised quality. So Durand milked by hand? Actually, no, but they were willing to overlook that small transgression and focus on the bigger point: Durand, with his thirty Holsteins and thirty Norman cows, merely had to step out the back door to collect his milk, and the result was better, more distinctive Camembert—a true farmhouse Camembert. "He is sure of the quality of his milk, and it gives his cheese its taste," said Rouchaud. But Durand was the only person in Normandy still making Camembert this way; he was a curio, something for tourists to see. Surely they weren't suggesting that there was a future for Durand's type of cheese making? "In the past, there were lots of farms making Camembert here," Rouchaud replied. "In the Auvergne, you have two hundred thirty-four farms making Saint-Nectaire. There are eighty-six producers making Reblochon. Farm production can be valuable."

We put sanitary booties on our shoes and went back to see the man himself. Durand, a tall, wiry forty-six-year-old wearing rubber boots, a plastic white apron, and a hairnet, was ladling curds into dozens of molds when we arrived in his atelier, which combined the fastidiously clean, all-white look of an operating room with the oppressive humidity of a hothouse. Years of practice had given his ladling a rhythmic quality, and as he leaned over the table, one hand dropping chunks of tofu-like white curds into the plastic molds, the other hand tucked behind him, the image that came to mind was of an Olympic speed skater. Durand was not what I had expected. Given all the press he had received, I had expected him to be an ebullient character and a tireless self-promoter—a carnival barker. Instead, he turned out to be a taciturn man who exuded a certain strangeness. He seemed to be of another time and place, and after a moment's reflection, I put my finger on it: There was something medieval about Durand. In fact, he was exactly what I imagined a fifteenth-century cheese-making monk would have looked like. His assistant, a sullen woman with an alarmingly full mustache, only amplified the feeling of having stepped into a scene out of the Middle Ages.

At any rate, Durand didn't seem especially interested in talking; fortunately for me, Roger and Rouchaud were happy to speak for him. They explained the Camembert-making process. Durand's cows were milked early in the morning. A small amount of rennet, an enzyme extracted from the lining of a calf's fourth stomach, was then added to each pail of milk to encourage the curdling process, and the milk was heated to 93 degrees Fahrenheit. Once optimal curdling was achieved, which took several hours, Durand would put the curds into the molds—six scoops in each. Depending on the amount of milk drawn in the morning, the farm typically produced four hundred to five hundred wheels of Camembert a day. The molds would later be salted, then spend two days in the *haloir,* or drying chamber, followed by fifteen days, give or take a few, in the *salle d'affinage*—the finishing room.

Rouchaud said that a twenty- to twenty-seven-day gestation period would be preferable, but demand was sufficiently strong that Durand needed to get the cheese out the door. Also, holding it back an extra week or two would create "a problem of money," as Rouchaud put it. Money already was a problem. Although his Camembert was far more labor-intensive, it fetched the same price as standard Camemberts: around $3.50 per wheel. "It's so much work and such a low profit margin," Rouchaud said. "But he's obliged to sell it at the market price." Charging five dollars per wheel would have eased the financial strain, perhaps enough to have allowed Durand to age the cheese for another week or ten days and possibly even have enabled him to invest in more Norman cows, which were less productive than the Holsteins but yielded better-quality milk.

We eventually ended up back in the office, where we talked a little longer. Rouchaud and Roger then said they had to leave; I told them I was going to stick around and try to chat with Durand. With his spokesmen gone, he was somewhat more forthcoming, if not exactly loquacious. He told me he had been born in L'Aigle, a nearby town, and had moved to the farm as a child. His father had produced only milk. When Durand took over, in 1987, he decided to begin making Camembert—to turn the farm into "a place for true Camembert." But it was not an easy pursuit, and circumstances were making it ever more difficult. The sterile work environment required by European Union regulations had scrubbed away some of the beneficial microbes that had previously lingered in the air and on the surfaces, and he admitted that even his cheese had lost some of its quality. These new regulations had not only affected the production of cheese, they'd made it very expensive—prohibitively so—for lots of small producers like Durand, and the cost of compliance was driving many of them out of business.

Durand said the French public, having grown up on industrialized Camembert, no longer knew what the good stuff tasted like, and the Réaux incident had convinced many consumers that they didn't want to know.

At this point, it was a sense of duty that kept him going. There were people like Rouchaud and Roger who cherished his Camembert, and he felt obligated to them. "I don't have a choice," he said, "and there is a satisfaction in making a product that pleases consumers, a cheese that pleases *amateurs*." He said that he sold his Camembert on site and at a few outdoor markets in the area. But he was a venerated figure in the world of Camembert, and he was only two hours from Paris; why weren't three-star restaurants coming to buy his cheese? It didn't work that way, he explained—maybe the distance was a deterrent. I said it wouldn't be in New York; chefs there would make the drive themselves to purchase his Camembert and to encourage his efforts. For that matter, lots of frustrated lawyers would probably quit their practices and move out to the countryside to produce Camembert alongside him. Refugees from the city had played a big part in the emergence of America's artisanal cheese movement, which was now flourishing. However, Durand and I both agreed that that sort of thing wasn't likely to happen in France; here, your chosen career, your *métier*, was considered your station for life, and you definitely did not give up a well-paying job in Paris to go milk cows in Normandy. But it was unfortunate that there weren't more people making Camembert the way he did and that he wasn't getting more support. Durand smiled and gave a slight shrug. "Eh, *oui*, it is a little sad."

All the attention that Durand had attracted naturally gave the war over Camembert the appearance of a morality play, one pitting a pair of soulless corporate giants against a single, stalwart artisan. The way the story had been spun by the media did not please the man responsible for spinning the media on behalf of Lactalis, company spokesman Luc Morelon. He and I met one night for a drink at La Coupole, the famous art-deco brasserie on the Boulevard du Montparnasse in Paris. Morelon, who had worked for Lactalis for sixteen years, was dressed in a rumpled blue suit, and this, combined with his unruly gray hair, suggested his day had been a long one. To hear Morelon tell it, every day had been a long one since Lactalis and Isigny Sainte-Mère had announced they would be quitting the appellation. "Lactalis is the bad guy," he said, morosely staring down at the small plate of black olives he was demolishing. "We're the bad guys."

Everything had been fine, Morelon said, until 1999, when a lab in Belgium had reported finding elevated levels of Listeria in Lepetit Camemberts. Further analysis had shown that the lab had been wrong, he said, but the French government had forced the company to recall one million wheels of the cheese, a financial and public relations disaster. Indeed, sales of Lepetit had never fully recovered. But why hadn't the government relented after it had been shown that the initial lab results were erroneous? "We are in France; the administration is always right," Morelon said with a sardonic laugh.

The Réaux incident six years later caused Lactalis unpleasant flashbacks, and with the French public increasingly mindful of food safety, the company ultimately decided that it needed to treat all the milk used in its Camemberts. "We cannot take the risk of putting children in the hospital," Morelon said. "It would be catastrophic. Raw milk may have E. coli, and that's a fact; it's not an invention by Lactalis. We make eighty thousand Camemberts per day in raw milk. If there is a risk of one per ten thousand, it makes eight per day. It is not acceptable for a company like Lactalis."

Intriguingly, Morelon suggested that the raw-milk issue was a red herring. He told me that the nature of milk had changed. Twenty years ago, raw milk typically had 200,000 to 300,000 bacteria per gram. Now, thanks to the increased hygiene standards mandated by the European Union, the milk had just 10,000 bacteria per gram, or twenty to thirty times fewer microbes, and this had completely changed Camembert production. With the old bacteria count, Morelon said, cheese makers could rely on the milk to mature itself. That was no longer the case:

Nowadays, they had to use special cultures adapted to the taste of Camembert to get the milk to mature. With other cheeses, such as Roquefort, the raw milk might still matter, but it was now largely immaterial to Camembert, he said. So there was no way to tell the difference between raw-milk Camembert and Camembert made from treated milk? "I will give a taste to anyone to see if they can find the difference," he confidently declared.

At this point I confessed to some confusion. If there now were so many fewer bacteria in the milk, didn't this mean the milk was safer, and if so, why did Lactalis suddenly feel the need to thermalize it? "Ah, that's a complicated issue," he said. He explained that when there had been many more bacteria in the milk, all those pathogens had had to fight for space, and it had created a stable environment. With fewer germs, there was less competition and more space for the bacteria to develop. "It's a paradox of food safety," he said. "With fewer germs, the danger may be worse." They were able to control for salmonella and Listeria, but E. coli was still a problem, and a growing one. The Réaux incident had been caused, he said, by a new strain of E. coli 026, one that had never been seen before in dairy products. They could test all the milk, but it would take thirty hours to get the results, and that was too long; delaying the process would change the milk and the taste of the cheese. Leaving the milk untested and untreated was not an option. "It is an impossible risk for us to accept," he said.

He paused to say hello to a group of businessmen leaving the restaurant. "They are from our Russia plant; they are in Paris for a meeting," he explained, helping himself to another olive. I asked him why, if all he was saying was true, the authorities didn't just agree to amend the rules. Part of it, he said, was political: Having lectured the world about the unique quality of its raw-milk cheeses, the French government didn't wish to appear hypocritical by giving in to Lactalis and Isigny. Here, Morelon began to mock French bureaucrats: " 'We have always defended raw milk in the international market. We are the champions of raw milk, and the Americans and the English don't understand anything about cheese. As usual, we in France are the best in the world. Others have to adapt to our genius.' " He broke into a belly laugh.

The other, perhaps larger, problem was that Lactalis was an industrial giant, and Morelon said there was a reflexive bias in France against corporations. "Lactalis is big," he said with a mordant chuckle, "and the first rule in France is that small is beautiful. The second rule is, small is beautiful, and the third rule is, small is beautiful." It didn't matter that Lactalis produced nine thousand of the thirteen thousand tons of raw-milk Camembert made each year in Normandy; it didn't matter that the company was offering bonuses to its seven hundred fifty milk suppliers in the appellation to shift more of their production to Norman cows. Lactalis was perceived as the enemy, and this impression had been reinforced by all the media coverage that the war over Camembert had attracted. "We're the big giant who wants to kill the small guys, and we're using food safety as the tool," he said, resuming his sardonic, slightly aggrieved tone. "It's a nice story for the newspapers."

Perhaps Lactalis wasn't trying to bury the little guys, but it plainly had an overwhelming economic advantage: It could compete a lot easier on price than a small producer like Durand, and in today's France, price matters greatly. This was a point emphasized to me by Christian Ligeard, an official in the French Ministry of Agriculture. Ligeard was talking not about Camembert, but rather, about Roquefort and its most notorious champion, José Bové. In his view, Bové was a demagogue whose battle on behalf of Roquefort producers had been as misleading as it was misguided. What threatened their livelihoods, said Ligeard, was not globalization and free trade; it was the fact that their cheeses were simply too expensive for most French consumers. "It is not a problem to sell these cheeses; the problem is the price," he said. "The working class here does not have the money to eat Roquefort every day. It's like Champagne; they can maybe afford to have it on Sunday."

The day after my meeting with Morelon, I paid a visit to Philippe Alléosse. A sinewy forty-six-year-old with intense blue eyes, closely cut dark hair, and a radiant smile, Alléosse owned what was considered by many to be the finest cheese shop in Paris. It was located on the rue Poncelet in the seventeenth arrondissement, home to one of Paris's most charming outdoor markets. But Alléosse didn't merely sell cheese; he was an *affineur* who bought unfinished cheeses and aged them in his own cellars. This was considered an art unto itself, and the genial Alléosse was one of its masters. He supplied a number of the city's top restaurants, including several three-stars, and the turnover at his small eponymous shop was always brisk.

For our meeting, Alléosse had invited me to his *cave d'affinage*, which was also located in the seventeenth, but at its northern edge, near the city limits. It was here that Alléosse received newly made cheeses from his network of producers and nurtured them to maturity. Before talking, he took me down to the cellar for a look (there, too, sanitary boots were obligatory). Alléosse carried one hundred fifty to two hundred different types of cheese, and the cellar normally contained around twenty thousand individual pieces, which gave the room a bracingly pungent perfume. The cellar was divided into four separate chambers, each given over to a particular family of cheeses. One room was devoted exclusively to goat cheeses. Another was for soft, surface mold–ripened cheeses, among them Camembert; a third was for hard cheeses, such as Comté; and the fourth was devoted to washed-rind cheeses, such as Muenster and Époisses. Most of the cheeses were arrayed on metal shelving racks with wheels, and as we made our way through each room, Alléosse, a man plainly in love with his work, kept pulling cheeses off the shelves and putting them under my nose. "Smell this," "touch this," "look at this." My resistance finally crumbled when we arrived at the dolly containing Saint-Marcellin, a tangy, deliriously runny cow's-milk cheese produced near Lyon. I told Alléosse of my fondness for Saint-Marcellin; he immediately handed me one of the puck-size disks, which I proceeded to scarf. It was sublime—as good a mid-morning fillip as you could ever hope to taste.

After finishing the tour, we went to the office that he shared with his wife, Rachel, an affable woman with short red hair who was doing the company's bookkeeping. She continued working as Alléosse and I chatted at his desk. He said that the battle over Camembert was indeed symbolic; if *lait cru* Camembert was allowed to be cast aside, then no cheese was safe. This was a fight over tradition, he said, but it was also a war over taste. I told Alléosse of my conversation with Morelon and how the Lactalis spokesman had insisted there was no way to distinguish raw-milk Camembert from that made with treated milk. At this, Alléosse shook his head, threw his hands in the air, and turned to his wife. "Can you believe this?" he said, his voice rising in indignation. "Can you believe what Morelon said?" She shook her head and assumed a look of disgust (a sincere one, too; she wasn't just humoring her husband). Pivoting around to look at me again, Alléosse said, "*That's* an insult; *that's* an industrialist speaking to you."

To Alléosse, the Camembert situation was nothing out of the ordinary; this was the way things worked in France now. "The industrial companies are such a powerful force here," he said. "The state just closes its eyes, and small producers are destroyed." But while the wrangling over Camembert didn't surprise him, he was perturbed by it; he was perturbed by much of what he saw happening around him. He had a habit of prefacing his remarks with the words, "Do you find it normal that …" The phrase was inevitably the lead-in to a rhetorical question, a way of underscoring his incredulity at the course of events in France—at the industrialization of agriculture and the demise of the artisan and the loss of good cheese and good taste. To hear him tell it, quality was plummeting everywhere; finding cheeses of character was increasingly difficult. "In France," he said, "we have a lot of cheeses, but a lot of them are without quality. Look at the large producers of Camembert. If you produce fifteen thousand Camembert a day, how do you control the quality? Impossible. You get quantity, but not quality." I didn't tell him that Lactalis was making six hundred thousand a day, but he probably knew that already.

What troubled Alléosse more than the fate of this one, totemic cheese was that his compatriots seemed unconcerned about its plight and the plight of raw-milk cheeses generally—that they just didn't care anymore. He understood that many French couldn't afford to make a daily diet of the kinds of cheeses that he sold, but the public's apathy about the continued existence of such cheeses dismayed him. Having dedicated his life to upholding France's gastronomic tradition, he naturally took the apathy as a personal slight, a statement that his work no longer had any value. And it wasn't just the attitude of the man on the rue; echoing Durand, Alléosse said that even the professionals seemed unconcerned with cheese. "No French chefs come to visit here," he said. "We get foreign chefs. [Japanese chef Hiroyuki] Hiramatsu came here with an entire team, but no French chefs." At this point, he said, it was the passion of his foreign clients that kept him going. "The French think that good cheese is too expensive," he said. "It is the Americans and other foreigners who support quality. I have Americans coming into the store saying 'Philippe, you must continue, you must protect *lait cru* cheeses, you have the best *métier* in the world.' I never hear that from French people."

Before leaving Durand's farm, I had purchased a disk of his Camembert, which I had brought back to Paris and opened that night. The cheese came in the familiar thin round wooden box and wrapped in paper, but that's where the similarities with other Camemberts ended. I knew Camembert to be a pale, somewhat rubbery, and very mild cheese. Durand's rendition was different. For one thing, it was incredibly creamy and had a richer yellow color than other Camemberts. But it was the aroma and flavor that really set it apart. The cheese had an almost feral bouquet, with a bracing whiff of fresh grass and mushrooms. It was once said that Camembert smelled like God's feet; I could only hope that He was so lucky. The cheese tasted as strong as it smelled: It wasn't as powerful as Époisses or Reblochon, but it bore a closer resemblance to those divinely stinky cheeses than it did to the anodyne Camemberts found even in some of the better *fromageries* in Paris. Here was a heavyweight cheese with an unmistakable *goût de terroir*, and as I cut wedge after wedge of Durand's handiwork, I found myself expressing mental solidarity with him and Rouchaud and Roger and others battling on behalf of *le véritable Camembert*. This was a cheese that needed to be saved.

"Without Wine, It Would Be a Desert"

O N MAY 15, 2007, the day before Nicolas Sarkozy was to be inaugurated as French president, a group called the Abu Hafs al-Masri Brigades, identifying itself as Al-Qaeda's European arm, issued a statement on an Islamist Web site warning of a terrorist campaign in France in response to the election of the "Zionist" Sarkozy. Several hours after Sarkozy took his oath, another group delivered a threat. In a grainy videotaped message sent to a French television station, seven balaclava-clad men, speaking in what appeared to be a cave, told the new president he had one month to satisfy their demands or "blood would flow." The ultimatum echoed the previous day's warning, but that's where the similarities ended. The men in the video were not Islamic extremists; rather, they were militant French winemakers, part of a shadowy organization known as the Comité Régional d'Action Viticole, or CRAV, which was waging a campaign of low-grade violence in the Languedoc-Roussillon region, the area hardest hit by an economic crisis decimating broad swathes of France's wine industry. They were wine terrorists.

La crise viticole, as it was known, was the greatest peacetime menace French winemakers had faced since the phylloxera root louse had chewed its way through the vineyards of Burgundy and Bordeaux in the 1860s. A sharp, decades-long decline in domestic wine consumption, combined with the emergence of robust competition from abroad, had led to a collapse in prices at the lower end of the French wine market, leaving thousands of vintners facing financial ruin. Across France, there were huge inventories of unsold Cabernet, Chardonnay, and

Syrah—what the French media referred to as "the wine lake." By 2005, the lake was overflowing and required draining: One hundred million liters of Appellation d'Origine Contrôlée (AOC) wine—which is to say, premium wine—were distilled into ethanol. In 2002, authorities in the Beaujolais region, another flash point, were forced to order the destruction of thirteen million unsold bottles, representing 7 percent of the previous year's total production.

The crisis didn't affect all French winemakers. For the country's most acclaimed producers, business had never been better. The global wealth boom that had begun in the 1990s had created ravenous demand for France's most prized wines and sent their already-high prices soaring. The 1982 Château Pétrus, from one of Bordeaux's most illustrious estates, had come onto the market for sixty dollars per bottle; within months of its release, the 2005 Pétrus was trading hands for five thousand dollars a pop. (And that '82 Pétrus? Twenty-five years later, it was fetching six thousand dollars). As the thirst for fine wine spread from New York and London to Beijing and Moscow, a bottle of Pétrus became a trophy—as much a totem of success as a Gulfstream or a Porsche. The French wine industry was increasingly divided among a tiny number of globally recognized luxury brands and a vast army of unheralded and economically pressed vintners, and as prices continued to surge at the top and plummet at the bottom, the distance separating them became a chasm.

Nowhere was the wine crisis more acute than in the Languedoc, a sprawling region that hugged the Mediterranean coast from west of Marseille down to the Spanish border. The Languedoc had always been a viticultural backwater, producing cheap wines for the French working classes, and the area had a tradition of agrarian militancy. In 1907, Languedoc winemakers staged one of the most serious rural uprisings in French history. Angered by falling prices and what they perceived to be the French government's indifference to their plight, eight hundred thousand vintners, their families, and their supporters waged several days of angry protests that very nearly sparked a civil war. French soldiers were sent in to quell the unrest, which they succeeded in doing only after six of the demonstrators had been shot dead.

One hundred years later, it was déjà vu all over again, except the only deaths to this point had been suicides: A handful of Languedoc vintners had brought the axe down on themselves rather than waiting for it to fall. But others, unwilling to surrender their livelihoods, had taken to violence, and the parallels between 1907 and 2007 were certainly not lost on them. CRAV's videotaped warning to Sarkozy urged winemakers to take up the old banner: "Wine producers, we appeal to you to revolt. We are at the point of no return. Show yourselves to be the worthy successors of the rebels of 1907, when people died so that future generations might earn their living from the land."

CRAV activists were doing their part to help history repeat itself. In April 2005, they hijacked a Spanish truck carrying wine across the border into France and dumped its thirty-thousand liter payload on the highway. Eight months later the group staged a daytime assault on a bottling facility near Montpellier, smashing open vats and sending 750,000 liters of French, Italian, and Spanish wines gushing out. In February 2006, CRAV turned a protest by several thousand winemakers in the city of Narbonne into a day of mayhem; its members damaged train and phone lines, disrupting rail service and communications across the Languedoc. More recently, it had detonated crude bombs at several Languedoc supermarkets, claiming they were deserving targets because they sold foreign wines. And now, with a new president in office, CRAV was threatening to take its campaign in a more lethal direction.

CRAV was said to have around a thousand members, and it appeared to be a well-disciplined organization; the police had been stymied repeatedly in their effort to apprehend those responsible for the attacks. Finding CRAV sympathizers was not as challenging. In standing up for destitute winemakers, those embattled sons of the soil, CRAV sent a message that resonated deeply. This was true even among people who deplored its tactics—even, it appeared, among people who had felt the brunt of those tactics. A manager of one of the bombed supermarkets told reporters, "They picked the wrong target; in this supermarket, we don't sell foreign wines. We understand the winegrowers' problems. My father is one of them."

By portraying its battle as one not just about vintners but also about vineyards, CRAV tapped a deep vein of French nostalgia. Agriculture held a sacred place in French life; the French considered themselves to be a nation of small farmers, and their reverence for the land and those who worked it seemed to grow stronger as more and more people abandoned the country for the city and French farming progressively declined. It was claimed that thirty thousand farms were now going out of business each year. In the 1960s, 20 percent of French workers were employed in agriculture; by the mid-2000s, the figure had fallen to just 3.5 percent. You couldn't keep the French down on the farm, but they still felt its tug, which was why thousands of Parisians turned up at the Salon International de l'Agriculture every year and why *la crise viticole* was seen not just as a wine problem, but as another milestone in the demise of French farming and the depopulation of rural France.

On a chilly, overcast day in November 2006, I traveled to Assas, a village near Montpellier, to visit with Pierre Clavel and his father, Jean. Pierre's winery, Domaine Clavel was one of the most respected in the Languedoc, producing savory, sun-splashed reds composed mainly of Syrah, Grenache, and Mourvèdre. It had a loyal following in France and could be found on retail shelves overseas, too. Jean, now retired, had been one of the most politically active and influential vintners in the region. He was also a historian of Languedoc wine making—and author of a book on the subject—whose expertise extended to the 1907 riots.

Lunch, served at a long table in the tasting room, consisted of lamb stew and salad, prepared by Pierre's wife, Estelle. She joined us for the meal, along with the couple's two young sons, Antoine and Martin. In deference to Estelle and the boys, we mostly made small talk while eating; as they cleared the table after lunch and Pierre uncorked a second bottle of his top cuvée, La Copa Santa, the conversation drifted to the problems in the Languedoc. I wondered about the human toll. How many of the Languedoc's ten thousand vintners would likely be put out of business? Jean prefaced his answer with some context: Around one third of the region's winemakers, he said, had traditionally depended on government subsidies to stay afloat, and the loss of those cash infusions (no longer allowed now under European Union rules) had put them in an untenable position even before the onset of the current troubles. He also noted that the vulnerable included a number of older vintners who were nearing retirement; they would just be *en retraite* sooner than they expected. Nonetheless, an enormous number of Languedoc winemakers would go under—"Thirty percent minimally," Jean said. At that, Pierre exploded. "This is murder!" he roared, pounding the table. "It's a tragedy!" His anger caught me off guard. I understood his concern for his friends and neighbors, but I pointed out that the crisis posed no threat to him—he produced good wines that sold well. "It's true; I'm okay," he said, his voice calm again. "But don't you understand? I don't want to work in a desert. I don't want my sons to work in a desert."

In 2004, a documentary called *Mondovino*, about the globalization of wine, was nominated for the Palme d'Or, the most prestigious award at the annual Cannes Film Festival. Several months after its splashy debut there, *Mondovino* was released in French theaters and garnered an equally enthusiastic response. Although the filmmaker, Jonathan Nossiter, was an American himself, the gist of the movie was that American interests were homogenizing the production and taste of wine and subverting French viticulture in the process. The critic Robert Parker with his vulgar palate, the Mondavis with their deep pockets and assembly-line Chardonnays: France's wine tradition was under assault from these avatars of globalization. The film's emotional high point comes when the acclaimed Burgundy producer Hubert de Montille tells Nossiter that the French have fallen victim to a fiendish American plot. "In the U.S., in California, they know all about marketing," de Montille explains. " 'Let's hide our lack of *terroir* with the taste of new oak. We'll explain that wine should taste like the vanilla of new oak ... And we'll convince the French, who really do have *terroir*, that that's what sells.' "

In fact, it was the French who popularized the use of new oak, a small point in the service of a larger one: De Montille's nefarious tale bore no relationship to reality, and the entire thrust of *Mondovino* was deeply misleading. It was certainly the case that wine was an increasingly globalized business, and that Parker and the Mondavis wielded enormous power; yet, to suggest that these were the main causes of the crisis roiling the Languedoc and other regions was just not true. But Nossiter didn't make that claim; he didn't even acknowledge the economic calamity befalling small French winemakers. Although *la crise viticole* was already ripping through French vineyards, it went unmentioned in a documentary supposedly meant to sound the alarm about French wine making. Nossiter's omission perhaps wasn't so surprising, though: Had he addressed the wine crisis, he would have been obliged to concede that the biggest problem facing French viticulture was the French themselves.

For one thing, French consumers were drinking less wine than ever before. Since 1960, France's per capita annual wine consumption had plummeted by more than 50 percent. Initially, the decline was driven by the same trends (health considerations, changing social mores) that led to the demise of the three-martini lunch in the United States and reduced alcohol intake in other countries. Now, though, there were uniquely French factors at work. In the mid-1990s, the government enacted some of the toughest drunk driving laws in Europe. The results were impressive: By 2004, alcohol-related road fatalities had declined 40 percent. But the French wine industry paid dearly for that progress: Restaurant wine sales fell sharply in response to the crackdown, and a critical source of demand for French vintners dried up accordingly.

However, the government wasn't just taking aim at drunk driving; it seemed intent on discouraging alcohol consumption, period. Indeed, French politicians on both the left and the right were increasingly demonstrating a neo-prohibitionist mindset. In 1991, a law was passed forbidding alcohol advertising on television and in movie theaters and barring liquor companies from sponsoring events like sports matches. Later, the government would seek to extend the ban to the Internet. In 2008, a court fined a Paris newspaper for publishing an article about holiday Champagnes: In a jaw-dropping display of adjudicatory jujitsu, it said the offending column constituted a form of advertising, in that it "intended to promote sales of alcoholic beverages in exercising a psychological effect on the reader that incited him or her to buy alcohol." Also in 2008, the government moved to bar all promotional activities involving free alcohol; among other things, the edict was meant to curb in-store wine tastings and—truly chilling—prevent winemakers from pouring samples for visiting journalists. All this, coupled with punishing inheritance taxes—up to 60 percent of the value of a property—that made it exceedingly hard to keep family wineries intact, suggested that France had a government that was at war with French oenology.

There was one development above all others that underscored the extent to which French wine culture was in retreat: America's enthusiasm for wine was beginning to eclipse France's. By 2007 the United States was in the midst of a wine boom that had seen consumption increase by 75 percent since the early 1990s, and it was now on course to surpass France in total wine consumption by 2015 (although on a per capita basis, France was still many bottles ahead). Thanks to the efforts of people like Robert Parker and the acclaimed Berkeley-based importer Kermit Lynch, vast numbers of Americans got hooked on wine in the three decades following the Judgment of Paris. And it wasn't just California wines that they embraced; the United States became home to the most ardent collectors of the finest French wines, and contrary to Hubert de Montille's conspiracy theorizing, many American oenophiles and vintners held France's wine-making tradition in the highest esteem. In 2005 Gallup reported that for the first time ever, Americans preferred wine to beer. This change in taste was reflected not just at the checkout counter, but in the proliferation of wine bars, wine schools, and instructional wine books. When it came to wine, it appeared that Americans were now the libertines, and the French, increasingly, were the puritans.

The precipitous decline of wine consumption in France was matched by a sharp fall in the sales of French wines abroad. The emergence in the 1990s of dynamic wine industries in places like Argentina and Chile, the advent of cleverly packaged New World brands like Australia's Yellow Tail (which in just three years of existence had become the biggest-selling imported wine in the United States), and the proliferation of good, inexpensive Spanish and Italian wines cut deeply into France's market share. In 1990, one of every three imported wines sold in the United States was French; by 2005, it was down to one of every six. Similar declines were recorded in Great Britain, traditionally the biggest market for French wines.

But increased competition alone didn't push French bottles off the shelves; French complacency played a big part, too. "We were totally blind to the emergence of these new countries," said Marc Sibard, the owner of the Caves Augé wine shop in Paris. "We didn't see it." While winemakers in other countries assiduously courted consumers, the French continued to believe that consumers would come to them—they always had. The prevailing wisdom was that French wines would find buyers simply by virtue of being French. "It was a question of attitude," says Sibard. "We always assumed that anything labeled 'France' would just sell." As one Burgundy winemaker, Patrick Hudelot, told the *New York Times*, "In France, there is a belief that you don't need to market your wine, that France's reputation is enough. And that way we are being left behind."

But France was also being left behind because it was producing a lot of bad wine. It had too many vintners who lacked the talent, ambition, or resources needed to make quality wines, and this, too, had contributed to the falling demand—possibly in the home market, certainly abroad. Moreover, the insipid stuff was no longer confined to the two lowest categories of French wines, *vins de pays* and *vins de table*. The highest classification, Appellation d'Origine Contrôlée, was now overrun with plonk, too, and many consumers, having learned the hard way that the AOC designation no longer guaranteed that a wine was necessarily even pleasant to drink, had taken their dollars, pounds, and euros elsewhere.

Controlled appellations were formally introduced in France in 1935. They were, firstly, an effort to map out the boundaries within which some premium wines, such as Châteauneuf-du-Pape, could be made and to keep these names from being used elsewhere. As such, they were a form of consumer protection—an assurance that what was on the label corresponded with what was in the bottle. More broadly, creating appellations was a way of codifying what centuries of trial and error had established: that wine was chiefly a product of the land, that some vineyards were superior to others, and that matching the right grape to the right site was the route to good wine. The aim, in other words, was to give the concept of *terroir* the force of law. The people who conceived the appellation system saw it as a quality-control mechanism, as well, and only the finest French vineyards were supposed to be eligible for AOC status.

As such, it was conferred sparingly in the early years. By 1940, there were only one hundred to one hundred fifty appellations (precise figures are hard to come by), and the number grew incrementally over the next several decades. Through the 1950s and '60s, fewer than 20 percent of French vineyards fell within AOCs. But in the 1970s, regulators decided that putting more vineyards (and therefore more wines) under the AOC umbrella was the way to ensure continued French domination of the global wine market. This proved to be a disastrous gambit. By the mid-2000s, there were more than four hundred fifty appellations, encompassing over 50 percent of all French vineyards and accounting for 45 percent of France's total wine production. Some of the newer appellations deserved the promotion, but others did not, and the AOC concept was debased as a result. A wine like Pétrus bore the AOC imprimatur, but many wines that weren't fit for a saucepan had it now, too.

Nor was this the only way in which the reliability of AOC wines was compromised. While the Institut National des Appellations d'Origine (INAO), in Paris, oversaw the appellation system, individual districts largely governed themselves, via local winemaker associations. Every appellation had its own particular set of rules, but they all tended to regulate heavily. Much of what a winemaker did in his vineyard—from how closely he planted his vines to when he could begin harvesting to how many grapes he could pick—was subject to regulation. In theory, the many rules promoted quality; in practice, however, they often served to undercut it. Self-governance meant majority rule, and in many appellations, the interests of the underachieving majority tended to trump those of the overachieving few. Permitted crop yields were often too high (generally speaking, the lower the yields, the better the quality of the fruit). Likewise, the boundaries of some districts were drawn too generously, extending into areas that were not suitable for making good wines.

Then there was the appellation taste test, the ultimate conflict of interest. A wine produced in an appellation was not automatically entitled to advertise its noble roots; in order to claim AOC status, it had to pass a taste test meant to ensure that it conformed to the standards of the appellation—that it exhibited sufficient *typicité*. Although the taste tests were done blind (with the identities of the wines concealed), they were conducted by appellation insiders, and in any given year, 95 to 99 percent of the wines submitted were approved. To reject a wine was to risk inadvertently shafting a friend or neighbor or maybe even yourself, and the tasting panels thus tended to err on the side of extreme leniency. As a result, a lot of bad wine was waved through. In a survey released in 2007 by the French consumer group UFC-Que Choisir, wine industry insiders acknowledged that as many as one third of all AOC wines were unworthy of the distinction. The AOC designation no longer assured even a modicum of quality, and consequently wine buyers in many markets had soured on French wines. Alain Bazot, UFC-Que Choisir's president, summed it up well: "For years, there has been a steady fall in the quality of many AOC wines which has completely undermined the confidence of consumers in the system."

Perversely, some appellations, rather than rooting out the

incompetent producers, seemed intent on driving away the good ones. In recent years, stars like Jean Thévenet, Didier Dagueneau, Eloi Dürrbach, Marcel Lapierre, Thierry and Jean-Marie Puzelat, Marcel Richaud, Georges Descombes, Jean-Paul Brun, and Philippe Jambon had all had wines turned down for being insufficiently typical. The reasons for the rejections varied; some of the wines supposedly had more residual sugar than allowed, others contained too much of one grape or another. These producers all made internationally acclaimed wines in appellations that mostly churned out swill and where scores of vintners were in financial distress. Given these circumstances, and the laxness with which the rules were otherwise enforced, it didn't require an especially conspiratorial mind to wonder if petty jealousies lay behind some of the snubs.

Whatever the case, the AOC system was rotting from within. To find out what if anything was being done to save it, I went to the INAO headquarters in the fall of 2006 to meet Hervé Briand, a senior official with the organization. A tall, genial man, Briand chose his words carefully—he was a bureaucrat—but he agreed that the appellation mechanism was in shambles. Dramatically increasing the number of appellations had been a mistake, he acknowledged, one that had badly damaged the reputation of French wines overseas. "Our image wasn't destroyed, but it was affected by the lesser quality of some of these wines," Briand said. He conceded, too, that the taste tests had been a problem. A jury comprised of local winemakers, local wine consultants, and local merchants was undeniably a recipe for mediocrity. "They know that if they say no, the wine is not AOC, it will be a very, very big economic cost for that producer," he said. "So there is a pressure in the mind to say yes." He said that "perhaps" 10 percent of AOC-designated wines were substandard.

Briand told me reforms were on the way; the INAO would use its authority to revamp the taste tests and try to eliminate or at least reduce the conflicts of interest, and it would also try to exercise more control over the production of wines. "The problems in the bottle are often the result of problems in the vineyard or the *chais* [winery]; we want to eliminate those problems," he said. But was more regulation really the answer? Suddenly, I put myself in the role of Milton Friedman, arch libertarian. Instead of adding more rules and making things even more complicated, why not reduce the number of rules, leave winemakers free to do their thing, and let consumers decide whose wines were worth drinking? Why not make the French wine industry a beacon of sensible, market-driven reform—a shining example for the rest of the country? Briand said that back in the 1930s and '40s, it had been lightly regulated. "The rules were not very numerous—they covered the boundaries and the grape varieties," he said. "Historically, people in these appellations made wine the same way as one another. Not the exact same wine, but similar." However, as the number of producers had grown, some of them had deviated from standard wine-making practices, and this had been unacceptable. "When you are in a collective way," he said, "you have to have rules for the important things, and you can't let someone make a wine completely differently." It was a revealing answer, and one that snapped me out of my reverie; I was in the office of a French *fonctionnaire,* not a lecture hall at the University of Chicago.

Briand was implying that the issue was bad winemakers breaking good rules, but it seemed to me that the bigger problem was good winemakers being forced to violate bad rules. I mentioned Jean Thévenet, whose difficulties with his appellation in the Mâcon region had been the subject of some press coverage. "The best producer"—at this Briand caught himself and rephrased his reply—"a producer with a good feel for the market can make a wine that will be a big success without being part of the AOC. Mr. Thévenet is not a bad man; he's a great man and makes great wine. But we have this problem everywhere in France—people making wine that is deeply different—but it can't be like that." The lack of conviction in his voice suggested that he wasn't buying his own argument.

I said that perhaps the original sin was not the decision to expand the appellation system, but rather, the now-discontinued policy of showering lavish subsidies on the wine industry, which had encouraged many unqualified people to get into viticulture and then had sustained them even when the market would not. Briand pointed out that the subsidies had not traditionally gone to AOC producers; rather, they had been given to vintners who produced *vins de pays* and *vins de table*. He said these payments had been motivated less by a desire to keep inept producers afloat than by a recognition that certain regions, particularly the Languedoc, had little else to offer people in the way of work. "The subsidies were to preserve a way of life," he explained. "These people—if they don't have viticulture, they would have nothing." He then invoked the same metaphor Jean Clavel had used. "Without wine, it would be a desert." .

Like a general inspecting his troops, Christian Moueix slowly made his way past a row of grapevines, looking each plant up and down and casting an approving glance at some, a dubious eye at others. We were in the vineyard of Château Bélair, in the Saint-Émilion appellation of Bordeaux, on a ridge overlooking the Dordogne plain, which on this cloudless late Saturday afternoon was bathed a brilliant shade of gold. Moueix, whose family owned Château Pétrus, in the neighboring village of Pomerol, and eight other wineries, all of them situated on what was referred to as the Right Bank of Bordeaux, had recently taken a 30 percent stake in Bélair and needed to check on the progress of its grapes. For Moueix, the harvest had started the day before at Château Trotanoy, in Pomerol, and he was now shuttling between vineyards, trying to determine where next to pick. After a cool, wet summer, the weather had turned brilliant in September, perhaps salvaging the 2007 vintage. However, rain was expected to return on Monday and Tuesday.

Two of Moueix's properties, Château La Fleur-Pétrus in Pomerol and Château Magdelaine in Saint-Émilion, were equipped with meteorological stations, from which he received frequent updates. But it was still unclear how much precipitation would fall, and in the absence of solid information, Moueix felt he had to gamble. Having concluded that the grapes at Pétrus were not ready, he would forgo picking there on Sunday and hope that the rain, when it came, would be light and brief. Pétrus, which sat on twenty-eight acres of land and produced twenty-five thousand to thirty thousand bottles annually, was the brightest star in the Moueix constellation. It had acquired its prominence chiefly through the efforts of Moueix's late father, Jean-Pierre, a legendary figure in the Bordeaux wine trade. The elder Moueix was a wine merchant who in 1952 became the sole agent for Pétrus, then wholly owned by the Loubat family. Although Pétrus had been making exceptional wines since 1900, it was largely unknown outside of Bordeaux, and the Pomerol appellation was a nonentity. That all changed thanks to Jean-Pierre; his tireless salesmanship gained Pétrus an international following (it became a favorite of the Kennedys) and helped turn Pomerol into one of the most prestigious wine districts in all of France. In 1964, having already bought Trotanoy and several other nearby châteaux, Moueix purchased a 50-percent stake in Pétrus, which he and Christian, who succeeded him in 1991, then propelled to even greater renown. In building up Pétrus and Pomerol, the Moueixs became among the wealthiest families in southern France and accumulated what was reputed to be one of the world's finest private art collections, replete with works by Picasso and Francis Bacon.

Pétrus was considered by many wine aficionados to be a masterpiece in its own right. It was certainly one of the richest and most profound wines made in Bordeaux. Several weeks after visiting with Moueix, at an auction in New York, I was treated to a glass of the heralded 1998 Pétrus. Although the wine was still an infant and wouldn't reach maturity for at least another decade, it was already sublime. Its bouquet was quintessentially Pomerol, with aromas of plums, raspberries, black truffles, flowers, and mocha. In the mouth, it was obscenely decadent; waves of lush fruit surged across the palate, pulled along by brisk acidity and voluptuous tannins. But typical of Pétrus, the heft was only one part of the equation; the wine also displayed an almost balletic grace and elegance. The aftertaste was so achingly good that I went to bed that night without brushing my teeth, in the hope that the flavors would linger till morning (sadly for me, and unfortunately for my wife, they didn't).

Insufficiently ripe fruit did not produce that kind of wine, and though the 2007 Pétrus would be no match for the '98, there was still a chance that it could turn out to be excellent in its own right, which was why Moueix had decided to hold off on harvesting the grapes despite the threat of rain. "With Pétrus," he said, "I'm obliged to take the risk."

At Bélair, the stakes were lower. Although the château occupied one of the most privileged sites on the Right Bank, the wines had not been impressive of late, and no one expected Moueix to engineer an instant turnaround, especially given the way 2007 was shaping up. He had purchased a share in Bélair in part to help his friend Pascal Delbeck, to whom the château had been bequeathed by its late owner. Delbeck was a popular figure in Bordeaux, but he was somewhat eccentric (in recent years, he had been using gypsies to harvest the grapes) and also lacked the financial resources to make a truly fine wine. Without an injection of capital, he likely would have had to sell. Moueix didn't want that to happen to Delbeck, and he also didn't wish to see Bélair end up in the hands of someone who might turn the wine into an inelegant fruit bomb of the sort that was now increasingly prevalent in Saint-Émilion. Moueix employed around one hundred twenty people, many of whom would now be put to work improving Bélair's production and distribution.

A courtly, erudite sixty-year-old, Moueix was Bordeaux royalty, and as he walked through the Bélair vineyard in his neatly pressed white shirt and stylish khaki shorts, Dolce & Gabbana sunglasses perched on his nose, he had an unmistakably aristocratic bearing. But then, he knelt down in the dirt. "Look at this," he said, beckoning to me. With one hand supporting his tall frame, he was using the other to caress a withered, gnarly grapevine. "This vine is about eighty years old—an old soldier," he said with a paternal smile. "You have to treat these old ones with care." He plucked a few Merlot grapes to sample; although lab analysis could tell him the ripeness of the berries, Moueix had spent his life in the vineyards and trusted his mouth more. Earlier in the day, he had told me that he didn't live in any of his châteaux because the sight of barren vines in winter depressed him, and as we stood there, admiring the octogenarian plant and spitting out grape skins, I suddenly understood that Moueix, although he didn't look the part, was at heart a farmer, as attached to the land as any other.

Two days later, another Bordeaux vintner, Bernard Richard, showed me around the vineyard of his winery, Château Fourton La Garenne. As we walked along a rutted path between long rows of tall, leafy vines, Richard periodically paused to inspect clusters of grapes. Like Moueix, he picked a few berries every time we stopped in order to check on the progress of the fruit. "They still need some time," he said, casting a worried glance at the sky. The expected rains had not materialized, but clouds were beginning to roll in. He said harvest was still at least a week away, and he would just have to hope for the best. Richard lifted up a large green leaf and plucked off several more dark berries, which he proceeded to pop into his mouth, one after the other. He then put his hand around the trunk of the vine. "They are like children, you know," he said, "and you have to look after them the same way."

Richard, too, was a farmer at heart, a fifth-generation winemaker, and his attachment to the land was as profound as Moueix's. It was so great, in fact, that in 2006, he sold his house in order to keep his winery. He now lived with his family in a pair of mobile homes parked on the lawn of the château. Richard was one of the thousands of French winemakers slowly going bust. Many had sad stories to tell, but few stories were as tragic as Richard's, and fewer still exposed so starkly the fault lines running through the vineyards of France. The reversals Richard had suffered—the evaporated demand for his wines, the forced sale of his house—were dismaying; the fact that all this had transpired fifteen minutes from Saint-Émilion and Pomerol, fifteen minutes from Christian Moueix and Pétrus and vineyards turning out five-thousand-dollar bottles of wine, beggared belief.

I had first met Richard three months earlier, when I was in Bordeaux for Vinexpo, a mammoth wine trade show. Some fifty thousand wine professionals and hangers-on from around the world had descended on Bordeaux in the middle of June for a week of sipping, slurping, and deal-making. The fair itself had taken place in three cavernous exhibition halls on the northern edge of the city of Bordeaux, but scores of private tastings and lavish lunches and dinners also had been held off-site. Many big-spending clients had come to Bordeaux for all or part of Vinexpo, giving the sprawling wine region the feel of the Hamptons in mid-August. Eager to bypass Bordeaux's clogged highways and streets, some of the visitors had hired helicopters to ferry them back and forth between châteaux, creating a daily airborne flotilla in the skies above the vineyards.

Located on the edge of a somnolent village twenty or so minutes from downtown Bordeaux, Fourton La Garenne sat at the end of a long, pockmarked driveway that eventually turned into grass. Approaching the château, I noticed the two mobile homes on the lawn. The château itself was in an advanced state of decrepitude. Its stone exterior was chipped and decayed, the corrugated roof completely rusted. The barrel room, located in the back of the château, was a small, dark chamber with crumbling walls and shards of rotten wood strewn about. Perhaps a dozen or so oak barrels sat in the unkempt yard behind the château, along with some stray farm equipment and cinderblocks. As I surveyed this scene, it occurred to me that I'd taken a wrong turn out of Bordeaux and somehow ended up in Appalachia.

One problem was immediately apparent: Fourton La Garenne was on the periphery of Bordeaux, in a place that probably wasn't very conducive to making wine—good ones, anyway. A few years earlier, in Burgundy, I'd spent several hours in the vineyards of Meursault with Stéphane Thibodaux, the estate manager for Domaine des Comtes Lafon, one of the region's most acclaimed wineries. As we had driven through the Goutte d'Or vineyard, Thibodaux had explained to me the lay of the land. "If you are on the left side of the road here," he had said with a wry smile, "you are a loser. If you are on the right side, you are a winner." This crude formulation got to the essence of French viticulture: Ultimately, you were only as good as the dirt you owned. Fourton La Garenne had a name that sounded every bit as distinguished as Pétrus and Bélair, but it didn't have the soil to match, and that was surely one reason for its troubles.

As I exited the car, Richard came out to meet me, along with his oldest daughter, Aude. Richard's three-year-old granddaughter, Leane, eyed me suspiciously and then scurried into the château. Richard, a trim, bearded fifty-eight-year-old with weather-beaten skin, was dressed in a blue mechanic's suit—a far cry from the tweed jackets and loafers worn in Bordeaux's more posh precincts. Richard's other daughter, Amandine, Leane's mother, was behind the château, laboring to push full barrels onto a wooden platform for racking. She was a strikingly pretty blonde, but she had an unsettling hardness to her eyes.

Using several different grapes—mainly Merlot, but also Cabernet Sauvignon, Cabernet Franc, Malbec, Sauvignon Blanc, and Semillon—the Richards produced around twenty-five thousand bottles of AOC-designated wines each year. Richard had started bottling his own wines only in 1994. Previously, he had sold his grapes to a nearby cooperative, which used them for wines that went out under its label. This was a common practice in France, but selling to a cooperative didn't have the cachet that selling wine under one's own name did. To do the bottling himself, Richard had to upgrade his facilities and had taken out a loan from Crédit Agricole, a major French bank. This was on top of a loan he had received from the same bank in 1991, when frost destroyed nearly his entire crop and he needed help covering his expenses.

He had still been repaying the loans when the crisis had struck in 2002 and the prices that his wines could obtain collapsed. Before, Richard had been getting two euros per liter wholesale; by 2007, the wholesale price was less than a euro. Adding to his woes, the local merchant who had previously distributed his wines dropped him as a client, forcing Richard to sell them himself. Then, the land values in his part of Bordeaux plummeted. A decade earlier, he could have sold one hectare of vineyard for the equivalent of sixty thousand dollars; now, the same patch of land could get maybe fifteen thousand. Suddenly, the Richards found themselves tending grapes and producing wines that were just about worthless. They pleaded with the bank to adjust the terms of the loans, but the bank refused; it wanted its money and began pressuring the family to liquidate assets. "I told them to stop strangling me," Richard recalled. He was eventually forced to choose between selling his home or the winery. He opted for the house. "It was a choice between dying and cutting off my arm," he explained. "I decided to cut off my arm."

We were talking in the yard behind the château, which I assumed had been the family's residence. Aude corrected me; they'd only ever used the château for wine making. She pointed to a large house visible just through the trees; that was their old home. It was now owned by "a rich Parisian who wanted a vacation place," Bernard said with a mordant laugh. He said the decision to sell the house had been painful. "It was the house we moved into when we married and where we raised our children," he said. (Richard also had a twenty-four-year-old son.) Why, I asked, hadn't they just sold the winery and kept the roof over their heads? Aude, who was rolling a cigarette, smiled wanly and answered for her father: "We love this property; we can't leave it." As we were chatting, now under a light rain, Amandine let out a groan. I looked over and saw her struggling to push a barrel of wine onto a slightly raised wooden platform in the middle of the lawn, her face flushed and contorted from the effort. Her sister and father didn't seem to notice. I commented to Aude that her family was in a sad situation. "Sad? No, just hard," she replied.

They were doing everything they could to bail themselves out, starting with plans to rip up around seven acres of vines and to use the land for vegetables and as grazing area for some cows and pigs. "We realized last year that we were producing too much wine," Aude told me. "Plus, the government will pay us a little money to uproot the vines." (Although subsidies were no longer available, winemakers were now being paid to tear out their crops.) She said that they would try to become a full-service farm for their neighbors: People would come and buy wine and fresh vegetables, and they could bring their children to pet the animals. In an attempt to carve out an additional niche for themselves, the Richards had also converted to biodynamic wine making, an ultra-organic approach to vineyard management. This would hopefully give them entrée to organic wine shops throughout France.

The rain had let up, and Richard opened a bottle for me to taste: the 2001 Château Fourton La Garenne Cuvée Fût de Chêne. The pale, washed-out color told me all I needed to know. The bouquet was just as feeble; it was a challenge to coax any aromas out of the glass. The wine tasted emaciated, with a strong herbal note that suggested unripe fruit and coarse, rustic tannins. Still, while it didn't deserve AOC status, it wasn't egregiously bad, and back when French factory workers would quaff a liter for lunch, there undoubtedly had been demand for such a wine. But those days were over. As we tasted, I asked Richard why he didn't have a booth at Vinexpo. He laughed. "That's just business," he said. "It isn't about wine." I said that there was a lot of money on display this year and mentioned the helicopter traffic. "Oh, yes, we hear the helicopters every night," Aude said with a bemused grin.

When I returned to Fourton La Garenne three months later, on the eve of the harvest, the Richards told me of a new outlet for their crop and a source of some possible short-term relief: They were now bottling and selling unfermented grape juice. As Bernard and I walked through the family vineyard, joined by Aude, we discussed the crisis and what had triggered it. They acknowledged that domestic consumption was a factor. "People in France just don't want to drink wine anymore," Aude said. They conceded, too, that the government and the banks had made it too easy for people to get into the wine business and that France had produced too much wine. Mostly, though, they blamed the crisis on foreign competition; against these mass-produced, shrewdly marketed Australian and Chilean wines, what chance did small French vintners have?

We talked about the growing economic divide in Bordeaux. I mentioned a recent remark made by Pierre Lurton, who was the scion of a prominent Bordeaux family and the managing director of two venerable wineries, Château Cheval Blanc and Château d'Yquem. In an interview with *Time* magazine, Lurton had expressed concern about the region's prosperity gap and compared it to the striking inequality that one found in many South American countries. Richard, who had been a study in serenity until this point, suddenly erupted in anger. "These are the people who are killing us!" he barked. "They are the ones who are telling us we make bad wines and that we need to become more like the New World producers." He noted, too, the irony of the South America comment, pointing out that Lurton had a winery in Argentina called Cheval des Andes. Aude nodded in agreement. "They should be helping the people here instead of going over there," she said.

Moueix was over there, too; in the early 1980s, he had started producing a wine in Napa Valley called Dominus, which had quickly established itself as one of California's finest. But Bordeaux was his home, and the wine crisis and the plight of small growers like Richard weighed on him. There was no escaping the crisis—not even in Pomerol and Saint-Émilion. His wife, Cherise, a beautiful Chinese-American woman whom he had met when she worked as an art dealer in Paris, had told me that Moueix was now routinely buttonholed in church by winemakers desperate for his help. He was doing what he could. In addition to Pétrus and his other properties, Moueix had a line of generic Bordeaux. He purchased wines from estates throughout the region, blended them, and sold them under the "Christian Moueix" label. He wasn't putting out plonk; he had a reputation to uphold and the wines he bought had to be good. But he felt the crisis keenly, and wanted to provide a lifeline to struggling neighbors. "Bordeaux has given so much to my family, and we have to give back," he said.

He knew, though, that his contribution was small; while it might buy a handful of winemakers some time, it wasn't going to change the grim prognosis. Bordeaux—France—had a surfeit of vintners and vineyards, and the crisis would only end when there were many fewer of both. "We were too lax in the seventies and eighties," Moueix said. "Things were too easy. There was no world competition, so we said, 'Let's plant more.' Terrible mistakes were made." But while the solution was obvious and unavoidable, that didn't make it any less wrenching. Finding new uses for former vineyards would be simple; finding new uses for former winemakers would not be. "Many of these people, this is all they know," he said. "Wine is the only thing they know."

King of the World

IN FEBRUARY 2007, Alain Ducasse hosted a tribute in Monte Carlo in honor of Paul Bocuse. The event was originally scheduled to coincide with Bocuse's eightieth birthday, the previous year, but his heart surgery had delayed the celebration. The weekend fête was held at the Hôtel de Paris, home to Louis XV, Ducasse's three-star restaurant, and at a handful of other venues in the tiny principality. Ferran Adrià, Juan Mari Arzak, Daniel Boulud, and Charlie Trotter were among the dozens of culinary eminences who took part in the festivities, which included a gala dinner, replete with magnums of Dom Pérignon, and a lunch prepared by an all-star ensemble of chefs. The gathering also featured the big-tent flourishes beloved by Bocuse: dancing girls in fishnet stockings, a performance by the Monte Carlo circus, and a fireworks display.

The occasion wasn't merely a chance to toast Bocuse. It was a symbolic passing of the toque—the moment the fifty-year-old Ducasse staked his claim to being the new godfather of French cuisine. Ducasse even donned chef's whites to pose for a picture with Bocuse, underscoring the significance of the moment: Unlike Bocuse, who had always sought to maintain the illusion that he was still a practicing chef by dressing up as one whenever cameras were nearby, Ducasse had long ago dropped any such pretense. His standard attire was a business suit, because he was now a businessman, and a very successful one. With over twenty restaurants on four continents, a prestigious cooking school, his own publishing imprint, and more than a thousand employees worldwide, Ducasse presided over a culinary empire of unprecedented size and reach. It even extended to the heavens: A few months before the Monte Carlo event, the Ducasse group had prepared meals for the astronauts aboard the International Space Station. (Among the items on the menu: roast quail and rice pudding.)

In the course of building *l'univers Ducasse,* the peripatetic chef had gained a reputation as a remarkably savvy manager, with an unerring eye for talent and a knack for putting people in the right jobs—in his own restaurants and in other ones, too. Top kitchens in France were crawling with Ducasse alums. All this had made Ducasse the most recognized chef of his generation and the logical choice to inherit the throne occupied by Bocuse—and by Point, Escoffier, and Carême before him.

It was a role that he was eager to assume. Six months after the Bocuse event, the newly elected Nicolas Sarkozy had lunch at Ducasse's three-star restaurant in Paris. Ducasse was there to greet him, but also to corner him. After exchanging pleasantries, he delivered a blunt warning: The 19.6 percent value-added tax was killing the restaurant industry, and if the government wanted him and other leading chefs to continue doing business in France, it was going to have to sharply reduce the rate. Sarkozy was later heard to remark to his guests, "Can you imagine if France were to lose Alain Ducasse?"

In the opinion of some critics, it would have been good riddance. To his detractors, Ducasse was a gastronomic bantamweight who had contributed little of lasting value to French cooking. François Simon called him a purveyor of "xeroxed" cuisine and a "sleek atomizer—spritzing his brand over you from a plane on his way to New York or Hong Kong." For Simon—and it was a view widely shared—Ducasse epitomized much of what was now wrong with high-end French fare: the absentee chefs, the relentless branding and self-promotion, the dearth of path-breaking ingenuity at the stove. In addition to being the best-known chef of his era, Ducasse also seemed to be the most unpopular.

A casual observer, stumbling upon the celebration in Monte Carlo, might have assumed that Ducasse was Bocuse's protégé. In fact, he had been a disciple of Alain Chapel, with whom he had worked in the late 1970s. By now, however, Bocuse had become his role model; it was even rumored that a deal had been struck for Ducasse to take over Bocuse's restaurant. If you believed that one reason for the malaise in French cuisine was too much Bocuse and not enough Chapel—too many chefs in airport lounges, too few in the kitchen—it was only natural to regard Ducasse as the embodiment of this unfortunate imbalance, and to perhaps also view him as something of a turncoat. But did Ducasse really betray Chapel's legacy to embrace Bocuse's, or did it only look that way?

Alain Ducasse grew up on a farm in southwest France; the aromas coming out of the kitchen on Sundays, when his grandmother cooked the family meal, aroused his interest in food, and in his late teens he went to work for Michel Guérard. It was 1975, the nouvelle cuisine movement was in full bloom, and Guérard's *cuisine minceur* was attracting widespread acclaim, which made it very difficult to land a position in his kitchen. But Ducasse, showing the moxie that would become a signature, talked himself into a job by offering to work for free. His talent so quickly manifested itself that within weeks he was on the payroll; he eventually ended up preparing most of the dishes that were photographed for Guérard's magnum opus, *Michel Guérard's La Grande Cuisine Minceur*.

In 1977 Ducasse left to apprentice with Roger Vergé at Moulin de Mougins, a three-star restaurant on the Riviera. It was there that Ducasse encountered Provençal cooking, which so enthralled him that he would eventually make it his own. He was especially smitten with the vegetables and the creative possibilities they presented. But while the Mediterranean became his reference point and abiding passion, he realized that his culinary education would be incomplete without a stint up north, in France's butter belt. So in 1978, Ducasse left the warmth of the Côte d'Azur and went to work for Chapel. The two years he spent there proved to be the most formative experience of his budding career. Ducasse immersed himself in his work and in mastering the Chapel way. From Chapel, he developed a reverence for quality ingredients and a bedrock conviction that the essence of good cooking was to present a few bright flavors in absolute harmony with one another. These were the ideas that would guide his career—or at least the cooking phase of it.

Having completed his training, Ducasse returned to the Riviera in 1980 to run the kitchen of another restaurant owned by Vergé, L'Amandier. Soon thereafter, he moved on to La Terrasse, a restaurant in nearby Juan-les-Pins, where he was installed as head chef. In 1984, La Terrasse was awarded two Michelin stars, an achievement that announced to the culinary world what had been instantly apparent to his mentors: The twenty-seven-year-old Ducasse was a very special talent. A third star was now regarded as a mere formality, and it was thought that Ducasse was on the cusp of one of those historic careers that would decisively influence French cuisine. Indeed he was, but no one could have anticipated the obstacle that yet lay in his path, or the direction that his career would take after he found his way past it.

In August 1984, Ducasse was the lone survivor of a plane crash in the French Alps. In the aftermath, he underwent multiple operations, spent months in the hospital, and emerged with a gimp that still hinders him. The accident and the long convalescence left a psychological mark just as profound. "Another person was born in that hospital," Ducasse's friend and fellow chef Jacques Maximin told me as we talked one morning in Paris. "I went to see him there, and it wasn't the same man. Before the accident, his ambition was just to be a big chef, to win three stars. But it was clear to me, in the hospital, that he was now after something more and that there was now an urgency that hadn't been there before. He was going to live his life with a vengeance."

Ducasse returned to La Terrasse, but he didn't stay long enough to earn a third star there. In 1987, he was hired as chef at Louis XV, the imposingly formal restaurant in Monte Carlo's Hôtel de Paris. He wasn't the first choice for the job: The hotel had tried to recruit several older, more established chefs but without success. Its determination to see Louis XV awarded three stars in a hurry (it didn't have even a single star yet) was one stumbling block; another was the poor reputation of the local workforce (which, given the resort location, was probably no surprise). Ducasse took the job, and he audaciously promised that the restaurant would have its three stars within four years. He delivered, and with time to spare: Louis XV was awarded a third star in 1990. Craig Claiborne, the feared restaurant critic of the *New York Times*, had earlier hailed Ducasse as "worthy of inclusion in the pantheon of great French chefs"; with the third star, the thirty-three-year-old wunderkind was officially installed. By now, his cooking was anchored firmly in the Mediterranean and incorporated Italian influences alongside Provençal ones. "He uses as much olive oil as butter in his cooking," wrote Claiborne, "and his repertory includes Provençal pumpkin soup with chicken quenelles along with zephyr-light ravioli filled with foie gras and an exceptionally well-made risotto with cheese, white truffles and cream. A firm believer in the freshest ingredients, Mr. Ducasse garners them from whatever source is at hand. In fall and winter, he buys his game from friends who hunt. His cheeses come from a small goat farm in the French town of Tende, just north of Monaco, and his fish are chosen from the morning hauls of nearby fishermen."

Ducasse remained in the Louis XV kitchen through the early 1990s, but just as Jacques Maximin had foreseen, he now had ambitions well beyond winning and keeping a third star. In 1995, he acquired La Bastide de Moustiers, a country inn located near the Gorges de Verdon in a rustic corner of Provence. He spruced it up, put one of his deputies in charge of the kitchen, and quickly turned the Bastide into one of the area's premier destinations. The following year, legendary chef Joël Robuchon announced his retirement. Reluctant to see his eponymous three-star restaurant in Paris close down, Robuchon approached a handful of chefs about taking over the property, but all demurred. The reluctance was understandable: The fifty-one-year-old Robuchon was considered the finest chef of his era, and moving into his old kitchen was bound to invite unfavorable comparisons. For Ducasse, though, this was catnip. The more daunting the challenge, the greater his interest.

In August 1996, Restaurant Alain Ducasse opened in the space previously occupied by Robuchon. Seven months later, it was awarded three stars. But Michelin, still under the direction of the imperious Bernard Naegellen and not yet comfortable with the idea of a chef operating a pair of three-star restaurants nearly six hundred miles apart, decided to express its concern by docking Louis XV a star. Point made, Michelin acquiesced the following year and awarded both restaurants its highest rating. Ducasse saw it as the triumph of the Bocuse-ian ideal. "Michelin has accepted that it's possible for a chef to do something besides get fat behind his stove," he tartly commented. (Ducasse would later move his Paris three-star from Robuchon's old haunt to the Hôtel Plaza Athénée, where it remains.) In any case, he had already moved on. In 1998, he started a casual restaurant in Paris called Spoon, which specialized in fusion food, and he was now also looking overseas. He traveled periodically to the United States to keep abreast of culinary trends there, and by the late 1990s he was toying with the idea of an American beachhead.

New York was the obvious destination, and in 2000 Ducasse opened a restaurant in Manhattan's Essex House Hotel. The timing was not ideal: The stock market was on the verge of a major correction, and heartburn on Wall Street inevitably meant indigestion for New York restaurateurs. It didn't help that Ducasse decided to create a luxury palace serving extravagantly haute cuisine in a town that no longer seemed to want either. Classic French fare was now considered passé and so were the restaurants that offered it; by 2004, the iconic Lutèce, La Côte Basque, and La Caravelle would all be out of business, with La Grenouille the last dinosaur standing.

Some unfavorable pre-opening publicity only steepened the odds against Alain Ducasse New York, or ADNY, as the restaurant would be known. New Yorkers were left with the impression that Ducasse was coming to teach them how to eat. Twenty years earlier, when the United States had still been a culinary backwater, this missionary impulse would have been warranted and maybe even welcomed. Now, it reeked of condescension and didn't endear Ducasse to his new clientele. Nor did the one-hundred-sixty-dollar prix fixe, which struck even spendthrift New Yorkers as cheeky. (Michelin wasn't happy, either: After Ducasse went transcontinental and opened in New York, the Guide registered its disapproval by again demoting Louis XV to two stars for a year.)

The initial reviews of ADNY bespoke an almost incandescent rage. Many critics felt the food came nowhere near to justifying the prices, and were outraged by the over-the-top flourishes, such as the dozen ornate knives that diners were asked to pick from in order to cut their meat and the dozen designer pens that they could use to sign their bills. *New York* magazine's Gael Greene was biting. "I'm not really amused being forced to choose my knife or my pen just so the house can show off how many it's assembled," she wrote. "I'm annoyed. It's an intrusion and it's vulgar. Were Ducasse to try that gimmick in Paris, I think they'd roll him through town to the guillotine ... The food has no emotion. If the emperor is naked, we will drape him in a tablecloth to give him time to get his ermine back from the Laundromat. Open to anything? Yes, we are. But in the end, we're not so easily fooled."

Unbowed, Ducasse decided in 2003 to double down his New York bet by opening a second restaurant, called Mix. This one had a more casual atmosphere and a menu that was a hybrid of French and American comfort foods. There was bouillabaisse alongside clam chowder, as well as macaroni and cheese and a French equivalent comprised of elbow noodles and chunks of ham bathed in butter and truffle *jus*. The reviews weren't quite as hostile, but with Mix, too, critics detected condescension. William Grimes of the *New York Times* complained that the elaborate serving dishes and the complicated menu explanations created a "visual and conceptual clutter" and reflected a patronizing attitude toward American diners—a belief that they required a circus with their bread. "Someone needs to tell Mr. Ducasse that Americans, even if they do watch a lot of television and have short attention spans, do not need to be distracted every second that they are in a restaurant," he wrote. "Mix is fun, but a little less fun might work just as well."

French critics were also turning on Ducasse, put off by his quest for mastery of the universe, which would soon take him to Africa and Asia. While François Simon, who years earlier had coauthored a cookbook with Ducasse but had since fallen out with him, was the most prominent detractor, he was hardly alone. The journalist Thierry Walton, who reviewed restaurants for French *Elle* under the pseudonym Léo Fourneau, was biting in his memoir, *Bon Appétit, Messieurs!* "In the game of ego," Walton wrote, "Ducasse is the winner ... He is a chameleon, adapting himself to his surroundings, reproducing but never inventing. Ducasse creates nothing."

More intriguingly, there were rumblings that Ducasse's wanderlust wasn't sitting well with Joël Robuchon. It was one thing for Ducasse to successfully take over his old restaurant; it was quite another for him to try to become king and eclipse Robuchon's reputation. When Robuchon came out of retirement in 2001, opening Robuchon a Galera in the casino-rich former Portuguese colony of Macao, it was seen as confirmation of the kitchen scuttlebutt. When Robuchon spent the next several years opening restaurants in cities around the world in which Ducasse was already present or on his way—including Monte Carlo, Ducasse's base—it was taken as a declaration of war.

But Ducasse plunged ahead. No longer content merely to be a chef and restaurateur, he was now attempting to establish himself as the next great codifier of French cuisine—the literary heir to Carême and Escoffier. In 1999, he started his own publishing business and released *Le Grand Livre de Cuisine*, a thousand-page, seven-hundred-recipe cookbook that evoked the desired comparisons with Escoffier's *Le Guide Culinaire*. An encyclopedic dessert book soon followed, along with a voluminous text on bistro and brasserie fare. Ducasse was also becoming an educator. In 1999, he opened Alain Ducasse Formation, a cooking school on the outskirts of Paris catering to professionals. Success was instant, and the enrollment, curriculum, and facilities all expanded rapidly. Four years later, Ducasse launched a widely publicized program called Fou de France, which brought young chefs from around the country to Paris for two-week stints at the Plaza Athénée. It was an opportunity for them to test their recipes on jaded Parisians, but it was also a way for Ducasse to underscore his own importance. He was now aiming to be the next godfather, and in receiving his favor, these chefs would be, in a sense, made men.

As if all this weren't enough, the Ducasse group was also turning into a culinary preservation society. In 2002, Ducasse took over Aux Lyonnais, a century-old bistro near the Paris Bourse specializing in the traditional cuisine of Lyon, France's other gastronomic hub. He gave the restaurant some needed repairs while leaving the essential look—the wood façade, the laced curtains, the zinc bar, the tiled walls—untouched, put one of his chefs in the kitchen, and quickly made it one of the city's most spirited and popular eateries. He later did the same thing with Rech, an old seafood restaurant in the seventeenth arrondissement, and would also take charge of Le Jules Verne, the landmark restaurant on the second level of the Eiffel Tower.

From a food perspective, his most important acquisition came in 2005, when he signed the deed to Benoit, arguably the most beautiful bistro in Paris and almost surely the best, with a long-held Michelin star to prove it. The restaurant, festooned in shiny brass, big mirrors, potted palms, and red velvet, had been opened in 1912 by Benoit Martray and had remained in the family. But after many years at the helm, Michel Petit, Martray's grandson, wanted to retire, and with no one to succeed him, he decided to sell to Ducasse. On the day the deal was to close, the imposingly tall (and badly misnamed) Petit walked through the door with the restaurant's keys draped around his neck like a noose and burst into tears. Ducasse told him to keep the keys and that he was welcome to eat at the restaurant any time he wished. Soon thereafter, Petit bought an apartment around the corner and began having lunch at Benoit every Tuesday.

In 1994, seven years after getting the job at Louis XV in part because other chefs didn't want to deal with the local workforce, Ducasse decided that the restaurant needed a shot of northern efficiency after all. The goal was to overhaul the wine service, and the dining room in general. He began pursuing Gérard Margeon, a talented young sommelier working as the wine steward at the Méridien Montparnasse hotel in Paris. The first time Margeon heard from Ducasse was during lunch service there. The conversation began: "Hello, this is Alain Ducasse. Can you come to Monaco?" Margeon politely declined; he was content in Paris and had no desire to relocate. He didn't yet know that once Ducasse had it in his mind to hire someone, no amount of rejection would dislodge the thought. Ducasse kept calling, and after much back-and-forth, Margeon finally agreed to pay a visit to Monte Carlo—not because he had any intention of taking the job but simply because he was now desperate to be rid of Ducasse. As soon as he stepped off the plane in Nice, the seduction began: He was escorted to a waiting helicopter and whisked off to the Hôtel de Paris, where he spent the weekend with Ducasse. Eventually, his resistance crumbled and he agreed to take the job. By then, he had come to understand that Ducasse was one of those bosses who inspired and exhausted in equal measure. As he told his wife on the morning he started at Louis XV, "You either work for Ducasse for one day, or you stay with him a long time."

Fourteen years later, Margeon was still with Ducasse (and now overseeing a team of more than fifty sommeliers worldwide), as were many other recruits. Quite apart from his culinary achievements, Ducasse seemed to have an almost preternatural ability to find, motivate, and keep the people he needed. He could sniff out talent in all sorts of places. In 1998, just as he was laying claim to six stars, he was introduced at a bar in Paris to Laurent Plantier, a young French entrepreneur. At the time, Plantier was pursuing an MBA at the Massachusetts Institute of Technology and had no particular interest in food. He'd never even heard of Ducasse. It didn't matter: Ducasse, impressed by his MIT education and his experience in the United States and in need of a CEO for his rapidly expanding group, immediately began courting Plantier, and the thirty-year-old Marseille native, like Margeon before him, eventually caved. His MIT classmates were baffled by his decision to take a job with a chef. "I think they just figured it was a French thing, that French people were weird," Plantier recalled.

The new hire hinted at where the Ducasse organization was headed; by the early-2000s, the company was said to be pulling in $16 million in annual revenues and had come to resemble, in its size, reach, and culture, a global investment bank. In return for working hellish hours and effectively signing over their lives, Ducasse employees were paid well and were further rewarded with a rich array of benefits. Chief among these was the chance to work abroad: Like an international financier, a Ducasse chef could do a stint in Paris, relocate to New York, spend several years in Tokyo, and then return to Paris to start the rotation anew. In some cases, the company covered moving expenses and provided housing allowances. It also offered language training: It retained the services of a firm that gave language lessons by phone, and employees could call in from anywhere in the world to work on their English or Japanese. For an Ivy League–minted Wall Streeter, such perks were standard fare; in the food world, they were unheard of, and for a barely educated young chef from the French countryside, they represented the opportunity of a lifetime.

It was partly for this reason that Ducasse commanded loyalty bordering on the fanatical. The Ducasse group was sometimes described as having an almost cultlike aspect, an impression reinforced by the Mao-like little red book of Ducasse aphorisms that was given to every new hire. Employees past and present spoke of Ducasse in awestruck terms. "He has this power—he knows people, he understands their character and the way they work, and he just knows where they belong," Jean-Louis Nomicos told me, sounding more like a disciple describing a Zen master than a chef describing his old boss. Nomicos had worked for Ducasse in Juan-les-Pins and Monte Carlo, and when, in 2001, he was offered the chef's position at Lasserre, a historic two-star in Paris, he sought Ducasse's counsel and blessing before taking the job. He and other Ducasse protégés appeared to literally consider his judgment to be infallible. "He just knows" was the mantra.

But by 2008, it was no longer clear that Ducasse was the most important person within his own organization. That distinction may have belonged instead to Franck Cerutti, who ran the Louis XV kitchen. With Ducasse no longer cooking, young chefs were sent to Monte Carlo to be schooled in the Ducasse ethos by Cerutti. Even Ducasse's harshest critics conceded that the forty-eight-year-old Cerutti was a brilliant chef—arguably the finest in France (even if he technically didn't work in France). François Simon described him as the "most Ducassian of [Ducasse's] students, who cooks, in my eyes, the true cuisine of Ducasse." But Simon also believed that the balance of power in the relationship had shifted. The true cuisine of Ducasse had become the cuisine of Cerutti, and if Ducasse ever went back to the kitchen, Simon wrote, it would now be Cerutti's food that he cooked.

For my taste, Cerutti was the best. He coaxed astonishing flavor out of every ingredient that crossed his cutting board, but especially fish and vegetables. I'd never experienced more sustained exhilaration at the table than my meals at Louis XV. A dinner one night began with a crudité of local vegetables—so fresh they glistened—with a black olive dipping sauce. It moved on to a seafood salad composed of clams, octopus, squid, and the most succulent gamberoni (local jumbo prawns) imaginable, then a lusty risotto of cèpes with baby spinach. The main courses included Mediterranean sea bass dressed with tomatoes, capers, lemon zest, and aged vinegar; an ethereal ragoût of stockfish tripe and salted cod served with red peppers, olives, and slices of Perugina sausage; and roasted lamb, cooked to a perfect shade of pink and accompanied by a medley of stuffed vegetables. For dessert, there was honey ice cream with roasted figs followed by Le Louis XV, the restaurant's signature chocolate-and-praline cake. Literally every bite had me tapping my feet in pleasure.

Ducasse and Cerutti first teamed up in the early 1980s at La Terrasse. In 1983, Cerutti left for a stint at the Hôtel Negresco, in his native Nice, and then went to Italy to work at the Florentine restaurant Enoteca Pinchiorri. For a French chef, this was an unusual, even heretical thing to do. Ducasse was flirting with scandal merely by putting pastas on his menu; the idea that a French chef would go to Italy to try to improve his cooking was akin to a world-class skier going to the Sahara Desert to work on his turns. But Cerutti didn't care. He had a measure of Italian lineage and was eager to explore this part of his heritage. More importantly, he didn't consider himself a French chef; in his mind, he was a Mediterranean chef, and as such he felt a stint in Italy was imperative.

Cerutti fell in love with Italian food, especially its simplicity. "Three olives, five capers, some garlic—that was all they used," he recalled. "They were parsimonious with the ingredients; they let things just be. The French are incapable of that—they always have to do something to it." A thin, soft-spoken man with a vague resemblance to Alfred E. Neuman, Cerutti might have made a career in Italy had the owner of the Enoteca not decided to Frenchify his menu in order to earn a third Michelin star. Cerutti didn't like the change and returned home. As it happened, Ducasse had just been hired as head chef at Louis XV; phone calls were exchanged, a deal was struck, and Cerutti became his deputy in the Monte Carlo kitchen.

Two decades later, they were still together, but their long association hadn't been continuous or necessarily always blissful. In 1990, Cerutti left Ducasse to open his own place in Nice; he had barely settled into his new life when Ducasse, eyeing Robuchon's restaurant in Paris, cajoled him into returning to Monte Carlo. Cerutti was rewarded for his sacrifice by being the guy in charge of the kitchen when Michelin took away Louis XV's third star for the first time, and again when Michelin punished Ducasse for going to New York. Nonetheless, Cerutti stayed on board; it was said that Ducasse was paying a lot of money to keep him happy—perhaps even helping to support the extended Cerutti family.

Driving to Monte Carlo with Cerutti after an early-morning visit to an outdoor market in Nice (like the Ducasse of old, Cerutti did a lot of his own shopping), I got the distinct impression that he was no longer interested in suffering for his boss's ambition. As we made our way along the Lower Corniche, the sun burning through the haze over the

Mediterranean, I asked about the collaborative process with Ducasse. Cerutti quickly made clear that he was the Decider; Ducasse merely stopped by every few weeks for lunch or dinner in the "aquarium" (the office in the kitchen), and that was about the extent of his involvement. So even if the kitchen was short-staffed or swamped, he wouldn't pitch in? "If he touched anything, he'd cut himself." Ducasse was strictly a *chef d'entreprise* now. But his name was still on the door; wasn't that frustrating? Cerutti shrugged. "People who know food know that it's my food."

That afternoon, I met with Ducasse in the aquarium. He had a large public relations apparatus, and one of his flacks was there to greet me. While we waited for Ducasse to arrive, she had the kitchen put out some cookies—not for me, but for him. "He always needs something to nibble on," she explained. I killed time by asking if she knew where her boss resided. "He has an apartment in Paris and a house in the Basque country, I think," she said. "But it's hard to say exactly where he lives." Moments later, Ducasse swept into the room in his trademark blue suit, minus a tie and minus a shave, too. He was trim, with receding gray hair, a gruff voice, and a slightly skeptical smile, and as he imperiously stretched himself across the small banquette, positioning himself at an angle with his back resting against the side wall, his demeanor did call to mind a Mafia don.

We first talked about his experience with Chapel and what he had taken away from Mionnay. "It was the perfectionism—the rigor of the techniques, the excellence of the dishes," he said. "The biggest thing was the importance Chapel placed on the quality of the ingredients and the need to preserve their integrity, to preserve their original taste. The food was extremely sophisticated, but it also had this fundamental simplicity." I noted that he had grown close to Bocuse and asked what he thought Bocuse's legacy was. "The *médiasation* of cuisine; he increased the visibility of French cuisine and the visibility of cuisine generally."

He claimed, unconvincingly, that he didn't see himself as Bocuse's heir; Robuchon or Pierre Gagnaire could just as easily fill that role, he said. But surely he was a bigger celebrity? "I don't know," he said with a shrug. "You should go check Googlefight." And weren't he and Robuchon blood rivals now, chasing each other around the world? "*C'est bullshit*," he said. There was no animosity: He and Robuchon were on the same team, pursuing the same objective—making French cuisine more popular. In fact, he was even planning to publish Robuchon's next cookbook. But if their imagined enmity generated media interest in chefs and cuisine, it was all to the good as far as he was concerned. Ducasse talked quickly, and though he apparently didn't speak much English, he sprinkled his conversation with English and Franglais expressions, such as *mixité* and *wow effect*, a phrase he used several times to describe, disparagingly, cooking he thought offered more sizzle than substance.

Ducasse told me he hadn't set out to conquer the world; it was just that one mountain always led to another, and he liked to climb. When he was awarded three stars for the first time it was "good for five minutes." The empire-building, he said, was a function of restlessness but also inquisitiveness. "If I weren't a chef, I'd be a traveler or an architect. It's necessary to have change. Every day, I want to learn something new, something that I didn't know and couldn't have imagined, to satisfy my curiosity," he said. His mouth was his compass: He was tasting his way around the world. He illustrated the point for me by rhapsodizing for a few minutes about some *yuba*—tofu skin— that he'd had recently in Kyoto.

I asked if he missed cooking. "I cook in my head," he said. I waited for a laugh, a smile—something to confirm that he was joking. But he was serious: He said that his travels gave him recipe ideas; he jotted them down and left it to his chefs to make it happen. It was best to think of him as the creative director for the Ducasse Group, identifying suitable locations for restaurants and conceptualizing them; after that, his lieutenants were in charge. "There's lots of delegation; it's a *grande démocratie*," he said. "I find the place and the idea, then I give them the keys. I decide the editorial line—I'm the one with the global vision." His use of the word *global* provided a good segue; I noted that some people viewed him as an avatar of globalization, doing for haute cuisine what Ray Kroc had done for hamburgers. "I am against globalization," he insisted, his voice rising. "I am for global, I am for local—I am glocal. I am for a culture of difference. I never do the same restaurant twice; I don't want to copy." Each of his restaurants was tailored to its location and relied as much as possible on local ingredients. Eating at Spoon in Paris was different than eating at Spoon in London.

Dumping a little more oil in the pan, I brought up Spain and the fact that many people believed it had eclipsed France. At the mention of *la nueva cocina*, Ducasse rolled his eyes. Then, quickly regaining his magnanimity, he said he adored Ferran Adrià and the rest of the Spanish armada but didn't think they posed any real challenge to French supremacy. "Tell me, where's the competition? How many Spanish chefs are overseas? My competition is Robuchon, Gagnaire, Guy Savoy, the Pourcel brothers, Jean-Georges [Vongerichten]." In other words, influence was a function of ubiquity. I wasn't going to argue the point, and he didn't give me the chance; he quickly dismissed the entire subject as another media concoction. "It's good for cuisine if the journalists think there is a war. It gives them a reason to talk about us. It would be terrible if they didn't talk about us."

We finished the interview, and Ducasse walked me to the door. As we stood in the entryway to Louis XV, three colorfully dressed, zaftig women came out. Ducasse gave them a warm greeting and ducked into the restaurant to personally retrieve their goodie bags. (Female guests were sent home with a brioche and cookies or chocolates.) After seeing them off, he turned back to me and said, "The woman in the floral dress was one of Chapel's most loyal clients."

In 2005, Mix in New York closed after just twenty-three months in business. That same year, ADNY was awarded three stars in the inaugural Michelin Guide to New York, and amazingly, Michelin didn't shaft Cerutti this time. But three stars no longer assured success in France, and they seemed to matter even less in New York. The restaurant continued to struggle, and in 2007, Ducasse decided to shutter it—a poignant commentary on the diminished power of Michelin and a big setback for him. Ducasse wasn't giving up on New York, though; he was just regrouping, and in 2007, he announced he would be opening two new restaurants there—an upscale, wine-oriented establishment called Adour, in the St. Regis Hotel, and a New York branch of Benoit.

A few weeks after our meeting in Monte Carlo, Ducasse was in New York to do a tasting of the menu at Adour. It was an opportunity for two of the hotel's executives to acquaint themselves with the food and for Ducasse, who'd already done several run-throughs on his own, to see how the kitchen, under the direction of Tony Ensault, a longtime protégé, was coming along. I was invited to take part in the tasting, which started at four P.M., the time the construction crew quit for the night. The four of us were shown to a table in an alcove of Adour's dining room, which was littered with construction equipment—ladders, electric cables, painting platforms, dumpsters. Our little nook had been cleared of all debris and set with a beautifully arranged, white-linen table. As soon as we sat down, Ducasse removed his blazer, placed a notebook at his side and, like a marksman fidgeting with his rifle, began intently fingering his fork. Each of us was given a menu listing the twelve dishes we would be served and the two wines that would accompany each course. With the menu we were given Champagne cocktails. Ducasse immediately found a fault. "It's not cold enough," he told the sommelier. He betrayed no anger; he was merely providing instruction, and the young sommelier nodded vigorously.

Ducasse and I shared one plate, the St. Regis executives shared the other. First up was an appetizer of raw, marinated *hamachi* and geoduck served with radish and green apple mustard. As soon as the plate was laid down, Ducasse attacked. Using his sauce spoon as a probe, he gently poked the fish, then carved out a healthy slab, slid it onto his spoon, carefully dabbed it in the mustard, and plopped it in his mouth. "It's not cold enough; the fish needs to be colder," he calmly announced. The hotel guys nodded in agreement while one of the waiters scurried back to the kitchen to relay the boss's verdict. Ducasse sized up dishes with the same alacrity that he apparently sized up employees.

He had no qualms with the concepts; the only flaws were serving temperatures and seasonings. The foie gras didn't have quite enough salt; "*trop timide*," he said. The short ribs also needed more salt. For the most part, though, Ducasse seemed thoroughly satisfied with the quality of the preparations, and several made him swoon. A plate of day-boat scallops served with diced black truffles, salsify, spinach, and a shellfish *jus* sent him into ecstasy. "This is great pleasure," he said excitedly, adding rather enigmatically that it wasn't "food for the tourists." While the dish was an involved one to make, he explained, it came to the table as a beacon of simplicity. This was truly great cooking—unlike the stuff produced by the Spaniards and their acolytes, which too often "lost the essence" of ingredients. "Who wants to eat marshmallow of pork with balsamic vinaigrette?" he said with a laugh.

Ducasse exuded gruff charm. He told us that he'd recently eaten at Grayz, the midtown restaurant of chef Gray Kunz, and had been dumbstruck by the number of plates they used. "The star there is the dishwasher," he quipped. It somehow came out that the wife of one of the hotel executives was a native Italian but didn't cook, which elicited faux indignation from Ducasse. "What's the point of marrying an Italian if she doesn't make pasta?" he asked. When he wasn't eating or joking, Ducasse was trying to anticipate how New Yorkers would respond to the food. He seemed eager to project an air of supreme confidence—"There is nothing like this on any other menu in New York" he boasted of a plate of autumn vegetables served with a simple vegetable *jus*—but anxiety periodically broke through. "I think New York will like that," he said quietly of one dessert, a *vacherin* served with mango marmalade, coconut, and a passion fruit emulsion. At times, he conveyed an earnest desire to impress American diners; at other times, he made fun of them. He joked about putting Caesar salad on the menu, and when I mentioned that Cerutti had complained about the ordering habits of Americans at Louis XV, Ducasse, in slow, mocking English, said, "I will have a lobster salad and beef, well-done."

It was seven P.M. when the tasting wrapped up. After twelve dishes and two dozen glasses of wine, the hoteliers looked like men desperately seeking pillows. Ducasse announced that he had a reservation in an hour at Le Bernardin. "Are you serious?" one of them asked. "*Oui*," said Ducasse, who seemed genuinely surprised by the question. "This was work; that's dinner."

A few weeks earlier, a press conference had been held at the Plaza Athénée to announce that Ducasse would be taking over a prestigious French pastry academy, the École Nationale Superior de la Pâtisserie. After mingling for a few minutes with the two dozen or so journalists in attendance, Ducasse stepped to the front of the room and read a prepared statement. He seemed strangely nervous; he read in a soft, halting voice, as if he were struggling with the words, and his eyes never left the paper. An assistant would later confide that Ducasse didn't like to read aloud in public. Gérard Margeon had told me that he and Ducasse were "just two country boys" and that Ducasse had the spirit of a "noble *paysan*." For all his bravado and seeming urbanity, was Ducasse a bumpkin at heart? With his rural upbringing and limited formal education, was he intimidated by having to read aloud to a bunch of hyper-educated journalists? And could it be that all those knives and pens in New York, far from being some cynical and cheesy ploy, had represented an earnest attempt to impress the city folk? Three months after I saw Ducasse at Adour, *New York* magazine ran a profile of the peripatetic chef which suggested that his problem was that he tried too hard to please. By then, I had come to pretty much the same conclusion.

Ducasse was certainly not above reproach. The world of food and wine would have been none the poorer without either Spoon or Mix, and by opening Benoit outlets in New York and Tokyo, it could be argued that Ducasse had devalued the original in Paris. For all his good intentions, Ducasse's first attempt to conquer New York had been a bust, and by 2008 he was grappling with a potential failure in London, where he had established a much-criticized luxury restaurant in the Dorchester Hotel. Far from affirming that unlimited horizons were available to talented, ambitious chefs such as himself, Ducasse had inadvertently demonstrated the near-impossibility of empire-building on a global scale: If a manager as skillful and diligent as he could suffer so many flameouts, what hope was there for other chefs trying to franchise themselves around the world?

It was also the case that the chef manqué approach, of which Ducasse was the most visible example, had not served French gastronomy especially well. It was an unquestionable factor in the diminished ingenuity, and perhaps also declining quality, of high-end French cooking during the 1990s and into the new millennium. True, the French were hardly the only ones to stray from the kitchen—top chefs in New York and London were doing the same thing—but the French had always been looked to for creative inspiration, and that position of intellectual leadership was being squandered. Contrary to Ducasse's claim, influence was measured not by the number of restaurants that a chef operated, but by how widely his efforts were imitated and his insights embraced, and on this score, the Spaniards were drubbing the French.

Even so, much of the criticism aimed at Ducasse was unwarranted. Most of his restaurants were excellent and maintained their quality even as he took on additional projects, a consistency that eluded other chefs with far-flung interests (in this way, too, Ducasse was the exception that proved the rule). Louis XV was brilliant, and while the Paris three-star didn't rise to the same standard, it certainly merited its rating. Under Ducasse, Aux Lyonnais wasn't just the best Lyonnais bistro in Paris; it was as good as any bistro in Lyon. And though it was a pity that an historic restaurant like Benoit ended up in the hands of a conglomerate, it was better that it be absorbed by Ducasse's empire than by a less quality-conscious group (of which there were many). François Simon, no fan of Ducasse, thought the food at Benoit had become even better under his watch; that was debatable, but it definitely hadn't slipped. And while Mix and Spoon were not Ducasse's best efforts, they at least represented attempts to put something different on the plate.

To claim, as some did, that Ducasse had no interest in innovation and had not distinguished himself as a chef was wrong. While he never produced that one canonical dish that can confer immortality, he helped elevate Mediterranean cooking to a level of respect in France that it had never before enjoyed; olive oil acquired the stature of butter and cream, and it became possible to put things like ravioli and risotto on the menus of starred restaurants in Paris without scandalizing the guests. And certainly, no French chef did as much as Ducasse to raise the image of vegetables—to make them, by dint of serious, passionate treatment, as integral to haute cuisine as meat, fowl, and fish. It was no accident that Ducasse earned a third star at the age of thirty-three, and although he quit the kitchen not long thereafter, his legacy at the stove is a formidable one.

Now, in his role as gastronomic impresario, he was trying to preserve some of the glories of France's culinary heritage while also attempting to give French cuisine renewed vitality. He was the head of a global enterprise, and profit was plainly a motive, but he was also serving a greater good. The food writer Emmanuel Rubin, a colleague of François Simon's at *Le Figaro*, made this point by drawing a rapier-sharp distinction between Ducasse and his erstwhile rival, Robuchon. "Ducasse cares about French cuisine," said Rubin. "Robuchon cares about Robuchon." Ducasse's crowning achievement is the fact that he has cultivated a small army of exceptional chefs, provided platforms for their talents, and given them the creative and financial freedom to fully realize their abilities, which are no small gifts at a time when the economics of the restaurant business in France isn't exactly favorable. And while Ducasse is no longer in the kitchen, he has inculcated his charges with the ideas that formed the cornerstone of his training—a reverence for good ingredients and a monomaniacal determination to express their flavors as purely and vividly as possible, the lesson that he learned from Chapel. "He is a businessman now, but he teaches us to be artisans and to cook with passion," said Jean-Louis Nomicos. Although Ducasse's career path had come to mirror Bocuse's rather than Chapel's, he didn't betray his mentor's legacy. Three decades after nouvelle cuisine's heyday, Ducasse had achieved a synthesis of sorts: He was using Bocuse's methods to transmit Chapel's values.

Toward the end of my conversation with Jacques Maximin, I'd asked what advice he'd give to a teenager considering a career as a chef. Maximin, a small, pugnacious man, took a drag on his cigarette, stubbed it out in the ashtray, and said, "I'd tell him to think hard about it." He paused for a moment, and then added, "Or I'd tell him to go to work for Ducasse." Not long thereafter, Maximin, whose two-star restaurant had run aground financially, took his own advice and became a consultant to the Ducasse organization.

The New French Revolution

THE FOOD FIGHT THAT broke out among leading French chefs in 1996, pitting self-styled traditionalists like Alain Ducasse and Joël Robuchon against modernists such as Pierre Gagnaire and Michel Troisgros, was good for a few headlines but quickly receded from view. However, the question that provoked it—which way forward for French cuisine?—never went away, and by 2008, with Spain now widely seen as having supplanted France as the world's gastronomic pacesetter, the divisions had hardened. One camp believed that the Iberian innovators were best ignored and that classic French cooking would brush aside this challenge and reassert its supremacy. The other was equally convinced that France desperately needed creative upheaval in its kitchens and—echoes of nouvelle cuisine—that this could only be accomplished by breaking free of the past. But even as the two sides pushed very different agendas, their paths were now converging in a most unexpected place: the kitchen. Whether traditionalists or modernists, French chefs were returning to the stove.

One of the people at the vanguard of this trend was Christian Constant. By rights, the fifty-seven-year-old Constant should have been a three-star chef by now and enjoying all the privileges conferred by this lofty status—above all, the privilege of not having to oversee the day-to-day functions of a kitchen. His talent had announced itself at a precocious age and he had set off in pursuit of Michelin glory, doing stints at two venerable Paris establishments, Ledoyen and L'Espadon, before being hired in 1988 as the chef at Les Ambassadeurs, the ornate restaurant in the Hôtel de Crillon, also in Paris. In 1997, he held a pair of Michelin stars and a third one was considered a virtual certainty. But it was at this moment, on the cusp of achieving the ultimate accolade, that Constant did something astonishing. Tired of having to respond to every new twist in culinary fashion, and wanting to work in a more laid-back setting, he walked away from the Crillon and a probable third star and opened a small place on the rue Saint-Dominique, a serpentine thoroughfare in the chic seventh arrondissement.

He named it Violon d'Ingres after the French painter Ingres, who was born in Montaubon, Constant's hometown in southwestern France. In its initial incarnation, Violon was a somewhat formal restaurant serving upscale fare at upscale prices (the set dinner menu was 590FF, or $115). Michelin liked what it found and gave Constant first one star and then a second. That was as high as Violon rose, and by the early 2000s, it seemed that the restaurant, and Constant, had become afterthoughts. It was during this period that Constant became convinced that the French food scene was changing dramatically. Luxury was out; the economy was bad and people didn't have the money to spend on exorbitant meals, nor did they care for ostentation. Constant knew that he had to adjust to the prevailing mood. "I didn't want to be some chef standing in the door looking up and down the street to see if anyone would be coming for lunch today."

So in 2004, he reinvented Violon. He revamped the décor, giving the restaurant a more relaxed look and feel, and he built an open kitchen (still a rarity in Paris) in order to create even greater intimacy between himself and the guests. More dramatically, he introduced a three-course, €45 ($60) set menu. He wanted to continue serving things such as foie gras and turbot but at a more agreeable price. To make the new formula work, he cut the extravagances—he decided not to hire a sommelier, for instance. ("People know wine as well as the sommelier.") But that was the beauty of it: He was saving money on things people no longer wished to pay for. "The clientele has changed," he explained. "People don't want that kind of formality anymore; they want something more convivial. Also, they want to spend less and return to restaurants more often."

The revamped approach proved wildly popular; getting a reservation became almost as challenging as winning a third star. By then, Constant had two other restaurants on the same block, both successful as well: Café Constant, a homey bistro serving homey fare (roast chicken, steak with mashed potatoes, profiteroles, floating island), and Les Fables de la Fontaine, a tiny, elegantly modern fish restaurant. Continuing his colonization of the rue Saint-Dominique, Constant opened a fourth place there in 2007: Les Cocottes de Christian Constant, an airy restaurant evocative of an American diner (counter seating ran the entire length of the restaurant) that specialized in casseroles (cocottes)—the ultimate in inexpensive comfort food. Parisians ate this up, too; Sarkozy even came for lunch one day.

But there was more to the Christian Constant story than the forsaken third star and the growing empire on the rue Saint-Dominique. During the years he had spent in high-end kitchens, he had earned a reputation not only as a talented cook, but as an exceptional mentor who cultivated a generation of exceptionally capable young chefs—a group that came to be known as Generation Constant. At L'Espadon, he had employed two gifted lieutenants, Yves Camdeborde and Thierry Breton, who had followed him to Les Ambassadeurs, where they had been joined in the kitchen by a bevy of other future stars that included Eric Fréchon, Thierry Faucher, Rodolphe Paquin, and Didier Varnier. It was a rare day at Les Ambassadeurs when the atmosphere around the skillets and salamanders was anything less than electric.

Constant had a rebellious streak, and although it would be several years before he acted on it himself, he imparted that contrarian spirit to his protégés. Fernand Point had prepared his *brigade*—Bocuse, the Troisgros brothers, Outhier, Bise, Peyrot—for the single-minded pursuit of those three Michelin stars; Constant set his men on a radically different course. He had already begun to suspect that the three-star model was in trouble (his suspicion would jell into a conviction after he opened Violon). He also knew that his young charges were truly in love with cooking and that at least some of them had temperaments better suited to small restaurants than to culinary temples.

So when it came time for Camdeborde and Breton to move on, Constant urged them to think inexpensive and small, which is what they did. "He understood my personality, and he also thought that the system was changing," Camdeborde would later recall. Camdeborde took his knives to the unfashionable fourteenth arrondissement, where in 1992 he opened a bistro called La Régalade. The setting and service were casual, but the cooking was as skillfully executed as that in most starred restaurants, and the prices were shockingly low for the quality on offer. La Régalade quickly became one of the toughest tables in Paris. In 2004, he would sell La Régalade and take over a charming hotel, the Relais Saint-Germain, off the Boulevard Saint-Germain in the sixth, to which he attached a pint-size restaurant called Le Comptoir du Relais. Le Comptoir followed the Régalade template and proved to be equally popular (and even harder to get into because it was that much smaller). Camdeborde began describing himself as an *aubergiste*—an innkeeper, right in the heart of Paris.

Breton followed a similar trail. In 1995, he started a restaurant called Chez Michel, specializing in the food of his native Brittany, in the gritty tenth arrondissement, near the Gare du Nord. He, too, skimped on the ambience so that he would have the money to buy the choicest ingredients but charge only a modest fee. (In 2007, his set menu was thirty euros, or around forty dollars.) Other Constant acolytes did likewise: Eric Fréchon opened an eponymous restaurant in the nineteenth (unable to surrender the three-star dream, he would later become the chef at the Hôtel Bristol). Thierry Faucher started a low-frills place in the fifteenth, and Rodolphe Paquin did likewise in the eleventh. Constant eventually took his own advice and set up on the rue Saint-Dominique, by which time the movement he had inspired had acquired a moniker—*bistronomie*, which could be translated as: everything on the plate, relatively little on the bill, and the chef in the house.

That's where Breton could be found, twelve years after opening Chez Michel. Although he had a second restaurant next door, Chez Casimir, equally casual and also inexpensive, he was at Chez Michel's stove for every service. Peering into the kitchen (the door was always open) and seeing the tousle-haired, solidly built thirty-eight-year-old standing over the flame was an arresting sight. A chef who cooks! The excellent salmon marinated herring-style, the rich, velvety lobster bisque, the succulent veal fricassee with root vegetables—it was truly Breton's food, and if the three-person waitstaff happened to be swamped, he would even deliver it to the table himself.

The intimacy went beyond the food and service. In the early evening, his wife would stop by with Breton's children for some pre-bedtime horsing around and hugs. And late-arriving guests who lingered over coffee were often treated to another unusual sight: Breton, dressed in Lycra shorts, carrying his bicycle from the kitchen and setting out on a forty-kilometer nocturnal workout. Breton had solicitations nearly every week to establish other restaurants, but he had no interest in expanding beyond his small corner of Paris. "Someone came to me recently and offered me the chance to open a restaurant in Asia," he recalled late one afternoon as the staff was setting up for dinner. "I said I'd go there maybe for a vacation, but that's it. I have a perfect arrangement. It works for me, it works for the clients. I don't want to conquer the world."

But the *bistronomie* movement was about more than just lifestyle; it also had an ideological dimension. Christian Constant and the chefs he had trained believed that classical French cuisine didn't need to apologize for itself and that avant-garde cooking was better left to those not fortunate enough to have the strong culinary tradition that France did. "I'm a bit chauvinistic, but France is the best country for food in the world," Camdeborde said over coffee one morning in the empty dining room of Le Comptoir. "I'm not against evolution, but it's important to preserve the art of living and eating, and gastronomy. Some of these young chefs are trying to copy the Spanish, and I look at some of what they are making and ask myself, Why are they doing that? Does French cuisine not have a personality? Why would you want to abandon true French cuisine? Does a globalized cuisine really interest you?"

It was of no interest to Constant. With his slick dark hair, stubbled face, and gravelly voice, Constant looked and sounded more like a mutinous sailor than the leader of a gastronomic revolt. (As it happens, he had met his Scottish-born wife while aboard a ship: He was doing a cooking demonstration on the QE2, for which she was a crew member at the time.) And it was a peculiar sort of insurrection that he was leading: It wasn't an attempt to tear down an existing order but rather, to validate one. Constant wasn't a reactionary, but he was worried about the Adrià wannabes in French kitchens and about the proliferation of McDonald's and pizza. "We're in danger of losing our identity," he said. He adored old-school cooking—"I love the traditional, things like béarnaise sauce, gratinées"—and was using his kitchens to keep it alive and to rekindle a passion for it in others. He was convinced the restaurant-going public was coming around to his way of thinking. "The French want to find the classic again," he said. "People are returning to the old values, reconnecting with the basics."

In an interview with *Food & Wine*, François Simon plaintively asked, "What happened to the notion of chefs as beloved community figures prowling the neighborhood shaking hands with suppliers?" Constant had become just such a chef, and as he made his morning rounds, dressed in a thick sweater and faded black jeans, he radiated contentment. He spent several minutes taking reservations at Les Cocottes, then darted into the Violon kitchen to check on the progress of the cassoulet. Although he was operating four establishments and employed a *chef de cuisine* for each, he kept a hand in every pot—if not quite literally, certainly figuratively. From Violon he stopped in at the neighboring vegetable stand. The owner had planned to retire, but Constant had persuaded him to keep going by promising to regularly purchase provisions from him. "I said to him, 'Eh, no, stop—stay in business. We're reinvigorating this street.'" He next dipped into Les Fables de la Fontaine to make sure everything was set for lunch service, helping himself (and me) to a quick white-wine aperitif. From there, it was off to Café Constant; a few regulars were at the bar, and Constant greeted them like the ward boss he had become.

Naturally, another round of white wine was in order. Constant told me he had no regrets about not having received a third star. "You spend all your time scared, your whole existence is simply about winning that third star," he said quietly. He wasn't against Michelin or the system of stars; Violon still had a star, and Les Fables had one, too. But he thought that Michelin needed to shower more praise on the chefs who stayed in their restaurants and cooked. "That's the one thing I criticize Michelin for—they need to defend the artisans more. I'm in my place every day, these other chefs are too. Michelin should give five stars to chefs who are in the kitchen."

Gilles Choukroun looked down at my coffee cup, paused momentarily, and picked up the small spoon that lay on the side of the saucer. He gently placed the spoon in my cup, its thin silver handle rising up out of the jet-black espresso. "Why does the spoon come on the plate; why can't it come to the table already in the cup?" he asked. It was a rhetorical question, Choukroun's way of illustrating the point that French cuisine was now in a period of revolutionary ferment, in which everything—from the composition of sauces to the division of labor in the kitchen to the placement of demitasse spoons—was open to reinterpretation. We were sitting in the stylish bar of Choukroun's restaurant, Angl'Opéra, located on the Avenue de l'Opéra, halfway between the Paris opera house and the Louvre. In contrast to its gray, tired neighborhood, the restaurant was arrestingly contemporary, with aluminum tabletops and a riot of brightly colored accoutrements: blue water glasses, orange and pink shades, zebra-striped banquettes. As we talked, dance music pulsated gently in the background—proof in itself, Choukroun explained, that the French dining scene was in a state of delicious upheaval. He said that when he had opened his previous restaurant, Le Café des Délices, in 2000, guests had been shocked to find music being piped into the dining room. "Clients and the press were completely surprised," he recalled. " 'What's happening?' It just wasn't done here." Seven years later, he said, restaurants all over Paris were making music part of the ambience, and younger diners, at least, were delighted. "There is a revolution going on. The chefs and the clients want a cuisine that is *très actuel, très fun.*"

Fun. If there was one idea that united younger French chefs, it was that French cuisine needed to loosen up. In their view, *fun* was not inimical to French cuisine; there was no requirement that French cuisine had to be served by morose waiters in somber dining rooms; and having good food and a good time were not incompatible desires. The stocky, handsome Choukroun, at age forty, was one of the chefs at the head of this movement. A few years earlier, he had founded a group called Générations C, a confederacy of young chefs committed to putting more fun into French food. The "C" stood for "cuisines" and "cultures," a dual meaning that spoke to the worldliness these chefs supposedly brought to the kitchen, in contrast to the insularity of their culinary forebearers. "The goal was to get the word out about all the great things that are happening with young chefs in France," said Choukroun. In his view, French cuisine had been wrongly depicted as hidebound and incapable of change. Choukroun cited Arthur Lubow's *New York Times Magazine* article about Spain's gastronomic ferment as the most damaging source of this misconception. "No question, Adrià is a great chef," he said. "But it would be very difficult to name ten truly great Spanish chefs. By contrast, I can name dozens of top French chefs, working in Paris and the provinces."

Even so, Choukroun and his peers were determined to show that they could be as eclectic and playful as the Spanish and just as open to ideas and flavors from other countries (if not necessarily open to the idea that other nations could produce food and chefs that were the equal of France's). Choukroun, for instance, offered rococo creations like crème brûlée of foie gras with peanuts, and salmon with lemon risotto accompanied by a shot glass of hot coconut milk. Some critics found his concoctions, and those of like-minded chefs, to be more incoherent than inventive. But to people like *Omnivore*'s Luc Dubanchet, this freewheeling style was reinvigorating French cuisine.

The desire for creative license was expressed most forcefully by a thirty-five-year-old chef named Alexandre Bourdas, who owned a restaurant called Sa.Qua.Na in the seaside town of Honfleur, in Normandy. The name suggested Bourdas's modernist leanings; he had run three-star chef Michel Bras's restaurant on the Japanese island of Hokkaido, and Sa.Qua.Na was a play on the Japanese word for fish, *sakana*. Like Camdeborde, Breton, and the *bistronomie* cohort, Bourdas had no interest in doing luxury fine dining when he returned from Japan in 2005. He wanted to have a cozy restaurant serving superior food at a decent price; he'd be in the kitchen, his wife would run the dining room, and he would be close to both his suppliers and his customers— "human rapport," as he put it while we chatted one Sunday morning on a cement wall in the middle of the cobblestone street in front of the restaurant. But where he differed from the Parisians was in his cooking, which, if not quite as outré as Choukroun's, was daring all the same— poached chicken, for instance, served with hazelnuts, a bouillon of baby turnips and onion tops, and a mix of chopped hard-boiled egg and Roquefort cheese. Bourdas said he personally felt unencumbered by the weight of France's culinary tradition and that this was true for many of his peers. "My generation wants freedom of expression," he said. "We find influences everywhere today. For us, there is no code." Au revoir, Escoffier.

Sa.Qua.Na had a single Michelin star; Boudras said it was a useful thing in a town popular with tourists, but he seemed otherwise blasé about it. Among many younger French chefs now, the hunger for fun was matched by a professed indifference to Michelin; they were happy to receive its benediction but were not seeking it. Even so, the stars were finding them, and the 2007 Guide elevated one of their number, Pascal Barbot of Astrance, a restaurant in Paris, to the highest rung. It was a startling promotion, and not just because Barbot was only thirty-four.

There was the restaurant itself: Tucked into a charmless residential block in the sixteenth arrondissement, within view of the Seine, Astrance's exterior suggested nothing more than a casual neighborhood bistro. So did its interior: It had a tiny, split-level dining room, with black walls, scuffed in some areas; track lighting; and contiguous mustard-colored banquettes. A small counter to the left of the entrance doubled as a reception desk and bar, and was also home to the coffeemaker. The stemware was arranged on glass shelves that had been built into one of the walls, next to a table, and the kitchen door opened directly to the dining room—a typical setup in most restaurants but unheard of in a three-star.

The dining room staff, overseen by co-owner Christophe Rohat, wore business suits, just about the only visual clue that Astrance was a restaurant with serious aspirations. The service was correct, but in a disarmingly casual way. The waiters, apparently NBA fans, had a habit of passing off plates to one another behind their backs. When guests went to the bathroom, they went unescorted, and their napkins were neither refolded nor reset—again, standard protocol in an ordinary restaurant, but a departure from the three-star norm. The relaxed service was matched by the informality of the clientele. Ties were nonexistent, jackets were optional, and so were jeans and sneakers.

Although Astrance's promotion was hailed by a number of top chefs and leading French critics, there were skeptics. Partly, it was the ambience: The idea of a three-star with this kind of setting and service simply didn't compute for some people. But there were also doubts about Barbot's cooking. No one denied that he had three-star potential, but was he really at the level now of someone like Pierre Gagnaire and Franck Cerutti? In truth, he wasn't—not yet. His food was good—innovative, very personal—and sometimes even great, but the talent was still raw. Barbot's signature dish was a foie gras and mushroom galette. The fungi were ordinary Paris mushrooms, which made for a clever, very contemporary juxtaposition of the luxurious and the quotidian. But it was also an aggressively unattractive dish; from a distance, it looked like a dried-out slice of grayish-white cake. The plate was brightened a bit by the dollop of lemon marmalade next to the galette, and a small puddle of hazelnut oil paired nicely with the foie gras, but the pleasure was more in the texture than in the taste. The dessert course I had at Astrance was thoroughly pedestrian: some ice cream, a sabayon with a few berries dropped in the glass, and a small dish of very ordinary clafoutis. The most arresting touch was the plate of fresh fruit that accompanied the desserts—a novel conclusion to a three-star meal, but not exactly taxing for the pastry chef.

It is possible that Michelin had promoted Barbot to make a statement—to demonstrate that the Guide, contrary to the accusations of people like Dubanchet and Pascal Remy, was not stuck in the past. It is conceivable that the third star taken from Taillevent was, symbolically and maybe even literally, the third star awarded to Astrance. In fact, Barbot and Astrance *did* have symbolic resonance, if not quite in the way that Michelin had perhaps intended. In terms of his background and the attitude he brought to his work, Barbot was a mold-breaker among top French chefs. In contrast to most three-star recipients, Barbot's interest in cooking had not been nurtured by his family: He had grown up in a household in which food was treated as mere sustenance. "I don't have the grandmother story," he told me with a laugh.

Instead, he got his early training at a cooking school. After doing his mandatory military service, which had him stationed in New Caledonia, he went to Paris and got a job with Alain Passard at his three-star restaurant, Arpège. He spent five years there, rising to number two in the kitchen. From Passard, Barbot came to understand the importance of "the product" and also acquired an egalitarian attitude toward ingredients. "Passard's philosophy was that a carrot mattered just as much as a lobster or a truffle, and that it is just as important to make wonderful carrots as it is to make wonderful lobsters." (True to his philosophy, Passard went to a predominantly vegetable menu in 2001.) It was also at Arpège that Barbot made the acquaintance of Christophe Rohat, who in time became the restaurant's maître d'.

In 1998, Barbot left Arpège and Paris and moved to Sydney, Australia. He worked there for two years, running the kitchen of a popular French restaurant. His time in New Caledonia had given him a love of the South Pacific, and he adored Australia. What he found most appealing was the sense of freedom. It was a young, dynamic country, where people were completely receptive to new ideas, not least at the table. This was particularly true of Sydney, which offered a dizzying array of cuisines and where an exuberant inventiveness held sway. The chefs wanted to surprise, diners wanted to be surprised. Barbot had never encountered such a spirited, progressive food culture, and he found it enthralling. Australia introduced him to new flavors and techniques, but what it mostly did was unshackle his mind. "Back in France, when I would try to create different kinds of dishes, I would question myself and worry about how people would react," he said. "But after Australia, I didn't ask myself those questions anymore. 'Is it okay to use scallops for something? What will people think?' I didn't care anymore. I was *décomplexe*"—free. In the past, French chefs had gone abroad to convert others; Barbot went abroad and returned home having been converted instead.

Barbot left Australia in 2000, lured back to Paris by an offer to take over the kitchen of Lapérouse, a Paris landmark, and to be reunited with Rohat, who would oversee the dining room. The pair lasted just three months there: Creative differences with the restaurant's owners led to a quickie divorce. Barbot decided to open his own place, one that would allow him to do more spontaneous cooking and to express the same freedom that he had experienced in Australia. "I wanted something very simple and very small," he said. He also wanted Rohat in the front of the house, and the two spent the next several months scouting locations. They finally settled on a small space on the rue Beethoven in the sixteenth, and because they both had good pedigrees in the business, the bank was willing to finance them almost completely.

Astrance opened in October 2000. Although the restaurant could have comfortably accommodated fifteen tables, Barbot and Rohat limited it to nine widely spaced ones, which meant no more than twenty-five diners per service. At the start, there were just five employees: Barbot and an assistant in the kitchen, Rohat and a waiter in the dining room, and a dishwasher. There was no à la carte menu, only a tasting menu that changed daily. In keeping with the prevailing fashion, Barbot sent a steady procession of smaller dishes to each table; a typical meal would consist of six courses.

Just days after receiving its first guests, Astrance was the subject of a glowing review in *Figaroscope*, and the reservation book filled up immediately. The demand for tables accelerated when Michelin awarded the restaurant a star in February 2001. Barbot was happy to receive it, but it was not something he had sought or especially cared about. "It is nothing against Michelin," he explained, "but I never worked to please the Guide. I worked to please the customers. I didn't want a three-star restaurant; it just wasn't my goal." He couldn't even recall the year Astrance had garnered its second star (it was 2005). His memory wasn't quite so sketchy regarding the third, though: The day before the 2007 promotions and demotions were to be announced, a colleague had walked into the kitchen and told him Jean-Luc Naret was on the phone. "I did something wrong?" he thought. It was a characteristically self-effacing reaction. As young as Barbot was, he looked even younger. He had a slight frame and pale, delicate features, and with his warm, guileless smile, he exuded a kind of boyish frailty and sweetness. *Sweet* was a word often used to describe him—and it's not a word often applied to three-star chefs.

By the time the third star was awarded, getting into Astrance had become even more challenging. In 2006, Barbot and Rohat had made the unusual decision to close the restaurant three days a week (two was standard for top restaurants in Paris). Despite the low number of covers, the quantity of plates coming out of the kitchen was brutal on the entire team—all the more so because the restaurant had been open six days a week. Also, Rohat had two children and desired more family time, and the unmarried Barbot wanted longer weekends to be able to go looking for new ideas. He also needed to more fully replenish his energy and enthusiasm. "I realized that I had to have a break," he said. "Cuisine is a pleasure for me, but I didn't want to be a slave. It was important to have a life, to have something that exists on the side." It was another way of saying that he wasn't going to let haute cuisine do to him what it had done to Alain Chapel and Bernard Loiseau.

In all these ways, Barbot was redefining what it meant to be a three-star chef. But in one important respect, he was a throwback. Like all big-time chefs, he had an extensive network of purveyors, but he was not content merely to receive daily deliveries at the restaurant; he wanted a closer relationship with the ingredients and the people who furnished them. For this reason, he made a weekly trek to Rungis, the famous (and famously sprawling) wholesale food market on the outskirts of Paris. (It had once been located in Les Halles, in the center of the city; in 1969, it was moved to a site just off the A6 highway near Orly Airport.) Barbot usually went on Tuesdays; driving a rented delivery van, he would leave Paris at 5:30 A.M., hoping to make it back by ten; heavy traffic coming into the city often made the return trip a two-hour odyssey. Barbot didn't need to go to Rungis; he sourced only around 10 percent of his supplies there. His visits were reconnaissance missions: He went to see what was in the market and to hear what the farmers were talking about—how crops were faring, how the growing season was shaping up. Barbot was not just the only three-star chef putting in a regular appearance at Rungis; insofar as he was aware, he was one of the few chefs who went there, period. In fact, he knew of just one other chef—a friend of his with a restaurant in Paris—who routinely made the trip.

Most of the people he did business with had no idea he was a chef of distinction, let alone one with three stars. This sometimes led to amusing exchanges. On the morning I joined Barbot, a beefy delivery man, upon being told that he was a chef, shrugged and said, "I work in a restaurant, too." Some of the merchants knew Barbot's identity and were flattered by his visits. "He doesn't delegate," Pascal, a fruit seller, told me. "He comes out, to see for himself. He's a great, great chef, but he's humble." Pascal was eager to have Barbot taste some lychees, just arrived from Thailand. With his pocket knife, he peeled and sliced several of them. He and I thought they were great; Barbot wasn't convinced, and as he continued to peruse the inventory, Pascal tried a few more, testing his impressions against the chef's. After careful evaluation, he reversed himself: "I think he's right." The lychees had good flavor, but they weren't as firm as they needed to be.

Barbot ended up spending nearly four hours at Rungis. He visited a half-dozen halls, picking up cherries, strawberries, white nectarines, apricots, melons, lemons, peas, *champignons de Paris* (the mushrooms for the galette), almonds, milk and yogurt (for staff meals), tarragon, coriander, basil, parsley, fennel, and several bunches of flowers. He paused only for cigarette breaks and to take a phone call from a fisherman on the Ile d'Yeu, off the coast of Brittany. The fisherman had just reached the dock and had John Dory and red tuna; Barbot told him to send it (the fish would arrive the next morning). Although the Rungis run was mostly just symbolic, Barbot applied forensic scrutiny to every product he inspected. He tasted enough fruits during the course of the morning to fill a small grove, and he agonized over nearly every purchase he made. Cost was no concern ("I never look at the prices"); quality was his only criterion. The apricots, just in from the south of France, were the primary source of indecision. Barbot went through perhaps twenty apricots, spread over three stands, before finally choosing several small baskets. At one point, as he wavered over one carton, he laughed at his own compulsiveness. "Can you imagine taking an hour to buy a box of apricots?"

"Better Than the Original"

IN 1862, A DELEGATION of Japanese diplomats visited France. During the trip, one of the emissaries, Shibata Teitaro, sent a letter home in which he described his difficulties with the cuisine. "We are troubled by the food, which is different," Teitaro wrote. "No matter where you go, you are served all the most prized dishes, most of which are based upon meat. If this meat is replaced with fish, it is cooked in oil. There is no variation in the vegetables and if, by chance, we are served some, they too taste like fat. As this cooking with butter does not suit us, we fixed ourselves a kind of sashimi during our stay in France, by cutting up raw fish and sprinkling it with the sauce we brought along. Since the beginning of our mission, that was the first time we found any food that satisfied us."

One can only wonder what Teitaro would make of Château de l'Éclair, set in the hills above Villefranche-sur-Saône, just north of Lyon. With its high, vaulted roof, latticed balconies, and weathered façade, the château looks like a typical French manor house—that is, until you notice the Japanese flag fluttering in the courtyard. Walking in the direction of the flag takes you past a building catty-corner to the château that contains a large, gleaming professional kitchen. A look inside will invariably prompt a double-take: All the young cooks are Japanese. If it doesn't quite rise to the level of Martians in Times Square, a kitchen full of Japanese cooks in the middle of the Beaujolais region is an arresting sight all the same, and one that probably would have given Teitaro a jolt.

The château is an overseas campus of L'École Hôtelière Tsuji, Japan's most prestigious professional cooking school. The Osaka-based academy was founded in 1960 by Shizuo Tsuji, a former journalist who held a degree in French literature and had a longstanding interest in French cuisine. Other cuisines, including Japanese, are also taught there, but with the encouragement of some leading French chefs, notably Paul Bocuse, Tsuji's school has become possibly the finest foreign-run French cooking program in the world. In 1980, with the help of Bocuse, Tsuji acquired Château de l'Éclair; nine years later, he added Château Escoffier, in the village of Reyrieux, several miles to the east. Around two hundred second-year students are sent to the châteaux annually, where they work at mastering classic French recipes and techniques. On the day I ate there, lunch consisted of cold marinated salmon, roasted lamb, a selection of cheeses, and tarte Tatin, all cooked and served by the students and all impressively done. The curriculum is supplemented by frequent visits from well-known chefs, bakers, winemakers, and pâtissiers. After graduating, many of the students do *stages* in top restaurants throughout France and then return home to cook or teach, lending their talents to what has become one of the great food stories of our time: the Japanification of French cuisine.

Nearly one hundred and fifty years after Teitaro starved his way through France, his compatriots have embraced French food with quasi-religious fervor. French restaurants, wine bars, bakeries, and cheese shops are ubiquitous in Japanese cities. Many are locally owned, but a number of leading French chefs also operate restaurants in Japan. Bocuse currently has six restaurants in Tokyo, Joël Robuchon has three, and Alain Ducasse and Pierre Gagnaire have two apiece. Michel Bras, Michel Troisgros, Marc Haeberlin, the Pourcel brothers, and Guy Martin all have outposts in Japan as well. Some of the most acclaimed names in French foodstuffs—cheese specialist Marie-Anne Cantin, baker Eric Kayser, pâtissiers Pierre Hermé and Gérard Mulot—have shops there, too. Japan has quite literally become a second home to French cuisine, a point that was underscored when Michelin published its first-ever Guide to Tokyo in 2007 and awarded three stars to three French restaurants and two stars to a half-dozen others. Robuchon was among the three-star recipients (his other Tokyo restaurants also received stars) and Gagnaire and Troisgros were both awarded two.

All this is an unintended consequence of four decades of French culinary imperialism. Starting in the 1960s, prominent chefs such as Bocuse, Raymond Oliver, and Pierre and Jean Troisgros began making regular trips to Japan, other chefs moved there to work, and French cuisine soon found a large and devoted following in the island nation. It was a development made possible by Japan's postwar economic boom; this new prosperity not only gave many Japanese the means to dine out luxuriously, but also the ability to travel abroad, and France proved to be an especially popular destination. In time, the Japanese became the savviest culinary tourists to France. They knew all the top tables, and thanks in part to a cluster of Japanese food writers living in France and reporting back home, they also seemed to know about up-and-coming restaurants even before many French did.

The Japanese also became ardent students of French cuisine and proved to be very adept at it. A few months before his death, Jean-Claude Vrinat told me that he found better baguettes in Tokyo than he did in Paris, and that the young Japanese cooks who came to work at Taillevent had a stronger grasp of French recipes and techniques than did most of the French chefs he hired. But there wasn't just mastery; there was also devotion. The Japanese had a reverence for France's gastronomic heritage that stood in dramatic contrast to the indifference of many French. In the late 1990s, when the Food Network aired the popular Japanese cooking show *Iron Chef*, a number of the Japanese chefs cited Alain Chapel as their inspiration. This was astonishing. By then, Chapel was largely a forgotten figure in France—chefs, of course, celebrated his memory, but the French public wouldn't have known him from Alain Châpeau. When I told Suzanne Chapel about the show and how often her husband's name was invoked, she nodded and told me that his enduring influence in Japan was one of the things that kept her going. "The respect the Japanese have for him and for French cuisine is very motivating," she told me. "They defend an ideal."

And not just in Japan. In a remarkable twist, some of the most acclaimed French cooking *in France* was now being done by Japanese chefs, three of whom even held Michelin stars: Hiroyuki Hiramatsu and Tateru Yoshino, both of whom had restaurants in Paris, and Keisuke Matsushima, who owned an eponymous restaurant in Nice. Hiramatsu was the most prominent of the three. With nineteen restaurants employing more than six hundred people, he was Japan's answer to Bocuse and Ducasse, and his restaurant group had served a turnkey function for some of the French chefs starting establishments in Japan. In 2001, he opened a nine-table restaurant on the Ile Saint-Louis in Paris, which quickly earned a Michelin star. Three years later, the restaurant relocated to a slightly larger space on the rue de Longchamp in the sixteenth arrondissement, where it retained its star.

It was there that I went to see Hiramatsu in April 2007. As our appointment wasn't scheduled until two P.M., I decided to have lunch beforehand. The dining room, decorated in a contemporary, vaguely Japanese style, was empty except for me and a dowdy British couple that was either a husband and his much older wife or a son and his mother. The waitstaff was entirely French, and the wine list was one of the best I'd encountered in France, studded with marquee names like Coche-Dury, Lafon, Roumier, and Guigal. The food—classic French, and fairly conservative at that—was good, if not quite as delicious as I'd hoped. An appetizer of sliced scallops and marinated salmon with celery rémoulade and tomato purée was very pleasant; my main course, roast veal, was cooked perfectly but could have used a little more flavor; ditto the chocolate cake that ended the meal.

I met with Hiramatsu in his small office overlooking the kitchen. A trim fifty-four-year-old with a full head of salt-and-pepper hair, he was dressed in slacks, an Izod shirt, and a windbreaker, his eyeglasses dangling around his neck by a cord. He spoke some French but not enough to be conversant, and his secretary, who was also Japanese, didn't speak any English. We decided that I would pose my questions in French, she would translate them into Japanese, Hiramatsu would reply in Japanese, and she would translate his answers into French. The office was very warm and I'd had two glasses of wine with lunch; between having to think and write in English, converse in French, and concentrate on staccato-burst Japanese, I felt as if my head would explode. After a few minutes, my mind finally came around, which was a good thing, because the soft-spoken Hiramatsu turned out to be a fascinating character—possibly the most interesting, erudite chef I'd encountered in France.

He had developed an interest in France as a teenager, he said. As a fifteen-year-old, he had read Jean-Jacques Rousseau's *Social Contract*, and it had been a life-shaping experience. "It was a shock for me—the appreciation of individualism, this idea of individual liberty," he said. "This was something that didn't exist in Japan." This was surprising. Rousseau, a Calvinist by birth and, later, by reconversion, abhorred gourmandism and would just as soon have had his taste buds extracted, which made him an unlikely source of inspiration for a chef. "My interest in Rousseau had no relationship with cuisine, just philosophy," Hiramatsu said. "This idea of respect for the individual—it hit me very hard. And I was attracted to France because it was the country that had this philosophy of individual freedom."

He had later learned about the School of Paris, and how foreign artists like Picasso, Chagall, and Modigliani had gravitated to the French capital and created some of the most innovative works of the early twentieth century. As Hiramatsu saw it, these men had been drawn to France by the liberty it offered—by the ideas that had animated Rousseau. At the age of eighteen, his head filled with what were, for a Japanese teenager, deeply subversive thoughts, Hiramatsu realized there was no choice but to move to France. "I needed to live there," he explained. "I saw that only in France could I be free." It was then that he decided to become a chef; food was a central part of French culture, and cooking would be his ticket to France.

Another eight years would pass before he set foot in the place that had so aroused his imagination. During that time, he trained at the

Hotel Okura in Tokyo, all the while studying Carême and Escoffier and immersing himself in the literature and culture of "the country of my dreams." When he finally reached France, at the age of twenty-six, he first worked as a cook at a two-star restaurant in the city of Nantes. Six months later, he moved to Paris, then in the throes of the nouvelle cuisine movement. There, he worked for two years in an unstarred but well-regarded restaurant called Claire Fontaine. But just as he was immersing himself in French life, Hiramatsu experienced another epiphany. "When I came to France, I was sure it would be forever," he explained. "But then I came to understand something Mr. Fernand Point had said. He said, 'Young chefs, return to your country and cook for your compatriots.' I realized that I had to return to Japan to share what I had learned in France and to teach the Japanese the real French cooking. I would be an ambassador, a missionary."

Twenty-five years later, with the Japanese having embraced French cuisine almost as if it were their own, Hiramatsu had accomplished his mission. "There is more passion in Japan for French food and wine than there is France," he said. "The Japanese are now very cultivated and knowledgeable when it comes to French cuisine, and when the food is good, they are very enthusiastic. On Saturdays and Sundays, they'll wait two or three hours to get a table! Even my mother will wait ninety minutes."

He told me that he had opened the restaurant in Paris not because he had wanted to conquer France but because he had needed a place where he could go to actually cook. "In Japan," he said, "I'm a *chef d'entreprise*. With all the restaurants I have there, I don't have the time or the energy to cook. Here, I can be a *chef de cuisine* again. This restaurant is a laboratory for me—a place to refine my cuisine, to create new dishes." By now, I was slack-jawed. No French chefs that I knew talked about Rousseau and the *Social Contract* and notions of individual liberty, and they definitely didn't open restaurants in other countries because they wanted to be in the kitchen cooking. Suzanne Chapel's words were ringing in my head: *They defend an ideal.*

Hiramatsu made eight trips a year to Paris, spending about one hundred days in total in France. He said that while the critics had responded enthusiastically to his Paris venture, the initial reaction among French diners had been cautious; they assumed, not without reason, that the food would reflect his Japanese roots. "At the beginning, the French clients thought of me as a Japanese chef," he said. "They were looking for the Japanese side to my cooking." But they now understood that while the chef was Japanese, the food was unabashedly French. "The other day," he said, breaking into a smile, "I had a client tell me that he finds the French cuisine we serve here better than what the French themselves do."

The Japanese weren't just passionate about French food; they were equally smitten with French wines. In 2005, the wine critic Michel Bettane, France's answer to Robert Parker, paid a visit to Japan and came away marveling at the connoisseurship and enthusiasm that he encountered. From the flawless stemware to the unfailingly perfect serving temperatures, he said, the level of respect accorded French wines in Japan was "unthinkable at home." Likewise, the Japanese wine writers that Bettane met exhibited a curiosity and knowledge that he felt put his French colleagues to shame. And just as young Japanese cooks migrated to France, Japanese wine experts also went to the motherland to ply their craft. Hideya Ishizuka, who was named Japan's Best Young Sommelier in 1987, relocated to France in 1991 and, without intending to, forced diners to reckon with the new face of French cuisine at their very table. He had set out intent on finding work with a Michelin-starred restaurant and quickly landed a position with a two-star in Brittany, where he spent a year. Then, in 1992, he met Jean-Michel Cazes, the owner of Château Lynch-Bages, a Bordeaux fifth growth. Cazes, one of Bordeaux's most respected figures, was impressed by the young Japanese man and hired him to work as the sommelier at an inn he had recently opened just down the road from his winery. In a part of Bordeaux largely devoid of good restaurants, Cordeillan-Bages had quickly established itself as the area's foremost dining destination. Because of its location, much of the clientele was in the wine business, which made the job of wine steward particularly challenging. Ishizuka's nationality, it seems, made it all the more so: Some French clients were not receptive to the idea of a Japanese sommelier. "For the first three or four years, it was very difficult," Ishizuka said. Cazes told him to ignore the skeptics and just go about his business. By 1999, the restaurant had won two Michelin stars and Ishizuka's knowledge and charm had won over the doubters; Gault Millau even described him as the dining room's star attraction.

Two years later, Ishizuka, now married with children, decided to move to Paris, where he took a job with Hiramatsu, who was just opening his restaurant there. In 2002, Ishizuka received a call from Alain Ducasse. At the time, Ducasse was making plans for his first restaurant in Japan, and having heard of Hiramatsu's talented and bilingual sommelier, he decided that this was just the person he needed for his Tokyo venture. In typical fashion, Ducasse swooped in on his prey, calling Ishizuka at regular intervals to try to lure him back to Tokyo. But Ishizuka was happy in Paris, and no amount of money or flattery could entice him. After several months, Ducasse finally surrendered. "He said that I was the only person who'd ever said no to him," Ishizuka proudly recalled. In 2005, Ishizuka left Hiramatsu to fulfill his dream of owning a classic Parisian wine bar-bistro. On the fashionable rue du Cherche-Midi, he opened Le Petit Verdot, named for one of the grapes used in Bordeaux. It was a jewel box of a restaurant with an appealing menu (warm terrine of rabbit and artichoke, roast rump of veal with sorrel and tomato) and a wine list rich in great French names, prominent among them Château Lynch-Bages. Ishizuka said that some locals were not especially welcoming of a Japanese *patron*: "There was some racism," he said. However, the bigots were a distinct minority, and a strong neighborhood clientele, as well as a fair number of Japanese and American tourists, had given the restaurant a promising start. Indeed, Ishizuka was now thinking of opening a second restaurant in Paris. Asked how the Japanese had come to so skillfully execute the flavors and forms of French cuisine, Ishizuka allowed a slight grin: "The thing about us Japanese is that we like to copy and are very good at it. In fact, we are so good at it that the copy eventually becomes better than the original."

The French, even if they weren't necessarily receptive to the idea of Japanese chefs assuming the mantle of Carême and Escoffier, could at least take pride in how successfully they had managed to implant their culinary tradition in a country six-thousand miles from France and a world apart culturally. But this also raised a question: If the French could turn Tokyo into a city of cassoulet lovers, why couldn't they do the same thing in the suburbs of Paris and Lyon, where many of France's ethnic minorities lived? It was a question that spoke to a broader issue—the failure of France to successfully assimilate huge numbers of the estimated five million immigrants who now lived there.

This failure was laid bare in October 2005, when two teenagers of North African descent were electrocuted in the Paris suburb of Clichy-sous-Bois. They had taken refuge in an electrical substation, apparently thinking that they were being chased by the police (whether they were being pursued has never been conclusively established and remains a source of controversy). News of the deaths sparked a night of violence in Clichy-sous-Bois, with immigrant youths vandalizing local businesses and burning cars. In the days that followed, the unrest spread, first to other Paris suburbs and then to other cities in France. By the time the violence subsided, three weeks later, one person was dead, nearly three thousand had been arrested, almost ten thousand cars had been torched, and more than three hundred million dollars in damage had been done in some two hundred communities across the country.

The spasm of violence shocked France, but it shouldn't have: It was the inevitable harvest of decades of failed integration. France had a large and growing population of predominantly Muslim émigrés from Algeria, Morocco, and Tunisia, three of its former colonies, and it was also home to scores of recent arrivals from other parts of Africa. But little effort had been made to absorb these newcomers. Many of them lived in blighted communities on the edge of Paris and other cities, out of sight and out of mind of both the French government and broader French society. Within these largely minority enclaves, there was little work to be found, and racial discrimination often prevented immigrant job-seekers from finding jobs in nearby areas. While the overall employment situation in France was abysmal, nowhere was it worse than in the *banlieues,* as these depressed suburbs were known; by some estimates, joblessness among minority youths was as high as 50 percent. The result was simmering resentment that finally boiled over in the autumn of 2005.

At the same time that the French suburbs were exploding in violence, the French hospitality industry was grappling with a dearth of workers. The shortage was mainly caused by onerous labor laws. But for some restaurateurs, the money wasn't an issue: They simply couldn't recruit willing people to fill all the positions they had to offer. During a morning that I spent with Christian Constant, a neighboring restaurateur stopped by to check out some of the furnishings at Les Cocottes, and the two men got to commiserating about staffing. "Impossible these days," said Constant. His colleague nodded and said, "We just can't find enough people to do the work."

This conversation took place less than ten miles from Clichy-sous-Bois—ten miles from a community with a huge number of able-bodied young men and women desperate for work. They needed jobs, and restaurateurs like Constant and his neighbor needed help. Yet no one seemed to have put two and two together. To an American, this failure was especially mystifying because the restaurant trade has been so central to the immigrant experience in the United States. For countless European, Asian, and Latin American immigrants, restaurant work had been a gateway to a better life. For France, wrestling with an ethnic minority crisis on the one hand and a restaurant manpower crisis on the other, the solution seemed obvious: Get the kids in the *banlieues* jobs as cooks, waiters, and runners.

True, McDonald's was providing them with work, but it was an American company specializing in fast food. Why weren't French restaurants offering similar opportunities? Doing so would not just be a means to a paycheck; it would be a way of connecting minority youths to French culture. Food was central to French identity, and for other, earlier immigrants, it had served an assimilative function; eating pot-au-feu and sipping a glass of Beaujolais was a way of being French and a statement of belonging. Gilles Pudlowski, the restaurant critic, has said that as a child growing up in Alsace, the son of Jewish émigrés from Poland, it was food that had made him feel French. "The only France I know is gourmet France," he wrote. "My exemplary French ... are master chefs ... master vintners, cellar men, and vine growers ... This country, as vast, multifarious, and well-fed as it is gourmand, is indeed a gigantic, convivial, perpetual, quotidian feast." Bringing the disaffected youths from the *banlieues* into the restaurant trade wouldn't just be a way of easing unemployment; it would be a way of alleviating their sense of alienation and more fully integrating them into French society.

Equally important, it would be a means of perpetuating France's gastronomic tradition. Every cuisine, in order to endure and flourish, needs a steady infusion of new blood—both new practitioners and new consumers. France was becoming increasingly multiethnic and multiracial; simply as a demographic matter, it seemed imperative that a knowledge of, and passion for, French cuisine take root in places like Clichy-sous-Bois. What sort of future would French cuisine have if 20 or 30 percent of the French population never touched the stuff? Non-immigrant French had embraced ethnic fare with some enthusiasm; in fact, couscous was said to be the most popular dish in France (admittedly, part of its appeal was that it was cheap). Cultivating a taste for French cuisine among France's ethnic minorities seemed no less important.

Yet nearly every time I raised this subject with eminent French chefs and pointed out the absence of dark-skinned faces—either clients or staff—in the kitchens and dining rooms of leading restaurants, I was met with quizzical expressions, as if the idea had never occurred to them. The only Michelin-starred chef who seemed genuinely interested in the topic was Alain Senderens, and his take on the issue was revealing. We were chatting one afternoon in his restaurant, and I noted that the swankier establishments in Paris didn't seem to reflect the city's changing complexion; there were few if any customers of North African descent, and it appeared to me that there were few if any North African employees. Senderens begged to differ. "All of the dishwashers here are Maghreb," he quickly replied. He then jumped out of his chair, left the room, and returned a few minutes later with his arm around a young North African dishwasher, who smiled sheepishly as he was put on display for me. "You see?" Senderens triumphantly declared.

But some restaurateurs readily acknowledged the problem and were willing to talk about it candidly. Gérard Allemandou owned a well-regarded fish spot, La Cagouille, near the Montparnasse train station. The restaurant was known not just for the quality of its food, but also for the diversity on display in its dining room and kitchen; the staff was largely composed of North Africans and sub-Saharan Africans. For Allemandou, a jovial bear of a man with unkempt hair and an even unrulier beard, the rainbow coalition in his restaurant was a necessity and a point of pride. "In France today, many of the young people don't want to work," he told me as we talked over coffee one morning at a corner table in the restaurant. "These people want to work, and without them, nothing is going to function. If you walk around Paris today, there are so many people of color. We need them."

It was clear that it was also personally important to him to have a restaurant that *looked* like modern France, and the satisfaction in his voice as he spoke of La Cagouille's *mixité* was unmistakable. "Some of the cooks have been here for fifteen years now," he said. "The number two in my kitchen is from the Ivory Coast. The number three is Malian. There is no relationship between my style of cooking and their native cuisines, but they make my cuisine better than I do." He conceded that he was still an exception among French restaurateurs. "Gastronomy is the last bastion of the reactionary spirit in France, and it's too bad," he said. The most upscale restaurants were the worst offenders. "The *grandes tables*—they are run by a certain caste that just doesn't realize the world has changed." But Allemandou was confident that reality would eventually catch up even with them;

it had to. "I think in ten or twenty years we will have a black or Maghrebian two- or three-star chef," he said. "Look at our soccer team, with its racial mix. We need restaurants that are like that. For our social cohesion, it is obligatory."

Fatéma Hal made a similar point over a dinner of chicken tagine and couscous at Mansouria, her restaurant in the eleventh arrondissement. Done in an Arabian Nights motif that managed to just skirt the edge of kitsch, Mansouria was Paris's most popular North African restaurant and its proprietor France's best-known Maghreb chef. A native of Oujda, Morocco, Hal moved to France in 1970 and opened Mansouria fourteen years later. In the beginning, she had three strikes against her: She was a woman, she was an immigrant, and she was serving ethnic fare. "They described it as 'Oriental cuisine,' " she recalled. "It was very difficult at first, because the French are just not as interested in other cuisines as the Americans and the English. They knew couscous, but that was it." It was only when Joël Robuchon, a fan of Moroccan cuisine, discovered her and began talking up the restaurant that attitudes began to change. Hal got her first book deal, and the book sold well; others followed, and she was now a beloved figure on the French food scene and abroad.

Even so, old attitudes hadn't entirely melted away. The French still didn't consider Maghreb cuisine to be their own; they continued to regard it as something imported and exotic. They also viewed it as inherently inferior to French cuisine. French chefs had embraced a few concepts and flavors from the Maghreb—preserved lemons, for instance—but the melting pot was more like a thimble. This chauvinism, Hal said, was particularly evident among critics and journalists, and she offered a hypothetical example to illustrate her point. "If a top French chef decided to open a Moroccan restaurant, the French journalists would assume that not only would he succeed, he would do it better than a native chef like me," she said. "They just assume that the French chefs know best. But if I announced that I was going to open a place serving traditional French cuisine—no way. They wouldn't accept it."

We talked for a bit about the riots in the *banlieues*. Hal thought the media had exaggerated the problem; there were certainly disaffected youths in these communities, but most of the residents just went about their business. She agreed, though, that there was a pressing need for jobs and that the restaurant trade was the obvious place to create them. Echoing Allemandou, she felt that food could be not only a source of work but a means of fostering social harmony. "Food promotes ties and encourages cultural understanding," she said, becoming more emphatic with each word. "It tells a story, and is a way of sharing that story with your neighbors." I asked Hal if she knew of any Maghreb chefs in the *banlieues* who were specializing in French fare. She said she had recently met a young cook from one of the suburbs who was interested in doing French cuisine, but she couldn't recall his name or where he worked.

I made some inquiries but had no luck locating him. But was it really possible that in all of France, there was not a single chef of North African or Middle Eastern descent doing star-worthy French cooking? On a visit to Bordeaux not long after my conversation with Hal, I discovered that there was at least one such person. While eating at Cordeillan-Bages, where Hideya Ishizuka had worked, I was introduced to a chef named Sylvestre Wahid, who was there having dinner with a woman whom I took to be his girlfriend. We talked only briefly, but it was long enough for me to learn that he had been born in Pakistan and raised in France, was a protégé of Alain Ducasse and was now the chef at Oustau de Baumanière, a two-star establishment in Provence and one of France's most famous restaurants.

A few months later, I went to visit the thirty-two-year-old Wahid at the Oustau. I arrived late on a warm, sun-splashed Sunday afternoon. I'd been to the Oustau several times, and its location—it was set in the middle of a haunting limestone rock formation known as Les Alpilles, in the shadow of Les Baux, a medieval village that had been carved out of the cliffs—was even more beautiful than I remembered it. Ducasse had told me that he thought the Oustau had the most spectacular setting of any restaurant in France, and standing beneath the craggy Alpilles and looking out over the Provençal plain toward the Mediterranean coast, it was hard to disagree.

I had assumed, with Wahid now in charge of the kitchen, that Jean-André Charial, the Oustau's longtime owner and chef, would not be around. But Wahid had apparently informed Charial of my visit, and shortly after I got to the Oustau, I was told that Charial would be joining me for a drink before dinner and that Wahid and I would talk at the end of the night.

I knew, from conversations with other chefs, that the sixty-two-year-old Charial was viewed within the profession as a somewhat tragic figure. Cooking was apparently not his first love, but duty had obliged him to take over the Oustau after the retirement of his legendary grandfather, Raymond Thuilier, who had founded the restaurant just after the Second World War. When the ninety-three-year-old Thuilier had stepped down, in 1990, Michelin had immediately stripped the restaurant of its third star, which it had held since 1954. Charial had never been able to win it back, a failure that over time had layered frustration on top of frustration.

Charial told me that he had hired Wahid for one reason: to get that third star. Recognizing that his opportunity had likely passed, he decided in 2005 that the best hope of regaining it was to cede the kitchen to a younger, hungrier chef. (More prosaically, Charial was also planning to run for president of the Relais & Châteaux group and knew that he would have to leave the kitchen if elected.) Wahid, then in his tenth year with the Ducasse organization, had heard from some friends that Charial was looking for a chef. He had expressed his interest to Ducasse, who had called Charial, and a match was soon made.

Charial said he was satisfied with the way things had turned out: "Sylvestre is very clever, and I think he's done a good job of keeping the spirit of the place." But he also made clear that the arrangement was not necessarily an open-ended one: If the Oustau wasn't awarded a third star in the next year or two, he might consider taking the restaurant in another direction, one that presumably would not include

Wahid. He mentioned Chez Bru, a nearby restaurant that also had two stars but was more casual (and therefore cheaper to operate). "I ask myself sometimes—more than sometimes—if this is the right way, all this effort to get the third star," he said. "I've invested twelve million euros in the last ten years, to renovate, to change the kitchen. I've got a brilliant chef now, so I don't know what more I can do. I can make it more profitable without Sylvestre, that's for sure. Maybe if in two years' time I still don't have it, maybe I'll just have to say that I'll never get it and change things."

I asked Charial about Wahid's background, and what he represented. "I didn't hire Sylvestre to make him a symbol," he replied sharply. "I hired him because of his talent and because we had the same idea about cooking. He's very classical." Charial allowed, though, that he himself was perhaps more progressive than many of his compatriots. He and his wife had adopted a thirteen-year-old Vietnamese refugee in the 1970s, an unusual thing to do in rural France at that time. (Their son now worked as a pastry chef in Los Angeles.) "I'm very open," he said. "For me, the color of the skin does not change a thing." But he acknowledged that Wahid's complexion was an issue for others. He said that Ducasse had told him that placing Wahid had not been easy—that some restaurants would not hire him because of his ethnicity. Charial said the French press also evinced a curious attitude. "I always have the impression, reading the French papers, that Sylvestre came from Pakistan yesterday," he said. "But he grew up here; he's French." What most disturbed him, he said, was the attitude of some clients. "I've had people say, 'You're using spice, I think your cooking is spicier because of your chef.' I've always used spices in my cooking. I've been to India many times and always came back with new spices and new ideas." Other guests were more direct. "They've said to me, 'Why did you take this Arab?' " I asked if these clients were foreign or French. "French."

A few minutes later, we said good-bye and I went into the dining room to eat. The food was impressive. I'd enjoyed my previous meals at the Oustau, and this one was certainly their equal. A

Bloody Mary sorbet, comprised of tomato, vodka, and spices, was an unusual and refreshing palate teaser. It was also visually striking: It came to the table in a cloud of smoke produced by liquid nitrogen, an Adrià-esque flourish that signaled the generational shift in the kitchen. But the first course was as traditionally French as they come: *oeuf en meurette*—poached egg served with cèpes and a red wine sauce, a deliciously earthy ode to autumn. Next came *rouget* with basil and thyme blossom, a Provençal (and Oustau) classic that was easily as sublime as Charial's rendition; line-caught sole with more cèpes and some of the sweetest prawns I'd ever tasted; a delicious roast pigeon with turnip, beetroot, and lavender essence; and a warm green-apple tart paired with roasted figs and vanilla ice cream. The food didn't quite have the polish and profundity of a three-star meal (or that a three-star meal was supposed to have, anyway), but Wahid was definitely headed in the right direction.

Make that Wahid and his brother: It turned out that his kid brother, Jonathan, was the pastry chef. Jonathan, thirty, had been hired by Charial at Sylvestre's request; he had previously worked at the Hôtel Ritz in Paris and had been crowned France's Champion of Desserts in 2005. Both Wahids, still in their chef's whites, joined me for coffee after dinner. By now, it was past eleven P.M., and the restaurant was empty except for a few waiters tidying up. Sylvestre was sinewy and tall, with a thin beard and mustache. Jonathan was clean-shaven and a little beefier. On this night, at least, Sylvestre was the more animated of the two, which probably owed something to the fact that the hour was late and Jonathan, in addition to his kitchen duties, had a wife and four-year-old child. (Sylvestre was single; "I'm married to my job," he said.) Sylvestre did most of the talking, and he told a remarkable story.

The Wahids were originally from Kohat, Pakistan, a city near Islamabad. Their father visited France in 1979 and decided, apparently on a lark, to join the French Foreign Legion. The family—Sylvestre and Jonathan, their mother, and two sisters—didn't see the senior Wahid for five years; according to Sylvestre, new recruits were required to be incommunicado for that length of time. Finally, in 1984, he brought the family to France, settling them in Nîmes. He immediately enrolled the children in Catholic school, which he believed was a way of hastening their integration into French society. "He didn't want us to forget our past, but he wanted us to feel part of the French community, to absorb the French spirit," Sylvestre explained.

By then, the father had taken a job overseeing food and beverage services for the Foreign Legion, and he had also acquired a taste for French cuisine and the bourgeois lifestyle. "My father liked the good things," Sylvestre said. "He cooked a lot of French food, and he liked to eat and drink well, and he shared that with us. We had Dom Pérignon, we had foie gras." I must have raised an eyebrow at the mention of drinking, because Sylvestre quickly brought up the family's Muslim faith. "My parents practiced, but not all things," he said. "They didn't think these things were prohibited in the Islamic religion; to them, the important thing was moderation. I drink wine, my brother drinks wine, my father drinks. My sisters do, too."

In 1990, when Sylvestre was fifteen, his father arranged for him to spend the summer working for a local pâtissier. (Jonathan would later get his start with the same man.) It was then that he discovered that he didn't just like eating good food; he enjoyed making it. Through the pâtissier, he landed a *stage* at a one-star restaurant in Nîmes called Cheval Blanc, whose chef at the time was Thierry Marx, now the chef at the Cordeillan-Bages. "Thierry showed me all about French food— the best meat, the best fish, the best everything," says Sylvestre. When he decided to pursue a culinary career, it came as unwelcome news to his mother: "She cried when I told her I wanted to be a chef. She said she [hadn't brought] her children to France to be cookers. In Pakistan, being a cooker is not a big job. I said to her that I would be somebody in this job."

After Cheval Blanc, Sylvestre went to Paris, where he worked at Les Élysées du Vernet, whose chef, Alain Solivérès, would later move to Taillevent. In 1996, Sylvestre was back in the south of France when he heard that Alain Ducasse was taking over Joël Robuchon's restaurant in Paris; Sylvestre sent over his résumé. "Ducasse is the best," he explained, "and I said I [would] only go back to Paris to work for him." He spent a decade with Ducasse. He worked first at the old Robuchon restaurant, then at the Plaza Athénée, after which Ducasse sent him to the Essex House in New York, where he was posted for nearly five years and fell in love with the city ("It's so cosmopolitan; Paris is cosmopolitan, but not like that").

In 2005, he was back in France, working at Ducasse's cooking school in Argenteuil, when he heard about the opening at the Oustau. Ducasse was completely supportive, he said, but also wanted to make sure that Sylvestre understood the pressure he would be facing. "With Mr. Ducasse," he said, "you can't hesitate, so when he asked me if I was ready, it had to be yes or no right away; I said yes, of course I'm ready." When he was formally offered the job, it was a pinch-me moment. "This was the most famous restaurant in the south of France," he said. "I'd never seen Oustau de Baumanière, but I knew the history of the house. I said to myself, 'Imagine—I'm going to be the new chef of Oustau de Baumanière at thirty years old. Are you crazy or what?' It was a dream come true."

Sylvestre said that while he had not encountered any overt racism in the restaurants in which he'd worked, he knew that some people could not see past the color of his skin. "Of course they looked at us differently," he said. "We feel French, we like this country, we appreciate what it has given us. But something we can never change is our face." At this point, Jonathan chimed in: "From the time we got to France, we knew that some people looked at us differently." Both agreed that this attitude had motivated them. "You have to work two or three times harder than someone else," Sylvestre said. "You don't want to give them the opportunity to say, 'You can't do this.' "

He was quick to add that he was not pursuing his career to make a point or to be a symbol. But he said he was happy if he and Jonathan were seen by other immigrants as role models, and he acknowledged that were they to win a third star, the story would be a compelling one. "Winning a third star makes you very French," he joked. "I can't wait to see how people will react." Mostly, though, Sylvestre wanted the third star for Charial. "Mr. Charial has given me such an opportunity," he said. "He doesn't judge anybody by how they look; I can tell just from the way he looks at me. He has taught me so much, and I feel I need to give him something back, and the only thing I can give him is the third star." A third star would also be a gift to his parents. They had both recently visited the Oustau; it was the first time they'd ever been in one of his restaurants. "They cried, they were so happy," Sylvestre said.

Conclusion

O<small>N A WEEKDAY AFTERNOON</small> in the spring of 2007, I found myself back in the Mâcon region, seven years after I'd made that regrettable return visit to Au Chapon Fin. Driving north on the highway, I passed a sign for Thoissey, where the restaurant was located. Surrendering once more to curiosity, I decided to go have a look. Maybe it was under new management and flourishing again; that was my hope, anyway. But the first indication was not an encouraging one: From a distance I could see that the parking lot was surrounded by a chain-link fence, and as I drew nearer I noticed that it was overrun with weeds. The building was still upright but was now abandoned, with much of its paint peeled off. By the looks of things, it had been a while since Chapon Fin had served its last meal, and I could only assume that a wrecking ball would soon be turning it into rubble. (There was already some collateral damage: I later discovered that with Chapon Fin gone, Thoissey had been removed from the Michelin Guide—literally taken off the map.) Chapon Fin had enjoyed a longer and vastly more successful run than most restaurants, and for all I knew, the circumstances that forced its closure may have had nothing to do with the weak economy or the state of French gastronomy. But as I stood there eyeing the skeletal remains of a place that had helped kindle my love of France and French food, I couldn't help but see its downfall as emblematic of theirs.

A few months earlier, in December 2006, Ferran Adrià, Heston Blumenthal, and Thomas Keller, along with the American food scientist and author Harold McGee, had issued a joint manifesto entitled

"Statement on the New Cookery," in which they laid out some of the core principles guiding their own efforts in the kitchen and that they believed should form the basis of a twenty-first-century cuisine. "In the past," they wrote, "cooks and their dishes were constrained by many factors: the limited availability of ingredients and ways of transforming them, limited understanding of cooking processes, and the necessarily narrow definitions and expectations embodied in local tradition. Today there are many fewer constraints, and tremendous potential for the progress of our craft. We can choose from the entire planet's ingredients, cooking methods, and traditions, and draw on all of human knowledge, to explore what it is possible to do with food and the experience of eating. This is not a new idea, but a new opportunity. Nearly two centuries ago, Brillat-Savarin wrote that the 'discovery of a new dish does more for human happiness than the discovery of a new star.' "

That not one French chef was among the manifesto's signatories was as telling as the French Culinary Institute not including a single chef from France in its gala celebration in New York that same year. But by then, some of the most eminent French chefs were pursuing an agenda of their own. In 2006, Alain Ducasse, Paul Bocuse, Guy Savoy, and a group of like-minded colleagues launched an effort to persuade UNESCO to formally declare French cuisine to be part of the world's cultural patrimony. Two years later, their effort won the backing of Nicolas Sarkozy, who said he supported it because "we have the best gastronomy in the world." The validity of that claim notwithstanding, the UNESCO bid was taken by some observers as a sign that the French had given up any notion of culinary progress and had ceded intellectual leadership in the kitchen—that French cuisine had, in the words of the *International Herald Tribune's* Mary Blume, entered "a gelid commemorative phase" and was looking inward and to the past rather than outward and to the future. François Simon put it more cuttingly; he said that if UNESCO agreed to enshrine French cooking this way, "opening the door of a restaurant, making a soufflé rise, shelling an oyster will become part of cultural activity like going to sleep at the opera, yawning at the theater, or slumping over James Joyce's *Ulysses*."

Given the state of things in France, the inclination to rest on former glory was understandable. In 2008, Sarkozy's government succeeded in amending the thirty-five-hour workweek to allow companies to negotiate or impose longer hours on employees, but apart from that, French labor laws remained as rigid as Mitterrand had made them and Chirac had left them. Especially distressing for restaurateurs, Sarkozy had failed to deliver on his promise to reduce the VAT, which remained a punitive 19.6 percent. With the onset of the global financial crisis in 2008, the French economy fell into recession, and the hospitality industry was hit hard. Some three thousand restaurants and cafés went bankrupt in the first half of the year, and profits for those that were able to keep the lights on declined by some 20 percent. 2009 promised more of the same.

But as devastating as the economic downturn was, some struggling restaurateurs knew that French cuisine faced an even graver long-term threat: Younger French seemed indifferent to what they ate and to the country's gastronomic heritage. Bernard Picolet, the owner of Les Amis du Beaujolais, a restaurant near the Champs-Élysées, told Britain's *Independent* newspaper, "Younger French people today don't understand or care about food. They are happy to gobble a sandwich or chips, rather than go to a restaurant. They will spend a lot of money going to a nightclub but not to eat a good meal. They have the most sophisticated kinds of mobile telephone but they have no idea what a courgette is. They know all about the Internet but they don't know where to start to eat a fish." I heard much the same from a twentysomething PR assistant to Alain Senderens when I interviewed the legendary chef in 2006. When I had asked Senderens if he was concerned about the dining habits of French youths, he had waved his hands dismissively and assured me there was nothing to worry about; the kids would come around—they always did. A few minutes later, after Senderens had stepped away to greet a client, his flack turned to me and in a hushed tone said, "It's true—my friends, they don't care anything about food; my generation just doesn't care."

But amid all the gloomy portents, there were some hopeful signs.

In 2008, regulators reaffirmed that appellation-designated Camembert could only be made with raw milk, and both Lactalis and Isigny Sainte-Mère eventually decided to continue making the *lait cru* variety rather than quit the appellation. True, this was a small victory in a war that was being lost, but perhaps it would help spark a raw-milk renaissance. That other staple of French cuisine, bread, was enjoying a revival. Its quality had plummeted through most of the twentieth century. The transition from sourdough-based bread-making to yeast-based panification, begun in the 1920s, was the initial and most significant factor in its decline. Two world wars didn't help matters, nor did the mechanization of *boulangeries* in the 1960s, which yielded a bumper crop of bad bread. But at the prodding of France's millers, whose businesses were suffering as a result of bread's diminished appeal, the bakers finally began to turn things around in the 1980s. Improvement came chiefly through the efforts of certain innovators, notably the late Lionel Poilâne, who reconciled "artisanal practices (long sourdough fermentation, baking in wood ovens, and so on) with production on a quasi-industrial scale" and whose entire genius was "summed up in the note of acidity that marks his fine round loaves."

Those words are taken from *Good Bread Is Back*, a book published in 2006 by Steven Kaplan, who has himself played a big part in French bread's revival. Kaplan, a historian who splits his time between Cornell University and the University of Versailles Saint-Quentin-en-Yvelines, has devoted much of his career to chronicling the role of bakers and bread in French society through the ages; he is now recognized as perhaps the world's leading authority on this topic. He is also a bread critic who, with his wife, wrote a guide to the one hundred best baguettes in Paris. Kaplan evaluates bread with the same full-sensory rigor that wine critics apply to Cabernets and Syrahs, and he has a gift for the descriptive: The first time I met him, he compared one loaf we tasted to Brigitte Bardot's posterior and proceeded to trace a voluptuous heart shape in the air to make sure I got the idea. His seamless blend of erudition and pugnacious, salty humor has made Kaplan a popular figure on French television and radio.

In the process, the Brooklyn native has become the conscience of French baking—a conscience that does not hesitate to tug. He carries a baguette with him whenever he visits restaurants for the first time, and if he finds the house bread substandard, he eats his own. He considers it a form of public shaming. Amazingly, this practice has never gotten him evicted from a restaurant. Indeed, he says, the waiters and owners often take the admonishment to heart; in some instances, they have sat down with Kaplan to talk about bread, confessed their sins, and vowed to have a better baguette waiting for him next time. He is close to some prominent bakers—Eric Kayser, Dominique Saibron—and seems to have liberty to enter their kitchens whenever he wishes. Kaplan is quick to acknowledge that the title of his book is slightly misleading; good bread is back, but only to a limited extent. By his reckoning, maybe 15 percent of French bakers produce bread worth eating these days, and constant vigilance is required, even with acclaimed producers. When he caught one *boulanger*, renowned for his supposedly all-natural approach, using additives, he made his displeasure known and their previously amicable relationship soured. But Kaplan was not about to sacrifice a good crust to the exigencies of friendship. "He lied to me, and he is far too talented to have to use the crutch of additives," he said.

Kaplan was ebullient proof that one man, even a foreigner, could make a difference. Perhaps other foreigners, similarly passionate about France and French cuisine, could follow his example. The Japanese were certainly doing their part, as were all those British, American, and German cheese lovers imploring Philippe Alléosse to continue his work. With or without a UNESCO declaration, France's gastronomic tradition was part of humanity's cultural heritage, and in the same way that people of many nationalities had contributed to the effort to protect Venice from the floods, there was no reason why food lovers the world over couldn't rally to the defense of French cuisine. Ultimately, though, its fate was in the hands of the French themselves, and while the outlook was not encouraging, there was still a chance that they might yet realize what was being squandered and resolve to prevent it.

Jean-Robert Pitte put it eloquently: "But all is not lost! Let the French convince themselves to eat well once again and they will remedy the disease of languor that sometimes affects them. They will salvage their optimism, and for certain, a great chunk of their economy, in a Europe and a developed world that have too willingly thrown their gourmandism out the window. A supplement to well-being is priceless; no one can lose by treating oneself to it."

Nearly a decade after Ladurée crossed itself off my list of favorite Paris lunch spots, it did continue to serve an exemplary praline mille feuille, much to my surprise and delight. In the meantime, though, I'd made a gratifying discovery. It turned out that Ladurée's praline mille feuille had been created by Pierre Hermé—widely considered France's most talented pâtissier—when he had worked as a consultant to the tea room in the 1990s. In 2001, Hermé had opened his own eponymous shop in Paris, on the rue Bonaparte in Saint-Germain-des-Prés. Although the line that perpetually snaked out the door of his tiny boutique affirmed that Hermé truly was the Hermès of pastry, it took me several years to set foot inside—a combination of habit and misplaced loyalty had kept me going to Ladurée for my mille feuille fix. When I finally visited Hermé's shop, I found that the praline mille feuille was also being offered there; he called it the 2000 Feuilles, and as sublime as the one he'd left behind at Ladurée was, the version at his own place was even better. The pastry was so impossibly light and flaky that I half feared it might float off into the next arrondissement if I didn't hold it tight, but what flavor it packed! This was the Platonic form of a praline mille feuille, so delicious that I immediately placed a triumphant call to my wife to let her know about it, rousing her from bed at six in the morning with the good news.

Soon after that maiden visit to Hermé, I had lunch for the first time at Le Comptoir du Relais, Yves Camdeborde's restaurant, which was located a few blocks away. There, I also made a discovery: Camdeborde served a sensational salade niçoise—better even than the one I used to eat at Ladurée. Not only that: The wine list included Marcel Lapierre's Morgon. And so an old, cherished routine was immediately reestablished. Now, whenever in Paris, I go to Le Comptoir for lunch and have the salad, which I chase down with the Morgon, Camdeborde's superb country bread, and possibly also a disk of insanely runny Saint-Marcellin. I then stroll over to Hermé, where I pick up a 2000 Feuilles (I am still limiting myself to one a day, but it's surely just a matter of time before I start doubling up). Pastry in hand, I cross the street to the small square in front of the Saint-Sulpice church and park myself on one of the benches. The pigeons, clearly recognizing the Hermé bag, start congregating at my feet before I even open it. I ignore them, just as I ignore the bemused looks of passersby who notice me gorging on the mille feuille. In that moment, sitting there on a bench in the middle of Paris and taking bite after blissful bite, I am just where I want to be: back in the France that I know and hope will endure.

Afterword

IN OCTOBER 2009, IT was announced that McDonald's would be opening a restaurant in the food court of the Louvre. The news came as a shock to many art lovers, who were aghast at the prospect of the Venus de Milo sharing space with the golden arches. In truth, the food court was already home to several other fast-food restaurants, and despite these affronts to good taste, the Louvre had managed to remain one of the world's preeminent museums. It would surely survive McDonald's. As a culinary matter, however, this latest conquest by McDonald's carried an undeniable symbolism: Allowing the American fast-food chain to peddle Big Macs and frites on the grounds of the Louvre—an institution as emblematic of France as the tricolor flag itself—marked another downward spike in France's food culture.

The global economic crisis that began in 2007 hit France hard, and not surprisingly, the recession was a boon for the fast-food industry. In 2008, a year that saw an estimated six thousand traditional restaurants go out of business and left thousands of others teetering, McDonald's France recorded an 11 percent annual jump in sales. The sharp economic downturn seemed to cement a shift in dining habits: More and more, the French just wanted to eat cheaply and quickly. According to a hospitality industry trade group, almost half the restaurant meals eaten in France were now enjoyed at fast-food establishments. In the face of this shifting culinary landscape, several eminent chefs decided to follow Alain Ducasse's lead, embracing the trend toward *restauration rapide*. In 2008, Paul Bocuse opened a fast-food joint in Lyon called Ouest Express, offering sandwiches, salads, and hot entrees. A second outlet opened in 2009, and there was talk of additional expansion and possibly even franchising. Marc Veyrat and Guy Martin, three-star recipients both, started sandwich shops of their own, and Thierry Marx, a two-star chef based in Bordeaux, planned to launch a cooking school devoted to "street food."

Traditional restaurants received some welcome news in March 2009, when the European Union gave France permission to cut the value-added tax on restaurant meals from 19.6 percent to 5.5; the same rate applied to fast-food establishments. The measure took effect July 1. France's finance minister, Christine Lagarde, said the change would "preserve and improve [France's] culinary reputation" and "revitalize its restaurant sector." However, restaurants were not legally obliged to pass along the savings to diners. In exchange for reducing the VAT, the Sarkozy administration had extracted a pledge from restaurant trade associations to create forty thousand new jobs, and had urged restaurateurs to "be generous with customers" and drop their prices. But the early indications were not promising. Some restaurant owners said they needed to keep the money if they hoped to stay in business, while others said they intended to use it to hire more staff or to raise salaries. A study released by France's tourism ministry several weeks after the VAT reduction was implemented found that while big restaurant chains had cut prices accordingly, only around one third of independent restaurants had done so, stoking fears that the government might revoke the tax cut.

But the VAT cut, no matter how effective, was unlikely to reverse the changes taking place at the highest levels of French cuisine. In late 2008, Olivier Roellinger, the chef and owner of a three-star restaurant in Brittany called Les Maisons de Bricourt, announced that he was renouncing his Michelin rating and closing the restaurant. This was perhaps an even more shocking development than Alain Senderens' decision to relinquish his three stars in 2005. In contrast to Senderens, whose best years were behind him, Roellinger had won his third star in 2006, and was at the peak of his creativity. In the summer of 2009, Jean-François Piège, one of France's most acclaimed young chefs, walked away from a three-star rating before he'd even achieved it. Piège, the chef at the Hotel Crillon in Paris and a protégé of Ducasse's, had been seen as a lock for three stars. But following the example of his predecessor, Christian Constant, he decided not to wait for Michelin's ultimate accolade and quit the Crillon. Not only that, he followed Constant to the rue Saint-Dominique, where he had taken over a famous old brasserie called Thoumieux. This charming street in the seventh arrondissement thus became the place where former Crillon chefs went to reinvent themselves, spurning the Michelin Guide in the process.

As of 2009, Bernard Loiseau's restaurant in Saulieu still had three stars, but those stars now seemed more like emblems of a bygone era of fine dining than symbols of France's gastronomic élan. Loiseau's suicide had helped spark the revolt among French chefs against Michelin, even though the Guide vehemently insisted that it had done nothing to provoke the chef to harm himself. But when I had interviewed Pascal Remy, the former Michelin inspector, he had alluded to two documents concerning Loiseau: the minutes of the meeting that Loiseau and his wife had had with Michelin in the fall of 2002, and a follow-up letter from Madame Loiseau, in which she said that the Guide's warning had been heard and that her husband would work to improve the performance of his restaurant. For legal purposes, I had to see those documents myself in order to be able to refer to them in the book, and fortunately, I was able to obtain them.

Just as Remy had said, the letter from Madame Loiseau had the word *warning* underlined and promised that her husband would henceforth dedicate himself to fixing things in his kitchen. The minutes of the meeting in Paris were especially revealing. They described Loiseau as being "visibly shocked" at the concerns being expressed about his food. There was no indication in the notes that Michelin had explicitly told Loiseau that his third star was at risk, but it wouldn't have had to: It would have been understood. Of course, Michelin didn't kill Loiseau; he killed himself. But what these documents show is that Michelin, in the period following Loiseau's death, was not forthright about what it had said to him and had, at the very least, contributed to the chef's emotional turmoil.

Michelin released its third annual restaurant guide to Tokyo in November 2009. Three-star ratings were awarded to eleven restaurants, putting Tokyo one ahead of Paris in that marquee category. Unveiling the new guide at a press conference, Jean-Luc Naret declared Tokyo the "capital of gastronomy" and "the world's best place to eat." It was a remarkable statement coming from the editorial director of France's restaurant bible, and while Michelin was perhaps not the most credible arbiter of the Japanese food scene (the first Tokyo guide, published in 2007, was widely ridiculed by Japanese chefs and critics, who objected to many of the specific ratings and thought it presumptuous of the French guide to pass judgment on Japanese cooking), the unspoken message was irrefutable: France was no longer the culinary epicenter of the world. It was now just one of a number of places where exemplary food could be found, and in contrast to Japan, Spain, and several other countries, France was falling, not rising.

We will never return to a time when France is the world's unrivaled gastronomic colossus. For aspiring American or British chefs, a stint in a top kitchen in France can still be an enriching experience and an important addition to the résumé. However, those chefs can now just as easily find instruction and inspiration in Spain or Italy—or in their home countries. Twenty-five years ago, culinary tourists could happily confine themselves to France; these days, the gastronaut's map extends from Paris to London to New York to San Francisco to Tokyo to Hong Kong to Singapore to Barcelona and numerous points in between. For the past decade, Spain has been the culinary pacesetter. In the coming decade, it could well be Japan that produces the most talked-about chefs and food trends. As China and India become economic superpowers, their influence will undoubtedly be felt in the culinary realm as well.

But amid the emergence of this New Gastronomic Order, there are yet reasons to be optimistic about France. For all the difficulties confronting the viticultural industry, France's finest wines—the likes of Pétrus, Haut-Brion, Romanée-Conti, and Chave—are still universal benchmarks and will surely remain so long into the future. Chefs like Christian Constant and Pascal Barbot are reinventing French haute cuisine—both its forms and its flavors. In this endeavor, they now have plenty of company. France, despite its problems, has not lost its ability to manufacture gifted chefs, and many of them can be found quietly toiling in kitchens throughout the country, creating new dishes and perhaps laying the groundwork for a culinary renaissance. Then there is that large and growing immigrant population, just waiting to be tapped. In an interview in 2009, Adam Gopnik, echoing the Parisian restaurateur Gérard Allemandou, pointed to the example of France's national soccer team—how players from immigrant backgrounds, notably the great Zinedine Zidane, had reinvigorated French soccer. Perhaps, he suggested, there was a boy "growing up in the slums of Marseilles" who one day would do the same for French cooking. Here's hoping that he does, and that French cuisine will once again flourish and enjoy a future as glorious as its past.

Acknowledgments

ALTHOUGH ONLY ONE NAME is on the cover, this book was a collaborative effort, and many debts of gratitude are owed.

In the course of researching the book, I solicited the views and enlisted the help of numerous people, and most of them could not have been more generous with their time and thoughts. There are far too many to name here, but my thanks to all. A handful of people were kind enough to read parts of the manuscript and to offer feedback and suggestions. Many thanks to Steven Kaplan, Colman Andrews, Mark Williamson, Nicholas Lander, Steven Jenkins, Rahul Jacob, Tyler Colman, David Schildknecht, Gwen Robinson, Tyler Cowen, and Guy Gâteau.

One of the smartest things I've ever done as a journalist was writing to Jacob Weisberg to broach the possibility of doing wine pieces for *Slate*. My association with *Slate* is a source of immense pleasure and pride. My editor, Julia Turner, is a joy to work with; my thanks to her, as well as to Jacob and to David Plotz. I am also grateful to the *Financial Times* and wish to thank the following people there: Rahul Jacob, Jancis Robinson, Nicholas Lander, Charles Morris, Tom O'Sullivan, and David Owen.

I was fortunate to work with several terrific people at Bloomsbury. I am indebted to Annik La Farge for the confidence that she showed in me, and to Nick Trautwein for his skillful editing and infinite patience. I knew, from the moment that I first spoke with Nick, that he was exactly the kind of editor I wanted: intelligent, low-key, and with a sense of humor. I feel very lucky to have had him as a partner in this project. Michael

Fishwick of Bloomsbury in London showed great enthusiasm for the book throughout its development and made some superb suggestions, as well. Many thanks also to Jenny Miyasaki for so masterfully guiding me through the production process, and to Janet McDonald, whose copyediting was amazingly thorough and much appreciated.

My agent, Larry Weissman, patted me on the back when I deserved it, read me the riot act when I needed it, and has become a very good friend along the way. His excitement about this book reinforced mine, and he has been an invaluable source of counsel and support. His wife and partner, Sascha, offered excellent advice with the proposal, and my thanks to her, as well.

Without Georges Martel, my wife and I might never have become romantically involved, the idea for this book might never have germinated, and researching it would not have been possible. Georges is family, and my debt to him is enormous. Nor would the book have been feasible without my in-laws, Joseph and Keiko Brennan, who were of great help to my wife during the many weeks that I was away researching the book and during the many months when I was sequestered in my office writing it. My brother, David Steinberger, offered much appreciated support and encouragement, as well. I also want to thank Brian Shames and Eric Tagliacozzo, dear friends both.

My grandfather, Dr. Laszlo Steinberger, died a few days after I turned in the manuscript. He was a month shy of his ninety-sixth birthday, and while I had hoped he would be around to see the book in print, he at least had the satisfaction of knowing that it was headed to the printer. This book is also dedicated to him, as well as to the memory of my other grandparents, Violet Steinberger and Dr. Max and Helen Alpert.

I wish to express my gratitude to my parents, John and Rita Steinberger. I left a promising job on Wall Street to pursue a career as a journalist. Most parents would have been horrified; mine encouraged me to give up investment banking for writing, and they have been a source of steadfast support ever since. I hope this book, in some small way, repays their faith in me.

Lastly, I want to thank my wife, Kathy Brennan, and my children, James and Ava. I long ago noticed that authors, in acknowledging their debts of gratitude, invariably speak of the burdens that book writing imposes on their families. I'd hoped to avoid sounding that hackneyed refrain by not allowing the book to be a burden on mine. No such luck: As challenging as this project was for me, it was doubly so for them. No young children should have to suffer the sight of their unshaven father pacing the halls like a zombie day after day, muttering to himself. As for what my wife endured—well, let's just say that Émile Jung was absolutely right: She is mango woman, and I can't begin to thank her enough for all that she did to make this book possible. Kathy, James, and Ava should know that they are my rock and inspiration, and this book is as much theirs as it is mine.

Selected Bibliography

I DREW UPON A NUMBER of sources while researching this book, including many newspaper and magazine articles. Rather than citing all of them, which would fill several pages, I have listed below only the ones that were particularly valuable to my reporting. But a handful of publications were especially useful to me: the *New York Times*, the *International Herald Tribune*, *Le Figaro*, *Le Monde*, the *Financial Times*, the *Times of London*, *Business Week*, the *Economist*, the *New Yorker*, *Time*, *Newsweek*, *Gourmet*, *Food & Wine*, and *Saveur*.

Abramson, Julia. *Food Culture in France*. Westport, CT: Greenwood Press, 2007.

Boisard, Pierre. *Camembert: A National Myth*. Berkeley: University of California Press, 2003.

Boulud, Daniel. *Letters to a Young Chef*. New York: Basic Books, 2003.

Brillat-Savarin, Jean Anthelme. *The Physiology of Taste: Or, Meditations on Transcendental Gastronomy*. Translated by M. F. K. Fisher. Washington, D.C.: Counterpoint, 1999.

Chapel, Alain. *La Cuisine: c'est beaucoup plus que des recettes*. Paris: Editions Robert Laffont, S. A., 1995.

Chelminski, Rudolph. *The Perfectionist: Life and Death in Haute Cuisine*. New York: Gotham Books, 2005.

Child, Julia, with Alex Prud'homme. *My Life in France*. New York: Anchor Books, 2006.

Colman, Tyler. *Wine Politics: How Governments, Environmentalists, Mobsters, and Critics Influence the Wines We Drink*. Berkeley: University of California Press, 2008.

David, Elizabeth. *The Best of Elizabeth David: South Wind Through the Kitchen*. New York: North Point Press, 1998.

Durand, Rodolph, Monin, Philippe, and Rao, Hayagreeva. "Institutional Change in Toque Ville: Nouvelle Cuisine as an Identity Movement in French Gastronomy." *American Journal of Sociology* 108, no. 4 (2003): 795–843.

Ferguson, Priscilla Parkhurst. *Accounting for Taste: The Triumph of French Cuisine*. Chicago: University of Chicago Press, 2004.

Selected Bibliography

Fischler, Claude. *L'homnivore*. Paris: Editions Odile Jacob, 1993.

Fourneau, Léo. *Bon Appétit, Messieurs!* Paris: Editions Grasset & Fasquelle, 2006.

Gergaud, Olivier, and Guzman, Linett Montano, and Verardi, Vincenzo. "Stardust over Paris Gastronomic Restaurants." *Journal of Wine Economics* 2, no. 1 (2007): 24–39.

Gopnik, Adam. "Is There a Crisis in French Cooking?" *New Yorker*, April 28–May 5, 1997.

Jenkins, Steven. *Cheese Primer*. New York: Workman Publishing, 1996.

Johnson, Hugh. *Hugh Johnson's Story of Wine*. Norwalk, CT: Easton Press, 1998.

Kamp, David. *The United States of Arugula: The Sun-Dried, Cold-Pressed, Dark-Roasted, Extra Virgin Story of the American Food Revolution*. New York: Broadway Books, 2006.

Kaplan, Steven Laurence. *Good Bread Is Back: A Contemporary History of French Bread, the Way It Is Made, and the People Who Make It*. Durham, NC: Duke University Press, 2006.

Kuh, Patric. *The Last Days of Haute Cuisine: America's Culinary Revolution*. New York: Viking Press, 2001.

Liebling, A. J. *Between Meals: An Appetite for Paris*. New York: North Point Press, 2004.

Lubow, Arthur. "A Laboratory of Taste." *New York Times Magazine*, August 10, 2003.

Mennell, Stephen. *All Manners of Food: Eating and Taste in England and France from the Middle Ages to the Present*, 2nd ed. Urbana: University of Illinois Press, 1996.

Mesplède, Jean-François. *Trois étoiles au Michelin: Une histoire de la haute gastronomie française*. Paris: Editions Gründ, 1998.

Ory, Pascal. "Gastronomy." In *Realms of Memory: The Construction of the French Past*. Vol. 2, *Traditions*, ed. Pierre Nora and Lawrence D. Kritzman, translated by Arthur Goldhammer, 442–467. New York: Columbia University Press, 1997.

Paterniti, Michael. "The Last Meal." *Esquire*, May 1998.

Pepin, Jacques. *The Apprentice: My Life in the Kitchen*. New York: Houghton Mifflin Harcourt, 2003.

Pitte, Jean-Robert. *French Gastronomy: The History and Geography of a Passion*. Translated by Jody Gladding. New York: Columbia University Press, 2002.

Remy, Pascal. *L'Inspecteur se met à table*. Paris: Equateurs, 2004.

Rosenblum, Mort. *A Goose in Toulouse: And Other Culinary Adventures in France*. New York: North Point Press, 2000.

Roux, Michel. *Life is a Menu: Reminiscences and Recipes from a Master Chef*. London: Constable & Robinson Ltd, 2000.

Sheraton, Mimi. *Eating My Words: An Appetite for Life*. New York: William Morrow, 2004.

Simon, François. *N'est pas gourmand qui veut: Un gastronome amoureux sur les routes de France*. Paris: Editions Robert Laffont, S. A., 2005.

Smith, Timothy B. *France in Crisis: Welfare, Inequality and Globalization since 1980*. Cambridge: Cambridge University Press, 2004.

Taber, George M. *Judgment of Paris: California vs. France and the Historic 1976 Paris Tasting That Revolutionized Wine*. New York: Scribner, 2005.

Wechsberg, Joseph. *Blue Trout and Black Truffles: The Peregrinations of an Epicure*. Chicago: Academy Chicago Publishers, 1985. G

Index

Index